D1603350

THE OLD ARMY IN TEXAS

THE OLD ARMY IN TEXAS

A Research Guide to the U.S. Army
in Nineteenth-Century Texas

BY THOMAS T. SMITH

Texas State Historical Association / *Austin*

Frontispiece: Jacob Hoffman, Troop F, Third Cavalry, Fort Hancock, Texas. *Photograph courtesy Lawrence T. Jones III, Austin.*

Library of Congress Cataloging-in-Publication Data
Smith, Thomas T., 1950–
    The old Army in Texas : a research guide to the U.S. Army in nineteenth century Texas
    / by Thomas T. Smith.
        p.   cm.
    Includes bibliographical references and index.
    ISBN 0-87611-170-3 (alk. paper)
        1. Texas—History, Military—19th century. 2. United States. Army—History—19th
    century. 3. Texas—History—Military—19th century—Bibliography. 4. United States.
    Army—History—19th century—Bibliography. I. Title
    F386.S63 1999
    355'.0097644'09034—dc21
                                                                        99-049712

Published by the Texas State Historical Association in cooperation with the Center for Studies in Texas History at the University of Texas at Austin.

Design by David Timmons

∞The paper used in this book meets the minimum requirements of the American National Standard for Permanence of Paper for Printed Library Materials, z39.84—1984.

This book is partially supported by a grant from the Summerfield G. Roberts Foundation, Dallas.

The views expressed herein are those of the author and do not purport to reflect the positions of the Department of the Army, or the Department of Defense.

Dedicated
to the memory of
Colonel Martin Lalor Crimmins (1876–1955)
Rough Rider trooper, medical scientist, regular army infantry officer,
and tireless Texas historian.

Lt. John Lampham Bullis in an 1872 pattern undress coat. Son of a New York doctor, Bullis was a twice-wounded Civil War corporal who built a remarkable military career in the Texas Indian Wars. He received four brevet promotions for his courageous leadership of the Seminole-Negro army scouts in eight frontier battles between 1873 and 1881. After his death in San Antonio in 1911 Camp Bullis was named in his honor. *Photograph courtesy Lawrence T. Jones III, Austin.*

CONTENTS

INTRODUCTION

In the process of research and writing on the regular army in nine-teenth-century Texas, I found myself again and again seeking the same historical compass points, benchmark information such as the date of a fort opening, the garrison of a post in a particular time, or the departmental commander for a specific period. Eventually I began to assemble an elementary data base of essential information, kept of course on odd bits of scrap paper in an old three-ring notebook, as I still consider the process of creating a computerized spreadsheet some-thing of riddle. That notebook became the basis for this project.

This guide is certainly not an all-encompassing reference work or even a complete bibliography for advanced scholars, nor was it intended to be. The fundamental purpose of this guide is to facilitate and encour-age both advocational and professional scholarship in Texas military his-tory. A second purpose of this publication is to provide the interested reader or the Texas historian with a basic outline for research on the U.S. Army in nineteenth-century Texas. Although some of it is raw data without analysis, it serves its function as primary information that is both reasonably accurate and logically organized.

This guide begins with a series of maps that sketch the evolution of the Texas military frontier in the nineteenth century. Part I, "U.S. Army Combat Operations in the Indian Wars of Texas, 1849–1881," is a reprint of an article I wrote for *Southwestern Historical Quarterly* in 1996. The article, slightly revised and updated for this publication, provides a detailed historical analysis of the characteristics of army tactical methods and the nature of combat on the Texas frontier, as well as a variety of data on the army-Indian conflict.

Part II provides a list of departmental commanders, the location of the headquarters for Texas, and the changes in the administrative organization or military title for the state. In the army's geographic organization for much of the latter half of the nineteenth century, the nation was divided into several military divisions commanded by very senior general officers. Each division contained military departments commanded by colonels or brigadier generals. Departments were usually composed of a single large state such as Texas, or a combination of smaller states or territories. Departments in turn were split into districts commanded by the ranking unit commander within its boundaries. Although the Department of Texas in turn was sub-divided into districts and sub-districts, capturing these multitudes of constantly changing internal military administrative boundaries and commanders is beyond the scope of this work.

Part III, "U.S. Army Sites in Texas 1836–1900," has a brief outline of 230 important posts, sites, and a number of better-known camps in the state, but does not include all the dozens of temporary outposts or subposts established by parent forts. Often the official designation of these temporary camps was simply a function of the approximate location or mood in which the nomadic unit commander found himself in when, on a whim, he filled out the "name of post" blank on the required administrative return at the end of each month. My personal favorite is from the droll appellation in 1852 of "Camp Lugubrious," as the original site of Fort Terrett, for which Lt. Col. Henry Bainbridge of the First Infantry received a blistering rebuke from an unamused departmental commander. As is often the case, there is seldom complete agreement among historians, or even in army records, on the exact founding or closing date for every fort or site. In selecting the dates for this guide I have attempted to cross-reference between primary and secondary sources to gain confirmation, or at least a general consensus.

To accurately locate over time every unit in Texas or to provided a complete list of garrisons at each post would require a separate volume. The list provided in Part IV, "Post Garrisons, 1836–1900," is a snapshot generally taken in October or November of each year. For a complete accounting of a specific post or regiment the researcher should consult the bibliography for access to the monthly Post Returns or the Regimental Returns.

Part V offers a chronological summary of 224 U.S. Army combat actions in the Texas Indian Wars for the period 1849–1881. The initial outline began with Francis B. Heitman's "Chronological list of battles, actions, etc., in which troops of the Regular Army have participated, and troops engaged," found in his invaluable *Historical Register and Dictionary of the United States Army . . .* (1903). Using a myriad of additional primary and secondary sources, as noted at the end of Part V, I have expanded the detail and scope of Heitman's work, but no doubt have missed a few actions, the particulars of which are still lurking in some overlooked post return or dusty letter buried in an old trunk.

The bibliography is divided into sections on biographical sources and regimental histories, histories of forts and garrison life, the Mexican War, and frontier operations. As the focus of this work is on the regular army on the frontier I have included but a few general references on the Civil War. The use of the term "selected" in the section heading is deliberate as it is not an exhaustive bibliography, but one limited to carefully selected sources that I have found particularly useful. It would be redundant to offer a complete repetition of such finely detailed bibliographic works as Joseph G. Dawson III, *The Late 19th Century U.S. Army, 1865–1898: A Research Guide* (Westport, Conn.: Greenwood Press, 1990) or Alwyn Barr's, "A Bibliography of Articles on the Military History of Texas," in volumes II, III, IV, and VI of *Texas Military History*. Considering the enclosed bibliography as a starting point, the reader should consult additional bibliographies of the works cited herein, for example Robert Wooster's excellent bibliographic essay in *Soldiers, Sutlers, and Settlers: Garrison Life On the Texas Frontier* (1987).

There are two important aspects of the bibliography that will be immediately apparent to Texas military historians. The first is that I have included a complete range of primary source microfilm material from the National Archives, including the roll numbers of specific periods of units and forts. The second is the fact that I have attempted to integrate archeological reports into the section on fort histories. In general, Texas military historians tend to ignore the valuable work of historic archeologists and, for the most part, archeologists do not adequately search for historical documentation of their site. I once read in an archeology report on a post, "Of the dozen or so books and articles on Texas forts, Fort _____ has had little attention." Within three hours at the Texas A&M library I cataloged eighty books and articles on Texas forts, including several on the fort in question. That event was actually the genesis of this selected bibliography, originally intended for the use of archeologists. As will happen, minor projects tend to take on a life of their own. Indeed, historians disagree if archeological reports are books, monographs, or articles, while archaeologists cannot agree on the spelling of archeology. Having been involved in the creation of both books and archeological reports I have usually listed them as the former because the degree of toil is the same whether mining from the record or the soil. What is certain is that military history and historical archeology need to form a more cooperative interdisciplinary bond than now exists, as the physical and paper record are complimentary, and at times contradictory, which is even more intriguing.

In closing, I would like to acknowledge the kind and gracious contributions, comments, and valuable suggestions offered in the course of this project by many friends and scholars, and in particular three great Texans and historians: Robert Wooster of Texas A&M at Corpus Christi, Jerry Don Thompson of Texas A&M International at Laredo, and the late Ben E. Pingenot of Fort Clark at Brackettville. Each has been most generous and amiable in offering wise counsel, and in giving of their time and energy. Although I have consulted subject matter scholars in each section of this work, any errors, omissions, or misinterpretations contained herein are entirely my own responsibility.

Maps

Texas Military Frontier
1848-1851

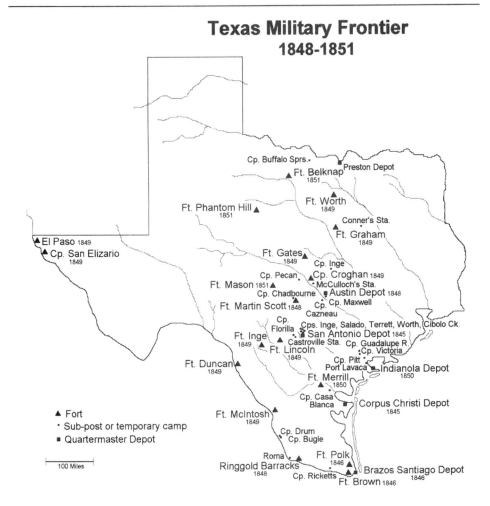

Cp. Buffalo Sprs.•
Preston Depot
▲ Ft. Belknap
1851

Ft. Phantom Hill ▲
1851

▲
Ft. Worth
1849

Conner's Sta.
•
▲
Ft. Graham
1849

▲ El Paso 1849
▲ Cp. San Elizario
1849

Ft. Gates ▲
1849
Cp. Inge
•
▲ Cp. Croghan 1849
Cp. Pecan •
• McCulloch's Sta.
Ft. Mason 1851 ▲
Cp. Chadbourne
Austin Depot 1848
Ft. Martin Scott 1848 ▲
Cp. Cp. Maxwell
Cazneau
Cp.
Florilla
Cps. Inge, Salado, Terrett, Worth, Cibolo Ck.
• San Antonio Depot 1845
Ft. Inge
1849
▲ Castroville Sta. Cp. Guadalupe R.
Ft. Lincoln
1849
• Cp. Victoria
Cp. Pitt •
Port Lavaca Indianola Depot
1850
Ft. Duncan ▲
1849
Ft. Merrill
▲ 1850
Cp. Casa
Blanca
Corpus Christi Depot
1845
Ft. McIntosh ▲
1849
Cp. Drum
Cp. Bugle
Roma •
Ringgold Barracks
1848
Ft. Polk
1846 ▲
Brazos Santiago Depot
1846
Cp. Ricketts Ft. Brown 1846

▲ Fort
• Sub-post or temporary camp
■ Quartermaster Depot

100 Miles

T. Smith 1999

Texas Military Frontier
1852-1854

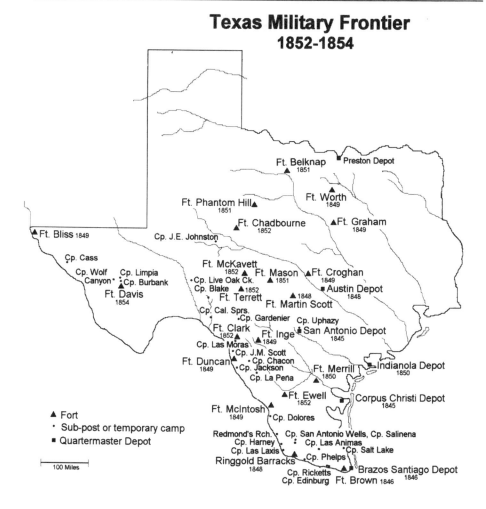

Ft. Belknap 1851
Preston Depot
Ft. Worth 1849
Ft. Phantom Hill 1851
Ft. Chadbourne 1852
Ft. Graham 1849
Ft. Bliss 1849
Cp. J.E. Johnston
Cp. Cass
Ft. McKavett 1852
Ft. Mason 1851
Ft. Croghan 1849
Cp. Wolf Canyon
Cp. Limpia
Cp. Burbank
Cp. Live Oak Ck.
Austin Depot 1848
Ft. Davis 1854
Cp. Blake
Ft. Terrett 1852
Cp. Cal. Sprs.
Ft. Martin Scott 1848
Cp. Gardenier
Cp. Uphazy
Ft. Clark 1852
Ft. Inge 1849
San Antonio Depot 1845
Cp. Las Moras
Cp. J.M. Scott
Ft. Duncan 1849
Cp. Chacon
Cp. Jackson
Ft. Merrill 1850
Indianola Depot 1850
Cp. La Peña
Ft. Ewell 1852
Corpus Christi Depot 1845
Ft. McIntosh 1849
Cp. Dolores
Redmond's Rch.
Cp. San Antonio Wells, Cp. Salinena
Cp. Harney
Cp. Las Animas
Cp. Salt Lake
Cp. Las Laxis
Cp. Phelps
Ringgold Barracks 1848
Brazos Santiago Depot 1846
Cp. Ricketts
Cp. Edinburg   Ft. Brown 1846

▲ Fort
• Sub-post or temporary camp
■ Quartermaster Depot

100 Miles

T. Smith 1999

Texas Military Frontier
1855-1861

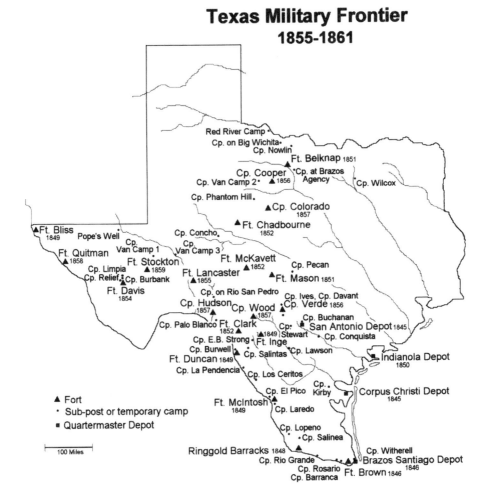

T. Smith 1999

Texas Military Frontier
1865-1881

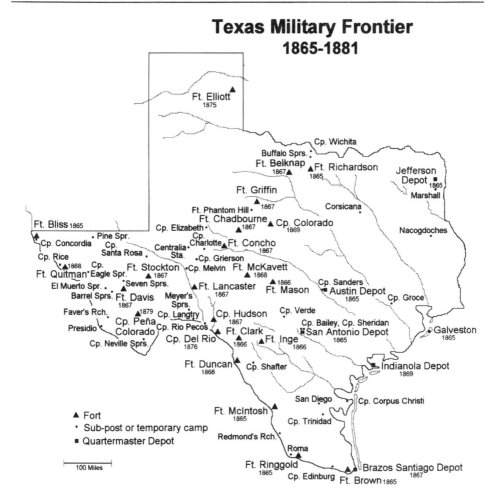

T. Smith 1999

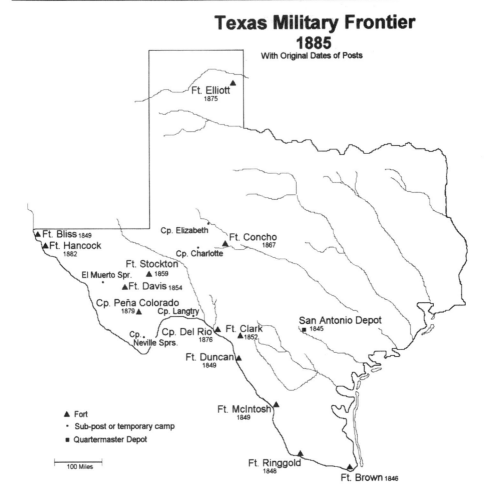

Texas Military Frontier
1885
With Original Dates of Posts

Ft. Elliott
1875

Cp. Elizabeth

▲Ft. Bliss 1849
▲Ft. Hancock
1882

Ft. Concho
1867

Cp. Charlotte

Ft. Stockton
El Muerto Spr.   ▲ 1859
▲Ft. Davis 1854

Cp. Peña Colorado
1879 ▲   Cp. Langtry

Cp. Del Rio ▲ Ft. Clark
Neville Sprs.   1876   ▲1852

San Antonio Depot
■ 1845

Ft. Duncan ▲
1849

Ft. McIntosh
1849

▲ Fort
• Sub-post or temporary camp
■ Quartermaster Depot

100 Miles

Ft. Ringgold
1848

Ft. Brown 1846

T. Smith 1999

Texas Military Frontier
1900
With Original Dates of Posts

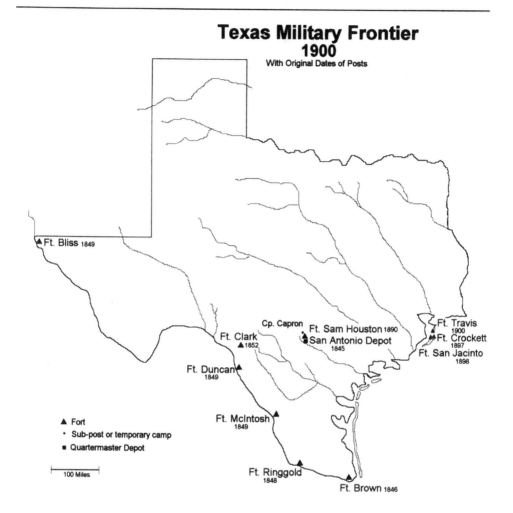

Ft. Bliss 1849

Cp. Capron

Ft. Clark
▲1852

Ft. Sam Houston 1890
San Antonio Depot
1845

Ft. Travis
1900
Ft. Crockett
1897
Ft. San Jacinto
1898

Ft. Duncan
1849

▲ Fort
• Sub-post or temporary camp
■ Quartermaster Depot

Ft. McIntosh
1849

100 Miles

Ft. Ringgold
1848

Ft. Brown 1846

T. Smith 1999

As a New York volunteer officer during the Civil War Maj. William Russell Jr. survived the bloody battles of Antietam, Gettysburg, and the Siege of Petersburg. On May 15, 1870, he died of wounds received May 14 while leading his Fourth Cavalry troopers in a skirmish at Mount Adams, one of twenty-five regular army officers killed in the Texas Indian Wars. *Photograph courtesy Lawrence T. Jones III, Austin.*

PART I

U.S. Army Combat Operations in the Indian Wars of Texas, 1849–1881

N July 1992 THE *Southwestern Historical Quarterly* published my "Fort Inge and Texas Frontier Military Operations, 1849–1869." That article treated Fort Inge as a case study in applying analytical methodology to study combat actions between the U.S. Army and the Indians on the Texas frontier. The purpose of this subsequent article, as reprinted from the April 1996 *Southwestern Historical Quarterly*, is to expand the database and methodology tested in that original study to include all of nineteenth-century Texas.[1]

The historical question is fairly straightforward: What was the nature of army combat operations against Indians on the Texas frontier? My goal is to produce a historically based analysis that will inform scholars and give general readers a solid foundation to replace the impressionistic, anecdotal history and the generalities found on television and in classic John Ford movies and revisionist westerns alike.

The database of this study is the historical record of the 219 actions and skirmishes between Indians and the U.S. Army units assigned to or patrolling in Texas between 1849 and 1881. Also included in the data are all actions of Texas-based army units that pursued Indians across the border into Mexico or into the Indian Territory, as well as actions of units stationed outside the state whose campaigns led them to fight on Texas soil. The basic information is found in Francis B. Heitman's *Historical Register and Dictionary of the United States Army* (1903).[2] From records in the Adjutant General's Office, Heitman compiled data on every action fought by the regular army from 1790 to 1902. For this study, I have fleshed out Heitman's data with various other sources, such as original reports in the National Archives; the annual *Reports of the Secretary of War*; published primary accounts; and additional information provided by secondary sources, usually on particular forts, units, or army officers.

The database has a number of inherent biases. It is extracted from reports representing the army and thus is one-sided. The Indian version of minor actions lacks substantial documentation, although I have used the few Indian accounts of major campaigns such as the Red River War. A second problem is skewed estimates of Indian opponents and casualties from the soldiers writing the primary accounts. However, there are several factors that tend to mitigate wild exaggeration. The army in the nineteenth century, as it does today, maintained a strict code of honor, particularly in official reports to superiors, which includes most of the combat reports. Even if the unit leader wanted to inflate the numbers in the public record he would face correction from the other soldier-witnesses, often veterans with a keen eye for detail. Nevertheless some bias must be assumed and the specific problem of accurate numbers is discussed in the section on the army count of Indian casualties.

The methodology of this analysis breaks the record of each engagement into component parts such as date, season, unit, parent fort, Indian tribe, Indian strength, weapons, army unit task-organization, type of operation, type of combat action, force ratio, results of engagement, logistics, and casualties. The statistical analysis for this study is not the sophisticated, computerized system of the cliometrician, but a simple stubby-pencil drill on a legal pad using basic math and percentage calculation.[3]

From 1849 to 1861 the U.S. Army fought two hundred engagements with Indians in North America, of which eighty-four (42 percent) involved Texas troops. In the post-Civil War period, from 1866 to 1881 (the year of the last U.S. Army battle with Indians in Texas), the army had a total of 873 Indian combats, of which 135 (15 percent) involved Texas. Thus the total of 219 army-Indian combats in Texas between 1849 and 1881 represents 20 percent of the 1,073 U.S. Army-Indian combats in North America during that period.[4]

At the close of the Mexican War in 1848 the War Department pulled its troops out of Mexico, then reorganized the army and its military geography to protect the vast new western frontier. Although the war had increased the national domain by one-third, Congress reduced the regular army to one-half of its wartime strength. Col. and Bvt. Maj. Gen. William Jenkins Worth, a veteran of the War of 1812 and hero of the Mexican War, was given departmental command of Texas and assigned 14 percent of the regular army. Worth's three regiments of infantry, two companies of artillery, and half a regiment of mounted troops amounted to 1,488 soldiers, the equivalent of one soldier for each 180 square miles of Texas.[5]

The first troops to take up station on the frontier arrived by sea from New Orleans on October 14, 1848, and occupied the old Mexican War post of Fort Brown. The First Infantry Regimental headquarters and three companies remained there while, in the next month, the regiment established a temporary two-company camp on Salado Creek, one company marched to Austin, another went to San Antonio, and two went to Davis' Landing (later Ringgold Barracks) on the Rio Grande.[6]

The following six months brought the remainder of the regiments destined for Texas, nearly all of which had been in the state during the war. Between 1848 and 1851 they established a string of company-sized posts up the Rio Grande to Fort Duncan and northeast along the frontier settlement lines on the Colorado, Brazos, and Trinity Rivers. In 1851 Col. Persifor F. Smith, a Princeton-educated lawyer and Mexican War hero, took command of Texas and made an extensive reconnaissance of the frontier. Smith decided that the thin First Federal Line was inadequate. He designed a new system of forts, eventually called the Second Federal Line, and sold the concept to the secretary of war. Smith wanted a new outer line of infantry-manned forts a hundred miles in advance of the settlement line, roughly at the edge of the Staked Plains and on the Edwards Plateau. The infantry would scout the great trails of the region, and when the Indians passed this line to raid the settlements the foot soldiers could warn the mounted troops stationed on the inner line, who would then take up the pursuit. Keeping the cavalry near the settlement line, where the settlers grew forage, would also prove considerably less expensive than hauling corn across the prairie. Additional posts would eventually be placed along the San Antonio-El Paso military road to guard this line of commerce.[7]

This new defensive strategy was thoughtful, systematic, and left the initiative entirely up to the bands of predatory Indians, who could choose their own time and place of striking while leaving their families safely hidden deep in the wilderness. This defect became apparent to a number of officers and War Department officials, who began lobbying before the Civil War for large-scale expeditions to seek out hostile Lipan and Comanche on their own ground in the winter, when their villages and families would be as vulnerable as the wives and children of Texas farmers.

Although the large-scale converging-column expedition was tried with limited results a few times in the antebellum era, the post-Civil War years saw the ultimate expression and success of this offensive strategy in Texas. In a single decade after the Civil War the Comanche military threat to Texas was shattered by five major U.S. Army expeditions into the *Comanchería*, culminating in 1874–1875 with the Red River War or Buffalo War, when five columns from three different departments converged on the Staked Plains. The Indian threat from sanctuaries in Mexico ended with six cross-border campaigns against the Kickapoo and Lipan in 1873 and in 1876–1878. Although a few minor skirmishes followed, the Indian wars in Texas effectively ended in 1880 with Col. Benjamin Grierson's defensive campaign in the Trans-Pecos against the remnants of the Apache band led by Victorio.

The first Indian combat involving U.S. Army troops assigned to guard the Texas frontier occurred on August 24, 1849, between a group of unidentified Indians, who had stolen horses from Fort Inge the night before, and a detachment of Company C, Second Dragoon Regiment, led by Lt. Lewis Neill, who pursued the raiders and recovered the animals. The last engagement occurred on May 3, 1881, when Lt. John L. Bullis and his Seminole-Negro scouts operating out of Fort Clark pursued a small band of Lipan Apaches into Mexico.[8]

The total of 219 engagements does not reflect the real level of army effort on the Texas frontier, for only a fraction of the patrols generated combat. From September 1878 to September 1879, for example, 128 patrols from thirteen Texas posts patrolled 40,100 miles and fought only two engagements.[9]

The number of army engagements involving army troops in Texas by calendar year are outlined in Chart 1. There were 84 army-led Indian battles involving Texas in 1849–1861 and 135 in 1866–1881. The total is 219, with 38 percent in the antebellum years and 62 percent in the post-Civil War era.

CHART 1: ARMY-INDIAN ACTIONS IN TEXAS,
1849–1881

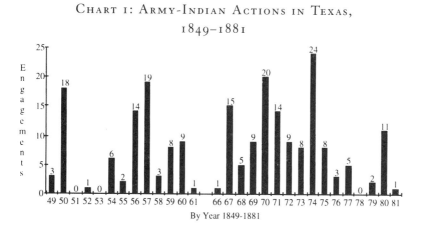

The year with the greatest number of engagements was 1874, with twenty-four engagements (11 percent), which marked the start of the great Buffalo War in the Texas Panhandle. Next is 1870 with twenty actions (9 percent), reflecting a sudden increase in raids into Texas from reservations in the Indian Territory as well as the operations of four regiments of cavalry in Texas. Next in numbers of engagements were 1857, 1850, and 1867. The nineteen engagements in 1857 and the fifteen in 1867 mark the first full years of the frontier operations of the two most aggressive regiments in Texas history, the Second Cavalry and Fourth Cavalry, respectively, while 1850 (eighteen actions) was a year of extremely aggressive operations by the Second Dragoons, the Eighth Infantry (mounted), and the First Infantry Regiment. It was also the year of the first large-scale Indian campaign by the army in Texas, in which Capt. William J. Hardee, Second Dragoons, directed the efforts of ten columns of soldiers and Texas Mounted Volunteers in clearing the Nueces Strip of hostile Indians. These five years are fairly balanced between the antebellum and post-Civil War eras, which might surprise scholars who have tended to focus on the latter.

The relatively quiet years of 1851–1853, with only one engagement, reflect a temporary treaty with a few powerful Comanche bands. During this period, the Comanche and Lipan raiders shifted their focus to easier targets in the border states of Mexico south of the Rio Bravo. Mexico paid a price for the improved military protection of Texas. The state of Nuevo León, for example, suffered 809 Indian raids between 1848 and 1870, with over one thousand casualties and four million pesos worth of lost property.[10]

In the antebellum period the four most active troops at posts were Fort Inge with eighteen actions (21 percent of 84), Fort McIntosh with nine, and Forts Clark and Davis with five each. In the post-Civil War era thirty-two actions (24 percent of the total of 135) were fought by detachments not directly associated with a fort. These were usually small groups of soldiers assigned to guard a road, mail station, or escort a supply train. In the post-Civil War years twenty-seven combats (20 percent of 135) involved larger expeditions composed of troops from several different posts and regiments usually out for a lengthy period of several months. The post directly associated with the most engagements in the post-Civil War era was Fort Davis with twelve (8 percent of 135), followed by Fort Clark with eleven. Not including the fifty-eight battles from large expeditions or small detachments the posts directly associated with the most actions for the entire period (1849–1881) of U.S. Army involvement in the Texas Indian wars were Fort Inge with twenty (10 percent of 219), Fort Davis with seventeen, Fort Clark with sixteen, and Fort McIntosh with nine.

Texas forts served as logistical bases in support of small-unit field operations rather than as formal points of defense. Although it had manuals dictating formations and methods for conventional warfare against European-style armies, the U.S. Army did not develop an institutional tactical doctrine for fighting Indians. Methods used in the irregular, decentralized warfare against Indians were largely up to the local commander. The tactics used in various field operations were a product of the mission of the unit, the type of unit, and the nature of the enemy.[11]

The mission statement is the official expression of the goals expected to be accomplished by the application of military power in a situation, and is the foundation for all operations. In February 1849 Bvt. Maj. Gen.

William J. Worth, then departmental commander for Texas, issued General Orders No. 13, the original mission statement for Texas troops. Worth instructed unit commanders to protect the lives and property of citizens, to prevent "as far as practicable" Indians from the United States crossing to raid in Mexico, and finally to protect non-hostile Indians against violence and injustice. The mission Worth outlined remained the basic operational task of army troops in Texas for the entire period of the Indian wars.[12]

The type of units sent to Texas to carry out the mission were regiments of infantry, a company or two of artillery, and mounted regiments variously labeled dragoons, mounted rifles, and, after 1855, cavalry. In the antebellum years (1849–1861) the War Department usually assigned to Texas two companies of artillery, four regiments of infantry, and two of the five existing mounted regiments. In the post-Civil War era (1866–1881) Texas typically had half an artillery regiment on the lower coast, four infantry regiments, and three of the ten existing cavalry regiments.[13]

Although mounted regiments were twice as expensive as foot soldiers, due to the cost of equipment, animals, and forage, in the summer of 1852 departmental commander Col. Persifor F. Smith once again impatiently informed the secretary of war that "Indians can only be pursued by mounted troops." While this would have seemed obvious to a Texan of the day, it was not apparent to Congress nor to the military establishment, and was, in fact, contrary to prior American military experience. Congress had authorized the creation of two mounted regiments in the 1830s and one in 1846, but the previous Indian wars of the Old Northwest, Southern interior, and Florida had been fought in heavy woodlands where the Indians campaigned on foot and the infantry proved the most effective arm. Always a ponderous institution more likely to base its actions on its most recent experience rather than its present one, the American military establishment embarked on a new learning curve on the Great Plains, and took three more decades to create and employ enough horse regiments to accomplish its goals.[14]

As illustrated in Charts 2 and 3, the two units involved in the most combats in Texas were the antebellum Second Cavalry Regiment and the post-Civil War Fourth Cavalry Regiment. The Second Cavalry, with thirty-six actions between 1856 and 1861, fought 43 percent of all ante-bellum actions in Texas and 16 percent of all engagements between 1849 and 1881. The Fourth Cavalry, with thirty-six battles between 1866 and 1875 fought 27 percent of the actions in Texas in the post-Civil War era and 16 percent of all engagements between 1849 and 1881.

CHART 2: ACTIONS IN TEXAS, 1849–1861

BY ARMY UNIT

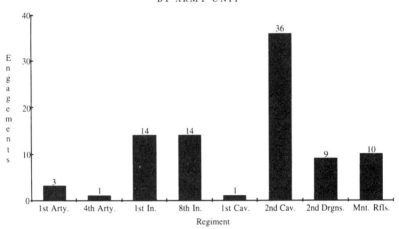

CHART 3: ACTIONS IN TEXAS, 1866–1881

BY ARMY UNIT

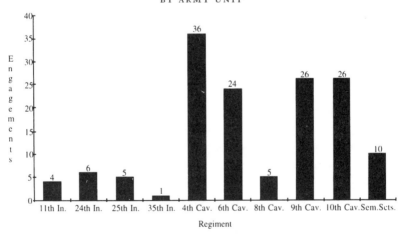

The buffalo soldiers of the post-Civil War black regiments of Ninth and Tenth Cavalry each had twenty-six engagements. Adding to these the eleven battles of the black Twenty-Fourth and Twenty-Fifth Infantry (six and five respectively) and the ten actions of the Seminole-Negro scouts results in a total of seventy-three engagements. This means that black soldiers fought 54 percent of the 135 post-Civil War engagements involving Texas troops.

In several cases more than one unit was involved in a battle, in which case both units received credit for the same skirmish. During 1849–1850 several companies of federally financed Texas Mounted Volunteers fought nine skirmishes while operating directly under army command, a short-lived arrangement for which neither party had much enthusiasm. The real significance of the unit charts is that the statistics indicate that horse regiments such as dragoons, cavalrymen, mounted rifles, or the sometimes mounted companies of the First and Eighth Infantry fought 85 percent of all engagements in Texas.

The principal tribes involved in the Texas Indian wars were the Comanche, Kiowa, and Lipan Apache, although a half a dozen other tribes, such as the Kickapoo, also raided in Texas. The *Comanchería*, the domain of the five major Comanche bands, stretched from the Edwards Plateau north to central Kansas. It was not the aboriginal homeland of the tribe, but was gained by military conquest after the arrival of the Spanish and the reintroduction of the horse in North America. The Kiowa Apache, with a long-standing alliance with the Comanche, seemed to be centered in the upper Texas panhandle between the branches of the Canadian Rivers. On the southwestern fringes of the *Comanchería* in western and southern Texas, the Lipan Apache hid their *rancherías* or small camps. The Lipan and Comanche tended to be blood enemies, but shared the general characteristics of the horse-mounted Plains Indian military cultures. In these societies horse raiding and warfare were the cultural norm, the pathway to local status for any ambitious young man.[15]

The Comanche warrior and the army cavalryman perhaps had more in common with each other than with the average Texas citizen. Both the warrior and soldier belonged to military societies that esteemed martial virtues, both had an appreciation for horseflesh and weapons, and both belonged to nomadic subcultures that depended on the horse for mobility. Indeed, in 1854 one young Second Dragoon officer became so bored with garrison duties at Fort Chadbourne, Texas, that he wrote his sister, "I have half a mind to join the Comanches and go to Mexico to steal horses . . . ."[16]

Although a number of soldiers were sympathetic toward the plight of the Plains tribes, most nineteenth-century Texans viewed Plains Indians much as citizens today might view a violent urban street gang— i.e., as a general menace to civilization, making little distinction between gangs, their sympathy for members directly proportional to the gangs' distance from their own front doors. Many of the Indians, especially the Comanche, seemed to view the Texans as a tribe apart, reserving for them a special fury not visited upon the army soldier, the Mexican, or other Indians.

In this clash of cultures, Anglos in the West tended to regard Indian society as homogenous and monolithic, with a policy-making hierarchy like republican white culture. A treaty with a Penateka Comanche leader meant, from the Texan perspective, that the treaty bound all Comanche. However, in the worldview of the Penateka leader, he, as an individual, was tied by the agreement, but his brother was not, nor were the Kotsoteka band or the implacable Kwahadi bound by the agreement. The whites failed to understand that effective peace would require a treaty with every individual warrior on the Plains.

Indians shared this cultural misunderstanding and sometimes viewed whites as a series of unrelated subgroups rather than as a mono- lithic culture. The Indians failed to recognize that the rancher killed in Texas was a concern of the farmer in Kansas. In the early 1850s the Lipan leader on the upper Brazos kept peace with the local Second Dragoon Regiment, but bragged to the soldiers that the Lipan were headed south to make war on the tribe of Mounted Rifles at Fort Inge.[17]

The statistics in Chart 4 support the anecdotal evidence offered by earlier generations of Texas historians who argued that the majority of combat was against the Comanche Indians. Forty-six of the antebellum reports and fifty-one of the post-Civil War reports name the Indian tribe engaged, a sample base of 44 percent of all 219 combats. Eighteen of these reports detail the specific Indian leader involved in the fight. Of the antebellum reports, almost two-thirds involved the Comanche and one-quarter the Apache (eleven Lipan and two Mescalero). Of the fifty-one tribes named in post-Civil War reports, more than one-half were the Comanche-Kiowa and one-third the Apache. Of the ninety-seven reports naming tribes during 1849–1881, just over one half named the Comanche-Kiowa and nearly one-third the Lipan and other Apache.

CHART 4: ACTIONS IN TEXAS, 1849–1881

INDIAN TRIBE BY % OF ENGAGEMENT

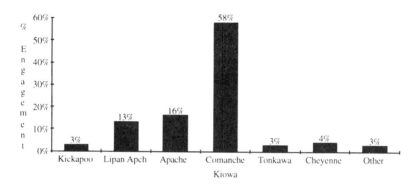

These statistics jibe with data offered by the commissioner of Indian affairs, who tabulated claims against the government for Indian depredations from 1812 to 1889. The commissioner reported 1,031 depredations blamed on the Comanche, 310 on the Kiowa, and 759 on the Apache, for a total loss of over eight million dollars' worth of property, probably a vastly inflated figure.[18]

The size of the Indian band was specified in forty-three antebellum Texas army reports and forty-three post-Civil War reports, a total sample of eighty-six or 39 percent. In the antebellum period 37 percent of the war parties consisted of ten Indians or less, while in the post-Civil War era this dropped to 20 percent. In the antebellum period only 7 percent of the Indian groups engaged involved more than one hundred warriors, compared to 20 percent in the post-Civil War era. In general, the Indians tended to fight in larger groups after the Civil War. Taking all of the engagements from 1849 to 1881, about 47 percent were with Indian war parties of twenty Indians or less, about 38 percent with war parties of twenty-one to one hundred warriors, and 13 percent with war parties of one hundred or more. Thus the statistics indicate that Indians of all tribes tended to raid in groups of twenty or less—no surprise considering the small-band societies and military culture of the nomadic Plains tribes.

Forty-three reports mention Indian arms by type, usually bows and lances. Of the seventeen antebellum reports that mention arms, only nine mention firearms (in the form of flintlocks, revolvers, or muzzle-loading rifles used by both the Comanche and Apache). In the post-Civil War twenty-six reports mention Indian weapons by type, and twenty-two mention firearms. In spite of concerns that the Indians might obtain repeating rifles, only one report mentions these weapons. On July 12, 1870, a group of 250 Kiowa under Kicking Bird, armed with the deadly seven-shot Spencer carbine, other rifles, and revolvers, engaged a Sixth Cavalry expedition out of Fort Richardson on the Little Wichita River. Two soldiers were killed and two wounded. The statistics indicate that the Indians used firearms, a fact important enough for soldiers to mention, in at least 16 percent of the engagements. Nearly all of these firearms seem to have been single-shot muzzle-loading or breech-loading rifles, or revolving pistols. Apparently repeating rifles were a rarity for Indians in Texas, as they certainly were for the soldiers.[19]

Due to the need of both the mounted Indians and soldiers for grass for their horses, only fifty-eight (26 percent) of the engagements took place during the winter months from December to March, with no appreciable difference between the antebellum and post-Civil War eras. Of the 161 grassy-month engagements, thirty-two (19 percent) took place in May and twenty-seven (17 percent) in September, the two highest monthly totals. March, with nine (4 percent), seemed to be the most unpopular month for fighting for either side.

The mission of the unit, the type of unit, and the nature of the enemy dictated the field methods the army used in Texas. The sub-components of each engagement are relatively complex but for purposes of this analysis are divided into the aspects of task-organization, type of operation, type of combat action, force ratio, results of engagement, logistics, and casualties.

The task-organization of an army operation includes such factors as leadership, size of the unit, and attachments such as scouts or volunteers. In the antebellum era officers led 80 percent of all U.S. Army-Indian battles with Indians in Texas. The 20 percent led by sergeants or corporals reflects both the shortage of officers on the frontier and the great skill of the army's noncommissioned officer corps. In the post-Civil War era officers led 88 percent of the combats and noncommissioned officers the remainder. Statistics of both eras combined indicated that officers led 83 percent of the combats and noncommissioned officers 17 percent.

Company-grade officers (lieutenants or captains) led 71 percent of all the army combats in Texas. In nineteenth-century army regulations concerning conventional linear combat, the regiment was the basic maneuver unit and the colonel of the regiment was the tactical decision-maker. Lieutenants and captains were expected to keep their unit's firing line aligned as the colonel directed and to march in the direction and formation dictated by the regimental commander, who usually had twenty or thirty years' service. In the irregular or unconventional circumstances of the Indian wars the junior officers, leading small units, were most often the tacticians, which gave them an extraordinary opportunity for decision-making under the extreme stress of combat. The payoff came in the rapid military expansions of the American Civil War and the Spanish-American War, when junior officers suddenly found themselves commanding regiments or wearing stars. Their conditioning as junior officers in the field and in combat during the Indian wars produced, on short notice, a remarkable set of field-grade and general officers for conventional warfare.

The exact size of the Texas-based army unit involved in an engagement is known in 122 cases, producing a sample of 56 percent of the total of 219. In the antebellum era 20 percent of the combats involved an army detachment of ten men or less. For the post-Civil War era this number is 13 percent, meaning that an average of 16 percent of all engagements during 1849–1881 involved a unit of ten soldiers or less. In the antebellum era 29 percent of the engagements involved a unit of from sixteen to twenty-five soldiers; the figure is 37 percent for the post-Civil War era. In the antebellum era only 7 percent of the skirmishes involved a unit of more than fifty soldiers, while this category increased to 49 percent in the post-Civil War years. The sample can be broadened to a total of 194 if we include reports that list the size as "detachment," meaning less than company strength, or note a company or a list of companies. In this case, for the entire period 1849–1881, 73 percent of the engagements were fought by an army unit of less than company strength and 27 percent by units of company strength or greater. A "company" included different numbers of men of in various periods, ranging from an average strength of thirty-five infantrymen or seventy cavalrymen in 1849 to as many as eighty men in 1870. The importance of the statistic is to demonstrate that in either era the small unit rather than the large column was the norm in Texas, but that after the Civil War the army tended to operate in larger units than in the antebellum era.[20]

The statistics also indicate that the army units often operated with civilian or Indian scouts but seldom with local civilian volunteers. In 18 percent of the antebellum engagements involving army troops from Texas, the unit had a Mexican or white guide or scout. In another 2 percent of the engagements the scout was an Indian, usually Delaware or Caddo. In only 6 percent of the post-Civil War engagements was the army scout a white or Mexican, while in 22 percent the guide was an Indian, usually either Tonkawa, Seminole, Lipan, or Delaware. Overall, the army had a scout or guide in 24 percent of the engagements. The clear trend was to make better use of Indian scouts after the Civil War than before.

Groups of local civilian volunteers temporarily aligned with the army to fight Indians in about 12 percent of the antebellum engagements in Texas but in only about 4 percent in the post-Civil War engagements. During the antebellum era, Congress occasionally authorized the army to employ federal provincial forces, usually called Texas Mounted Volunteers. These organizations were sometimes existing units of Texas Ranging Companies brought into federal service for a three- or six-month period, and they operated under army control in nine engagements (11 percent) before the Civil War.

Distinct again from either local civilian volunteers or from Texas Mounted Volunteers were the Texas Ranging Companies, often called Texas Rangers. These were the state-paid and state-controlled provincial mounted organizations for frontier protection that occasionally operated in concert with the U.S. Army before the Civil War, but practically never afterward, with the exception of Grierson's 1880 campaign against Victorio. The Texas Rangers were unquestionably effective but often worked at cross-purposes with federal military policy. In spite of the central position of the Rangers in Texas mythology, the concept was not invented in Texas, but appears to have been imported into Austin's old colony from Virginia, South Carolina, and Georgia. In fact, there were Georgia Rangers a century before there were Texas Rangers.[21]

The various types of army operations on the Texas frontier include the movement to contact, the pursuit, large-scale expeditions, the escort, and the defense of an area or point. In the antebellum era seventy-seven reports have enough information to determine the type of operation conducted by the army. This provides a strong sample base of 91 percent of all the antebellum engagements. The pursuit was the most common operation of Texas troops (43 percent). In this type of operation the commander of a fort or detachment received word that Indians had raided nearby. He immediately led or sent a patrol to the scene of the raid to try to pick up the trail or gather intelligence. The patrol then followed the Indians, often for days and several hundred miles, until they caught the raiders or abandoned the chase.

The second most common operation to produce an engagement in the antebellum era was the movement to contact or "scout" (36 percent), in which a routine security patrol moved along likely avenues of approach or infiltration routes such as trails and streams, or patrolled favorite water holes or river ford sites. These routine interdiction patrols were analogous to a policeman's beat, and the Texas fort served as the logistical base. The engagements resulting from these operations occurred when the patrol picked up a fresh trail and began a pursuit, or when the soldiers literally bumped into and fought an Indian war party.

Only 12 percent of antebellum Texas army engagements with Indians involved large expeditions of several companies operating over a wide area over a lengthy time, usually several months. In this era 8 percent of the Indian engagements stemmed from guarding a specific point such as a mail station, or from escorting a supply train, paymaster, or other such party.

In the post-Civil War years these statistics changed considerably. Of a total sample of eighty-one engagements, 43 percent resulted from the movement to contact or "scout" type of operation. This is a reflection of the fact that the army now assigned twice as many mounted regiments to the Department of Texas as it did in the antebellum years. The army also conducted many more large-scale expeditions in the post-Civil War years, resulting in 32 percent of the engagements. In this era the pursuit, so dominant in the antebellum years, accounted for only 15 percent of the battles. Escort and guard missions still resulted in about 10 percent of the engagements.

The antebellum and post-Civil War eras combined produce a sample of 158 reports (72 percent of 219 engagements) with enough detailed information to generalize about the type of operations conducted by U.S. Army troops in Texas. The most common type of operation resulting in a battle with Indians was the routine scout or movement to contact (40 percent of all engagements). This is followed by the pursuit (28 percent) and the large-scale expedition (23 percent). Guard mission and escort operations resulted in only 9 percent of all engagements.

Once the army unit made contact with hostile Indians and combat became inevitable, the unit leader had three basic tactical options: he could attack, defend, or try to withdraw. If he decided to attack his alternatives became more complex. If he had the advantage, he could conduct a hasty attack, an immediate assault that sacrificed coordination and capitalized on speed, initiative, and perhaps mass or surprise. Or he could conduct a deliberate attack by halting, taking time to plan and organize his assault force and supporting force, and synchronizing the assault on the enemy. If it was a cavalry unit the leader also had to decide, in either case, if he wanted to go in mounted. A mounted attack retained mobility but risked injury to his mounts; attacking dismounted, like the infantry, risked having the enemy capture his horse herd.

Reports from 138 engagements involving Texas troops have enough information to determine the type of action that occurred during the battle. The hasty attack was the most common type of action on the Texas frontier, conducted in 70 percent (65 percent mounted and 5 percent dismounted) of the combats during 1849–1881. In the antebellum era 84 percent (74 percent mounted and 10 percent dismounted) of the engagements were hasty attacks. In the post-Civil War years 59 percent (58 percent mounted and 1 percent dismounted) of the actions were hasty attacks. Only four antebellum engagements and one of the post-Civil War engagements were the sort of linear combat where the opposing battle lines formed and fought it out face-to-face. Most of the engagements were wild melees or scrambles through the brush that degenerated into an assortment of unconnected small-group struggles. Of the 70 percent of hasty attacks during 1848–1881, 27 percent were against Indian camps or villages and 43 percent were meeting engagements, the results of catching up with raiders or bumping into an Indian war party.

Perhaps the most extraordinary mounted hasty attack occurred on November 8, 1874, during the Buffalo War. Lt. Frank D. Baldwin, with one company each from the Sixth Cavalry and Fifth Infantry, was escorting twenty-three empty wagons to pick up supplies for Col. Nelson A. Miles's column. Near McClellan Creek, they suddenly came upon the Cheyenne camp of Gray Beard. Baldwin tossed his infantry in the wagons and launched a hasty attack in two wagon columns with the cavalry on the flanks, stormed the Indian war camp, and pursued the fleeing Cheyenne for ten miles. In the process Baldwin recovered two female captives, Adelaide and Julia Germain (or German), and earned his second Congressional Medal of Honor—one of the fifty-nine awarded during the Indian wars in Texas.[22]

The deliberate attack, with detailed army planning and coordination, was rare on the Texas frontier, occurring in only 2 percent of the engagements. However, the last combat action against Indians by an army unit from Texas was just such an attack. On April 24, 1881, five Lipan stole horses and murdered Mrs. McLauren on the Rio Frio near Uvalde. Word reached Fort Clark and Lt. John L. Bullis, with thirty of his Seminole-Negro scouts, started in pursuit, following the trail of the raiders for six days across the Rio Grande into the Burro Mountains of Mexico. Bullis found the Lipan camp late one evening and spent the night planning his attack and quietly deploying his forces. At daylight on May 3 he led a mounted assault on the camp, killed four Lipan warriors and captured an Indian woman, a child, and twenty-one stolen horses, all without a single casualty among his own troops.[23]

The defense is naturally more powerful than the attack because the defender is normally sitting still, usually behind cover and concealment, and the unit leader has better control of his forces. But the defense is reactive rather than proactive, giving up the initiative to the attacker. The attack can fail many times and still eventually win, but the defense need fail only once to lose. The hasty dismounted defense by army forces occurred in 28 percent of the engagements on the Texas frontier. It was less common in the antebellum period (nine reports) than in the post-Civil War years (twenty-nine). Of this 28 percent, 11 percent occurred when Indians attacked a wagon escort, 10 percent when Indians attacked an army unit in camp, 5 percent as a result of a meeting engagement when two forces collided, and 2 percent as the army defended a specific point such as a Texas mail station or water hole.

An example of a hasty defense occurred on October 10, 1871, the day after Quanah Parker and his band of Kwahadi Comanche made a daring night raid against Col. Ranald S. Mackenzie's cavalry column on the upper Brazos River. They stole sixty-six mounts, including Mackenzie's gray charger. A detachment of pursuing soldiers caught a small group of raiders driving the horses and chased them over a hill, directly into the path of a much larger force of advancing Comanches. The detachment commander, greatly outnumbered, dismounted his troopers and formed a hasty defense in a ravine. This group of Fourth Cavalry soldiers had the seven-shot Spencer carbine, carried by a few units from the Civil War years until 1873. Rapid firepower and the force-multiplier of protective cover and concealment saved the command until Mackenzie's column could come to its rescue. In this action 2d Lt. Robert G. Carter earned the Congressional Medal of Honor, one of only four officers to do so during the Indian Wars in Texas.[24]

In summary, of the types of combat actions conducted by army troops in the Texas Indian wars between 1849 and 1881, the immediate hasty attack was the most common (70 percent of the actions). The dismounted hasty defense was rarer (28 percent), and the deliberate attack was least common (2 percent).

Force ratio is a measure of the relative strength of opposing combatants. Force ratio, in modern tactical doctrine, is an important factor in the decision of the unit leader to conduct an attack, to defend, or to withdraw; generally, the attacker needs a three-to-one advantage for a successful offensive action. In ninety-one reports of army actions on the Texas frontier during 1849–1881 there is enough detail to determine the relative strengths of the two sides engaged. The ratios were an even 1:1 in 21 percent of the actions, a 2:1 advantage or greater for the army in 41 percent, and an army disadvantage of 1:2 or worse in 38 percent. The interesting fact is that in almost half of cases where the army was outnumbered, and in three-quarters of the cases where the odds were even, the leader chose to attack, a decision that would be frowned upon in modern doctrine.

Certainly personal ambition had a role in some leaders' decisions to launch an attack against superior numbers. Officers such as Mackenzie, Bullis, and William B. Hazen cultivated a reputation for daring and aggressiveness. However, army leaders who immediately attacked regardless of the odds may also have had an intuitive understanding of the importance of initiative in a combat situation. Seizing the initiative allows one side to dictate the terms of the battle and makes the other side conform to actions not of its choosing. Initiative might be gained by surprise, direction of movement, audacity, or violence of execution. Initiative can be determined in ninety-eight cases of army-Indian combat on the Texas frontier. In eighty-eight of those cases (sixty-five army, twenty-three Indian) the side that made the first move and gained the initiative retained that initiative throughout the battle. In only 10 percent of the battles did one side or the other overcome the initial disadvantage and gain the initiative.

Determining the victor in these battles is often difficult, and depends entirely on a subjective definition of "victory." For purposes of this analysis the conditions for an army or an Indian victory are one or more of the following: stolen property is recovered by the army or retained by the Indians; the casualty exchange ratio is lopsided; the Indians escape serious military punishment during the engagement; an Indian village or camp is destroyed; an army or Indian attack fails; an army or Indian defense succeeds.

The army could claim victory in 80 percent of a sample of seventy-two antebellum combats, the Indians in 18 percent (2 percent could be considered a draw). In the post-Civil War period fifty-eight reports have enough information to conclude that the army could legitimately claim victory in 76 percent of the engagements, the Indians in 21 percent (3 percent resulted in a draw). The data for both periods is remarkably similar. Of an overall sample of 130 cases during 1849–1881, 78 percent resulted in an army victory, 19 percent in an Indian victory, and 3 percent were draws. These calculations do not included the many times Indian war parties raided and got away without a pursuit. These, if the numbers were known, might also be considered Indian victories and army failures. In any case, the data is clear on one point: when there was a fight, the army usually won.

The next logical question is: what was the key element that led to victory in an engagement on the Texas frontier? In twenty-six victories (twenty-three army, three Indian) the element of surprise seemed to be decisive. Surprise is an advantage gained by striking the enemy in an unexpected manner, time, or place, which confuses the opponent and diminishes his ability to react effectively. Surprise was not always the decisive factor in these combats. Surprise was achieved by one side or the other in fifty-nine army-Indian engagements, forty times by the army, nineteen times by the Indians. The fact that Indians were so often surprised is a reflection of their notoriously lax security. The Indians rarely placed guards around their camps or flankers on their columns to provide early warning of an enemy attack.

There were other decisive factors for victory in Texas frontier battles. In thirteen victories the army had accurate intelligence on the exact location and disposition of Indian camps, overcoming the fundamental problem for any army commander in the Indian wars—finding the enemy. In nine cases (five army, four Indian) victory was a result of one side having such overwhelming numbers that the opponent could not overcome the odds. In only four cases victory came to the army through superior firepower, two involving the Colt six-shot pistol in the early antebellum era, and two involving the Spencer seven-shot rifle in the post-Civil War era. In all four cases the army detachment was badly outnumbered and the Indians broke off the action when they began to take significant casualties. However, the army seldom had a firepower advantage. The Indians often used firearms as well, and at close range in the Texas brush the bow and arrow, with its rapid rate of fire and accuracy, was as dangerous as the Colt pistol, and was probably more effective than the single-shot army rifles of the period. In four cases (one army, three Indian), the decisive element of victory was the advantage of a limited-visibility situation, usually a night attack to steal army horses and escape well-aimed direct fire, or the use of night as a cover to get into an advantageous position for a dawn attack. In three cases (one army, two Indian), the unexpected arrival of reinforcements turned a certain defeat into a victory.

A common characteristic of these engagements was the army's failure to follow up a tactical victory by exploiting the weakness of a beaten and disorganized foe. Small-unit skirmishing however, usually left the victor as disorganized as the defeated. Momentum was lost in the time it took to reconsolidate and reorganize the small unit after the friction of combat. Exploitation and pursuit after victory was normally a luxury only of larger units with fresh subunits in reserve for the follow-on mission. Seventy-five reports of engagements involving army troops in Texas offer specific information on why the army unit failed to pursue and annihilate a beaten Indian enemy after an engagement. In 28 percent of the cases the Indians scattered on multiple trails as individuals or small parties. This tactic of immediate dispersion after a battle has been routinely used throughout history by forces conducting irregular warfare. The army unit seldom had enough combat power to pursue in every direction. If the army leader split his unit to do so, it would become vulnerable.

In 20 percent of the engagements involving Texas soldiers the army leader determined his horses were too spent to continue a rapid pursuit. In 16 percent of the cases the army unit was overburdened by wounded and dead or had suffered the loss of key leadership. In 13 percent of the engagements the burden of taking care of recovered horses or other property prevented a pursuit. In 13 percent of the cases the unit leader was precluded from pursuing because the Indians escaped across a restricted border, either the reserve border with the Indian Territory or, in the vast majority of cases, the international border with Mexico. The remaining 10 percent of reports cite other reasons such as darkness, sudden bad weather, or the army patrol's lack of rations for the failure to continue the action.

Tactical sustainment is the army leadership's attention to the logistics of an operation, keeping the unit armed and fed. This was done through the basic load carried by each soldier, as well as through the unit supply train. A few Texas units used army wagons; others used pack mules. The pack mule gave army patrols more mobility than the wagon and is mentioned in ten reports, the earliest in 1849. However, the typical engagement involved no unit train. The command sustained itself on whatever the soldiers could carry, augmented with hunting for game. The level of sustainment is evident in thirty-six antebellum reports and in thirty-nine from the post-Civil War era. In 58 percent of the antebellum reports the level of sustainment could be considered good to fair and 42 percent poor, meaning the soldiers were out of rations and water during the engagement. For the post-Civil War period 64 percent would be considered good to fair, while 36 percent might be called poor. For both eras combined, the level of sustainment was good to fair in 64 percent of the engagements and poor in 36 percent. It is evident that logistics was a real problem in frontier operations.[25]

Logistics was a major factor in determining the duration of an operation. The exact length of time away from the fort or logistical base can be determined in ninety-three reports. In the antebellum era 82 percent of the operations or patrols lasted ten days or less, 9 percent between eleven and twenty days, and 9 percent more than twenty days. In the post-Civil War years 54 percent of the operations lasted ten days or less, 7 percent eleven to twenty days, and 18 percent more than twenty days. The average for both eras was 78 percent lasting ten days or less, 9 percent between eleven and twenty days, and 13 percent more than twenty days. There were more of the longer operations after the Civil War, but certainly the short operation of ten days or less away from the logistical base was the norm on the Texas frontier for both eras.

Fourteen reports give a good account of the number of miles traveled during a patrol or pursuit that resulted in an engagement. While the sample is too slim to draw solid conclusions it does demonstrate the range of possibilities, which include the following: 1,250 miles in thirty days, 333 miles in thirty days, 750 miles in twenty-five days, 417 miles in nine days, 110 miles in twenty-five hours, and finally one offhand remark about thirty-three straight hours in the saddle.

For the army unit leader in Texas the recovery of property from the Indians was physical proof of the success of his mission. Much of this property, particularly livestock, was in fact stolen by the Indians and truly "recovered" by the army, as could be determined by cattle and horse brands. However, the automatic assumption that any horses taken from the Indians during an engagement were recovered property is not necessarily true, as the Comanche especially were known to breed and raise large horse herds on their own. Nevertheless, fifty-one antebellum reports of engagements list the total recovered property as 1,052 horses and mules, 4 oxen, and 2 captives—a Mexican boy and a slave. For the post-Civil War years the thirty-three cases of recovered property include 1,758 horses and mules, 350 cattle, and 10 captives. These figures do not include the 1,000 Indian ponies killed by Colonel Mackenzie's troops after the Palo Duro Canyon fight in September 1874.

For the entire period 1849–1881, eighty-four Texas army reports list property recovered from the Indians after a battle or skirmish. The total includes 2,810 horses and mules, 350 cattle, and 12 captives; among the latter were two white boys, seven Mexican boys, one slave, and two white girls (the Germain or German sisters).

According to the 219 reports, army casualties during the Texas Indian wars from 1849 to 1881 totaled 180 soldiers. Of these, sixty-four were killed and 116 wounded. Additional casualties in army operations include ten civilian volunteers (two dead, eight wounded), three scouts (one dead, two wounded), and five Texas Mounted Volunteers (one dead, four wounded). While these numbers, incurred over a thirty-two-year period, would barely qualify as a hard skirmish in the American Civil War, they were not insignificant to those soldiers directly involved.

The majority of the soldier casualties (59 percent) came in antebellum Texas, with a total of 107, including eighteen officers (three dead, fifteen wounded), and eighty-nine enlisted men (twenty-eight dead, sixty-one wounded). In the post-Civil War era there were seventy-three soldier casualties, consisting of seven officers (one dead, six wounded), and sixty-six enlisted men (thirty-two dead, thirty-four wounded).

The twenty-five officer casualties represent a casualty ratio of about 14 percent, more than three times the 4 percent officer-to-soldier ratio in Texas in the period 1849–1881. In the antebellum period the 107 soldier casualties compare to an average yearly troop strength of 3,200 (3,084 enlisted men, 116 officers). The seventy-three casualties of the post-Civil

War period compare to an average yearly troop strength of 4,200 soldiers (4,002 enlisted men, 198 officers). This meant that a Texas soldier of the antebellum period had a 1 in 30 chance of becoming a casualty, much higher than the 1 to 58 chance of his post-Civil War counterpart. The worst casualty figures in all of the Texas Indian wars were for army officers in the antebellum years. They took 17 percent of the casualties in the period 1849–1861 while representing only 4 percent of the average troop strength.[26]

The U.S. Army in nineteenth-century Texas had its fair share of casualties when compared to the army-wide figures of the same period. From 1820 to 1861 thirty-five U.S. Army officers were killed in the Indian wars; 9 percent of these were in Texas, all in the last decade of the era. From 1866 to 1891 the U.S. Army suffered 137 officer casualties (sixty-nine killed, sixty-eight wounded) in Indian battles, 5 percent of these in Texas. In the same period the army had a total of 1,869 enlisted casualties (879 killed, 990 wounded), of which about 4 percent occurred among Texas troops. For the entire period 1789 to 1891 the best estimate of all army casualties in Indian battles is 2,125 killed and 2,156 wounded for a total casualty count of 4,281. Army casualties in Texas 1849–1881 account for 4 percent of this total.[27]

The battle dead-to-wounded ratio of army soldiers fighting Indians in Texas was 64:116 or a mortality rate of about 36 percent. This is better than the army-wide battle death rate of the period (47 percent) but worse than the rate in other conflicts such as the Civil War (33 percent), the Spanish-American War (18 percent), or the Vietnam War (23 percent).[28]

Indian casualty figures are more difficult to ascertain due to the irregular character of the conflict and the nature of the skirmishes. At best, army leaders' reports of the numbers of Indian casualties were estimates, as the Indians went to great lengths to recover their dead even in the midst of battle. The Indian casualty figures are taken at face value in reports where the army controlled the battlefield and had good evidence from blood trails or bodies. In reports where the situation seemed vague or confused the figures offered by the army report have been reduced by half. The body count apparently had little importance for the Indian-fighting army in Texas, for there is little emphasis on it in reports or in army correspondence.

Antebellum reports list 261 Indians killed, eighty-eight wounded, and fifty-three women and children captured. Post-Civil War reports list 163 Indians killed, twenty-four wounded, and 214 women and children taken as prisoners. The total Indian battle casualties from 1849 to 1881, according to army estimates, were 536 Indians (424 killed, 112 wounded). The antebellum era produced 65 percent of these casualties, indicating the deadly nature of Indian warfare in Texas during 1849–1861.

Although the Comanche and Lipan routinely killed enemy women and children and did not return soldier prisoners alive, only three army reports mention Indian women being killed in battle, and all three incidents appear to have been accidents. It is possible that the soldiers considered the death of an Indian noncombatant too insignificant to mention, and the officers were certainly aware that their reports became a matter of public record, but primary accounts from soldiers of the era indicate that it was not the policy of the regular army in Texas to kill women. In hasty attacks women were sometimes accidentally killed because, as a Tenth Cavalry officer from Fort Griffin explained, from a galloping horse Indian men and women "were scarcely distinguishable from each other, as all wore long hair and similar clothing." There are a few army documents from the early 1850s in which local commanders established a "no prisoners" policy, but by the post-Civil War era army leaders had discovered that capturing a band's women and children was a powerful leverage to force the warriors onto the reservations. Of course, keeping them there was another matter.[29]

Measuring Indian casualties against Indian population totals is very difficult. For example, in the antebellum era Indian Agent Robert S. Neighbors estimated there were twenty thousand Comanches in the *Comanchería*, while other estimates were as low as three thousand.[30]

Capt. William J. Hardee's Texas Indian census during an 1851 army expedition, in a period of relative peace, visited great assemblies of Indians on the Llano, San Saba, and Brazos Rivers. Hardee based his report on a careful head count and on intelligence from other Indians on the various bands that were not present. He reported 3,952 Indians, including 2,200 Comanche and 350 Lipan Apache. His census, he wrote, "I consider a tolerably accurate general knowledge of the number of Indians on the Texan frontier. This number has been greatly exaggerated: the general belief is, that there are ten thousand Comanche warriors on the frontier, while in fact, there are *not half as many hundred*" (original italics). Between the lines of this statement Hardee was telling the departmental commander and the secretary of war that he believed the Texans were inflating the Indian threat to gain army dollars.[31]

Hardee's smaller Indian population numbers make military sense in light of the two greatest Indian offensives in nineteenth-century Texas. When the wrath of the Comanche-Kiowa coalition came down on Texans in the Linnville Raid and Plum Creek Fight of August 1840, they put at least four hundred and possibly as many as one thousand warriors in the field. In the great alliance of the Buffalo War of 1874 the Comanche, Kiowa and Southern Cheyenne fielded about 1,200 warriors in the various battles. This is not a very effective marshaling of combat power if the Comanches alone had a large population base.

In 1877, three years after the Comanche military power was broken at Palo Duro Canyon and surrendered to the reservation, the agent census listed 1,545 Comanche (706 males) and 1,090 Kiowa (443 males) on the Kiowa and Comanche Agency in the Indian Territory. This head count may represent 8 percent of a once-powerful tribe of twenty thousand Comanche, or it may mean that about half of an original tribe of around three thousand survived the Indian wars of Texas.[32]

The U.S. Army in Texas, by its own estimate, killed about 424 Indians in battle while losing 64 of its own soldiers. Some modern historians, usually not scholars of the nineteenth-century military frontier, generalize about army genocide/extermination/annihilation of the Indians. If this was the mission of the army in Texas, the casualty figures indicate they did a poor job of it. It can been seen from the discussion of the engagements that a fundamental characteristic of army operations in Texas was that the army unit usually failed to follow up a small tactical victory with a complete battle of decision. The Indians would not stand still to be annihilated, which is what a strategy of annihilation means—risking all on a single decisive battle, like Napoleon.

Although not a nineteenth-century military term, the modern definition of a strategy of attrition more aptly describes U.S. Army frontier operations over three decades in Texas: a slow grinding down of Indian combat power, a willingness to trade man for man until ultimately the side with the greatest number of reserves wins. One could also apply to the situation the concept of a strategy of exhaustion, defined in modern terms as an orchestrated campaign against the resource base that keeps enemy military power in the field. Mackenzie and the Fourth Cavalry's campaigns against Comanche and Kiowa home villages is an example of this strategy, as is the deliberate destruction of the buffalo herds practically sponsored by the state governments of Texas and Kansas. Army combat operations and the destruction of buffalo are two of the five major factors that frontier scholars catalogue as erasing the power of the Plains Indian tribes. Additionally, diseases such as cholera depleted the Indian population base, and the inexorable tide of Western settlement gradually decreased the tribal territorial areas and options. Finally, the pace and intensity of all other factors exploded with the coming of the great railroad lines that eventually bisected the frontier.

In closing, it is useful to summarize the nature of Indian wars combat for army units on the Texas frontier and construct a typical model for the different periods. In the antebellum era the most active year was 1857. The army unit involved in an engagement was usually associated with a post, most likely Fort Inge, McIntosh, Clark, or Davis. The pursuit was the most common type of operation. A group of ten or fewer Comanche or Lipan Apache, probably without firearms, would raid the area; the soldiers would receive word of the raid, pick up the trail, and begin a chase. The army unit would be a mounted detachment of between sixteen and twenty-five soldiers led by a lieutenant or captain. If they caught up to the raiders the unit commander normally launched an immediate mounted hasty attack that turned the action into a confusing melee with little command and control. The army would usually be the victor in the tactical engagement, and after a few casualties the Indians would scatter in a multitude of directions. The army detachment would fail to pursue because of worn-down horses or the burden of wounded and dead comrades. If there was an army casualty the odds are it would be an officer. The patrol would be gone from the fort ten days or less and would probably have a fairly good level of logistical sustainment.

In the post-Civil War years the most active year was 1874. The army unit would be most likely not come directly from a fort, but be a detachment of fifty or so mounted soldiers, led by a lieutenant or captain, and assigned to a temporary camp at a water hole, river ford, or dangerous pass. The type of operation most typical for the era was a movement-to-contact or scout of an area in which the army unit would run into a Comanche or Lipan Apache band on the move, or would find a fresh trail and follow it. In this era the Indians would be more likely to have firearms and be a group of more than ten warriors. Upon sight of the Indians the detachment leader or company commander would order a mounted hasty attack, and the odds are he would win the engagement, but again, as before, fail to follow up the victory. After ten days or so the unit, at a good level of logistical sustainment, would return to its camp.

The combined statistics of the antebellum and post-Civil War eras yield a typical model of an engagement for an army unit assigned to Texas in the period 1849–1881. In the grassy months between April and November a mounted army detachment of less than company strength, led by a lieutenant or captain, would conduct a routine patrol or scout of an area, probably without a local guide or scout. The patrol would be out about ten days, covering several hundred miles, but would have enough coffee, beans, and hardtack biscuits along to avoid starvation. This would have been one of two dozen patrols they had made without glimpsing an Indian. The detachment would come upon a fresh Indian trail and follow and surprise the raiders, or unexpectedly meet a war party of twenty or fewer Comanche or Lipan Apache. The officer would order a mounted assault before the Indians could split into small groups and race for every point of the compass. In the wild charge that ensued the army unit would begin to fragment as small teams of soldiers chased small groups of Indians. The soldiers killed in these affairs often outraced the support of their comrades. After a while the officer would regain control of his unit but, because of the burden of recovered property, soldier casualties, or worn-out horses, he would elect not to follow up his tactical victory and pursue the Indians. He would then continue his patrol or return to his logistical base.

Although some of the statistics from this article might surprise the reader with an interest in nineteenth-century Texas frontier military operations, the final model of the "typical" Texas frontier army engagement probably will not. The final results is more or less what one would expect after a close reading of Texas military history. The model is unique primarily because it is constructed from the calculation of empirical evidence and historical analysis rather than cobbled haphazardly from a subjective assessment and general impression of the historical record. This analytical approach might prove useful for other Texas problems. For example, an interesting, and as yet unanswered, question of Texas military history is the exact nature of Texas Ranger operations on the frontier. This in turn could lead to a solid comparative analysis between the campaigns of state-controlled Ranger provincial force and regular army operations in order to test the old saw that in the frontier Indian wars the Rangers were a more effective military organization than the U.S. Army. Perhaps this legend is true; possibly it is myth.

NOTES

1. Thomas T. Smith, "Fort Inge and Texas Frontier Military Operations, 1849–1869," *Southwestern Historical Quarterly,* 96 (July, 1992), 1–25; Thomas T. Smith, "U.S. Army Combat Operations in the Indian Wars of Texas, 1849–1981," *Southwestern Historical Quarterly,* 99 (Apr., 1996), 500–531.

2. Francis B. Heitman, "Chronological list of battles, actions, etc., in which troops of the Regular Army have participated, and troops engaged," in *Historical Register and Dictionary of the United States Army . . .* (2 vols.; Washington, D.C., Government Printing Office, 1903), II, 400–446.

3. To list the sources for the details of each of the 219 U.S. Army-Indian skirmishes associated with Texas would require a footnote of many pages, but they include the following: letters and combat reports in *Report of the Secretary of War* for the years 1849–1881 as found in House of Representatives Executive Document 1 for each session of Congress; Returns From United States Military Posts, 1800–1916, Records of the United States Army Adjutant General's Office, 1780–1917, RG 94, Microfilm Publication M617 (National Archives; cited hereafter as NA); Records of United States Army Commands, 1784–1821, Letters Received, Department of Texas, RG 98 (NA), and Records of United States Army Continental Commands, 1821–1920, Department of Texas and the Eighth Military Department, Letters Received, 1866–1868, 1868–1870, Tabular Statements of Expeditions and Scouts 1869–1890, RG 393 (NA); General Orders No. 14, Headquarters, United States Army, Nov. 13, 1857, RG 94 (NA); General Orders No. 22, Headquarters, United States Army, Nov. 10, 1858, ibid.

See also: Capt. Robert G. Carter, *On the Border with Mackenzie; Or, Winning West Texas from the Comanches* (Washington, D.C.: Eynon, 1935), 349–372; Robert G. Carter, *The Old Sergeant's Story: Fighting Indians and Bad Men in Texas from 1870 to 1876* (1926; reprint, Mattituck, N.Y.: John M. Carroll, 1982), 72, 82–87, 97, 104–110; John Bell Hood, *Advance and Retreat: Personal Experiences in the United States and Confederate*

Armies (New Orleans: G.T. Beauregard, 1880), 11; Brig. Gen. Richard W. Johnson, *A Soldier's Reminiscences in Peace and War* (Philadelphia: J.B. Lippincott Co., 1886), 109–111, 125–126; Gen. Philip Henry Sheridan, *Personal Memoirs of P.H. Sheridan, General, United States Army* (2 vols.; New York: D. Appleton and Co., 1904), I, 22–23; Jesse Sumpter, *Paso del Águila: A Chronicle of Frontier Days on the Texas Border as Recorded in the Memoirs of Jesse Sumpter*, comp. Harry Warren, ed. Ben Pingenot (Austin: Encino Press, 1969), 18–20.

Other sources include: Lt. Col. William H. Carter, *From Yorktown to Santiago with the Sixth U.S. Cavalry* (1900; reprint, Austin: State House Press, 1989), 137–169, 277–278; Maj. Edward L. N. Glass, *The History of the Tenth Cavalry, 1866–1921* (1921; reprint, Fort Collins, Colo.: Old Army Press, 1972), 21–22, 96, 100; Joseph I. Lambert, *One Hundred Years with the Second Cavalry* (Fort Riley, Kan.: Capper Printing, 1939), 264–267; John H. Nankivell (ed.), *History of the Twenty-Fifth Regiment United States Infantry, 1869–1926* (1927; reprint, Fort Collins, Colo.: Old Army Press, 1972), 23–30; George Frederick Price, *Across the Continent with the Fifth Cavalry* (New York: Van Nostrand, 1883), 44–96, 650–651; Theo. F. Rodenbough, *From Everglade to Cañon with the Second Dragoons . . .* (New York: D. Van Nostrand, 1875), 165; Harold B. Simpson, *Cry Comanche: the 2nd U.S. Cavalry in Texas, 1848–1861* (Hillsboro, Tex.: Hill Junior College Press, 1979), 53–64, 83–93; Thomas Wilhelm, *History of the Eighth U.S. Infantry* (2 vols.; Headquarters, Eighth Infantry, 1873), II, 43, 48, 80–90.

See also: William Y. Chalfant, *Without Quarter: The Wichita Expedition and the Fight on Crooked Creek* (Norman: University of Oklahoma Press, 1991), 80–90; John M. Carroll (ed.), *The Black Military Experience in the American West* (New York: Liveright Publishing Corp., 1971), 71–72, 335–336, 390, 403–404; James L. Haley, *The Buffalo War: The History of the Red River Uprising of 1874* (1976; reprint, Norman: University of Oklahoma Press, 1985), 50–51, 127–137, 154–164, 192–197; Allen Lee Hamilton, *Sentinel of the Southern Plains: Fort Richardson and the Northwest Texas Frontier, 1866–1878* (Fort Worth: Texas Christian University Press, 1988), 23–24, 54–63, 83, 125–126; Herbert M. Hart, *Old Forts of the Southwest* (New York: Bonanza Books), 47; San Antonio *Herald*, May 9, 1857; William H. Leckie, *The Buffalo Soldiers: A Narrative History of the Negro Cavalry in the West* (Norman: University of Oklahoma Press, 1967), 150–151; Col. W. S. Nye, *Carbine and Lance: The Story of Old Fort Sill* (Norman: University of Oklahoma Press, 1937),152–153; Rupert Norval Richardson, *The Frontier of Northwest Texas, 1846 to 1876 . . .* (Glendale, Calif.: Arthur H. Clark Co., 1963), 190–193; Carl Coke Rister, *The Southwestern Frontier—1865–1881 . . .* (Cleveland: Arthur H. Clark Co., 1928), 114–121; Carl Coke Rister, *Fort Griffin on the Texas Frontier* (Norman: University of Oklahoma Press, 1956), 74–76; A.J. Sowell, *Early Settlers and Indian Fighters of Southwest Texas* (2 vols.; 1900; reprint, New York: Argosy-Antiquarian, 1964), II, 696–698; Robert M. Utley, *Frontier Regulars: The United States Army and the Indian, 1866–1891* (New York: Macmillan Publishing Co., 1973), 227.

Other sources include: Paul H. Carlson, *"Pecos Bill": A Military Biography of William R. Shafter* (College Station: Texas A&M University Press, 1989), 57–60, 81–84, 94, 101–102; James T. King, *War Eagle: A Life of General Eugene A. Carr* (Lincoln: University of Nebraska Press, 1963), 15–16; Ernest Wallace, *Ranald S. Mackenzie on the Texas Frontier* (1964; reprint, College Station: Texas A&M University Press, 1993), 34,

50–54, 64, 77–91, 98–104, 118–120, 136–146, 155–156, 197; Martin L. Crimmins (ed.), "Colonel Robert E. Lee's Report on Indian Combats in Texas," *Southwestern Historical Quarterly*, 39 (July, 1935), 21–32; Marvin E. Kroeker, "William B. Hazen," in *Soldiers West: Biographies from the Military Frontier*, ed. Paul Andrew Hutton (Lincoln: University of Nebraska Press, 1987), 193–212; Kenneth F. Neighbours, "Tonkaway Scouts and Guides," *West Texas Historical Association Yearbook*, 49 (1973), 90–112; Martin L. Crimmins, "Notes on the Establishment of Fort Elliott and the Buffalo Wallow Fight," *Panhandle-Plains Historical Review*, 25 (1952), 45.

4. Heitman, *Historical Register*, II, 400–446.

5. General Orders No. 49, War Department, Aug. 13, 1848; General Orders No. 58, War Department, Nov. 7 1848, RG 94 (NA).

6. National Archives Microfilm Publication M665, Returns From Regular Army Infantry Regiments, June 1821-Dec. 1916, Records of the United States Army Adjutant General's Office, 1780–1917, roll 3, Regimental Returns, First Infantry, Jan. 1844-Dec. 1848.

7. Smith to Secretary of War Conrad, Oct. 6, 1851, May 24, 1852; Smith to Division AAG Lt. Col. W. W. Bliss, Oct. 6, 21, Nov. 3, 1851, "Letter Book, Headquarters, Department of Texas, 1851–1854," Persifor F. Smith Papers (Historical Society of Pennsylvania, Philadelphia); Robert Wooster, "Military Strategy in the Southwest, 1848–1860," *Military History of Texas and the Southwest*, 15, no. 2 (1979), 5–15; Frank M. Temple, "Federal Military Defense of the Trans-Pecos Region, 1850–1880," *West Texas Historical Association Year Book*, 30 (Oct., 1954), 40–60.

8. H. Exec. Doc. 1, *Report of the Secretary of War*, 31st Cong., 1st Sess., 1849 (Serial 549), 34; H. Exec. Doc. 1, *Report of the Secretary of War*, 47th Cong., 1st Sess., 1881 (Serial 2010), pt. 2:128; Heitman, *Historical Register*, II, 446.

9. H. Exec. Doc. 1, *Report of the Secretary of War*, 46th Cong., 2nd Sess., 1879 (Serial 1903), pt. 2:114.

10. David B. Adams, "Embattled Borderland: Northern Nuevo León and the Indios Bárbaros, 1686–1870," *Southwestern Historical Quarterly*, 95 (Oct., 1991), 205–220.

11. On the army's failure to develop a tactical doctrine for the Indian wars see Utley, *Frontier Regulars*, 45–59, 147–167; William B. Skelton, *An American Profession of Arms: The Army Officer Corps, 1784–1861* (Lawrence: University Press of Kansas, 1992), 305, 326; Russell F. Weigley, *The American Way of War: A History of United States Military Strategy and Policy* (New York: Macmillan Publishing Co., 1973), 153–163; John M. Gates, "Indian's and Insurrectos: The U.S. Army's Experience with Insurgency," *Parameters: Journal of the U.S. Army War College*, 13 (Mar., 1983), 59–86; Perry D. Jamieson, *Crossing the Deadly Ground: United States Army Tactics, 1865–1899* (Tuscaloosa: University of Alabama Press, 1994), 36–53, 120–124; Thomas T. Smith, "West Point and the Indian Wars, 1802–1891," *Military History of the West*, 24 (Spring, 1994), 25–55.

12. General Orders No. 13, Feb. 14, 1849, Headquarters Eighth and Ninth Departments, Maj. Gen. William J. Worth, RG 94 (NA).

13. Average regimental assignments to Texas are from the annual departmental returns as reported by the adjutant general in the annual *Report of the Secretary of War* for the years 1849–1881.

14. Smith to Secretary of War Conrad, May 24, 1852, "Letter Book, Headquarters, Department of Texas, 1851–1854," Persifor F. Smith Papers.

15. W. W. Newcomb Jr., *The Indians of Texas, from Prehistoric to Modern Times* (Austin: University of Texas Press, 1961), 103–130; Ernest Wallace and E. Adamson Hoebel, *The Comanches: Lords of the South Plains* (Norman: University of Oklahoma Press, 1952), 33–17; T.R. Fehrenbach, *Comanche: The Destruction of A People* (New York: Alfred A. Knopf, 1974), 94–99, 133; William T. Hagan, *United States-Comanche Relations: The Reservation Years* (1976; reprint, Norman: University of Oklahoma Press, 1990), 8–26.

16. Lt. George H. Steuart to Miss Mary Steuart, August 16, 1854, Lieutenant George H. Steuart Correspondence, 1853–1855, Eberstadt Collection (Center for American History, University of Texas at Austin).

17. Dabney Herndon Maury, *Recollections of a Virginian in the Mexican, Indian and Civil Wars* (New York: Charles Scribner's Sons, 1894), 76.

18. H. Exec. Doc. 1, *Report of the Secretary of Interior*, 51st Cong., 2nd Sess., 1890 (Serial 2814), pt. 5:cxxxiv.

19. Heitman, *Historical Register*, II,435; Carter, *From Yorktown to Santiago with the Sixth U.S. Cavalry*, 141–146; Hamilton, *Sentinel of the Southern Plains*, 59.

20. For example, the Army Authorization Act of 1870 set the legal strength for a cavalry company at eighty-four enlisted men while an infantry company was authorized sixty. Due to desertion, sickness, death, extra duty, and other factors, by 1873 the actual strength of the average Fourth Cavalry company in Texas was only sixty-seven men while an average company of the Twenty-Fourth Infantry was only fifty-seven. H. Exec. Doc. 1, *Report of the Secretary of War*, 42nd Cong., 2nd Sess., 1871 (Serial 1503), pt. 2:1; H. Exec. Doc. 1, *Report of the Secretary of War*, 43rd Cong., 1st Sess., 1873 (Serial 1597), pt. 2:27, 37.

21. For an excellent study of the origins and early use of these provincial ranger companies in the colonial South see James M. Johnson, *Militiamen, Rangers, and Redcoats: The Military In Georgia, 1754–1776* (Macon, Ga.: Mercer University Press, 1992), 8–10.

22. Carter, *From Yorktown to Santiago with the Sixth U.S. Cavalry*, 169, 278; Haley, *The Buffalo War*, 192–193; Utley, *Frontier Regulars*, 233; Public Information Division, U.S. Army, *The Medal of Honor of the United States Army* (Washington, D.C.: Government Printing Office, 1948), 206–238.

23. H. Exec. Doc. 1, *Report of the Secretary of War*, 47th Cong., 1st Sess., 1881 (Serial 2010), pt. 2:128.

24. Public Information Division, U.S. Army, *The Medal of Honor*, 216; Wallace, *Ranald S. Mackenzie on the Texas Frontier*, 50–51.

25. For an interesting analysis of the logistical restrictions on frontier operations see Robert M. Utley, "A Chained Dog: The Indian-Fighting Army," *The American West* , 10 (July, 1973), 18–24, 61. For a good study of army use of pack mules see John Morgan Gates, "General George Crook's First Apache Campaign: (The Use of Mobile, Self-Contained Units Against the Apache in the Military Department of Arizona, 1871–1873)," *Journal of the West* , 6 (Apr., 1967), 310–320.

26. I calculated average troop strengths for Texas in the period 1849–1881 using the annual departmental returns as reported by the by the adjutant general in the annual *Report of the Secretary of War* for the years 1849–1881.

27. Army-wide casualty figures are from Skelton, *An American Profession of Arms*, 60, 409 n.86; Heitman, *Historical Register*, II, 13–42; Utley, *Frontier Regulars*, 423 n.19; Don Russell, "How Many Indians Were Killed? White Man versus Red Man: The Facts and the Legend," *The American West*, 10 (July, 1973), 42–47, 61–63.

28. Army-wide casualty statistics are from Utley, *Frontier Regulars*, 423 n.19. Battle casualty statistics from the other wars are from "Service and Casualties in Major Wars and Conflicts," *Defense 89: Department of Defense* (Sept.-Oct., 1989), 47.

29. Richard Henry Pratt, *Battlefield and Classroom: Four Decades with the American Indian, 1867–1904*, ed. Robert M. Utley (New Haven: Yale University Press, 1964), 58 (quotation). On the "no prisoners" policy see Rodenbough, *From Everglade to Cañon with the Second Dragoons*, 165–166.

30. For a discussion of Comanche population estimates see Wallace and Hoebel, *The Comanches,* 31–32; Fehrenbach, *Comanche*, 383. Hagan estimates there were about three thousand Comanche. Hagan, *United States-Comanche Relations*, 8.

31. "Hardee to Deas, Aug. 29, 1851," H. Exec. Doc. 2, *Report of the Secretary of War*, 32nd Cong., 1st Sess., 1851 (Serial 634), 122–123 (emphasis in original).

32. Kiowa and Comanche Agency census figures are from H. Exec. Doc. 1, *Report of the Commissioner of Indian Affairs*, 45th Cong., 2nd Sess., 1877 (Serial 1800), pt. 5:688. Robert M. Utley writes that in the period 1866–1891 army reports for all engagements by the army in North America show 4,371 Indians killed and 1,279 wounded. If true, the 187 reported Indian casualties from Texas troops in the post-Civil War era would be about 3 percent of the total of 5,650. Don Russell's research puts total Indians killed at 4,957 from 1850 to 1891. If this is true the 424 Indian dead from Texas battles for the period 1849–1881 would be about 9 percent of the total. Utley, *Frontier Regulars*, 423 n.19; Russell, "How Many Indians Were Killed?," 47.

Earning renown for his 1863 Civil War cavalry raid through Mississippi, for a quarter of a century Brig. Gen. Benjamin Henry Grierson was the regimental commander of the Buffalo Soldiers of the Tenth Cavalry. Grierson came to the Texas frontier in 1875 and served with distinction for a decade as commander of Forts Concho and Davis. *Photograph courtesy Lawrence T. Jones III, Austin.*

COMMANDERS AND ORGANIZATION, DEPARTMENT OF TEXAS, 1848–1900*

Military Department No. 8 (Texas) created August 31, 1848

Headquarters, Galveston, November 1, 1848

Bvt. Maj. Gen. David E. Twiggs, November 1, 1848

Headquarters, San Antonio, December 26, 1848

Bvt. Maj. Gen. William J. Worth, Colonel, Eighth Infantry, December 26, 1848

Bvt. Brig. Gen. William S. Harney, Colonel, Second Dragoons, May 14, 1849, assumed command upon Worth's death

Bvt. Maj. Gen. George M. Brooke, Colonel, Fifth Infantry, assigned May 26, 1849, assumed command July 7, 1849

Bvt. Maj. Gen. Persifor F. Smith, Colonel, Mounted Rifles, assigned February 22, 1851, assumed command September 16, 1851

Headquarters, Corpus Christi, November 11, 1852

Bvt. Brig. Gen. William S. Harney, Colonel, Second Dragoons, December 3, 1852, temporary command

Bvt. Maj. Gen. Persifor F. Smith, Colonel, Mounted Rifles, May 11, 1853, returned to command

Name changed to Department of Texas October 31, 1853

Headquarters, San Antonio, October 1, 1855

Col. Albert S. Johnston, Second Cavalry, April 1, 1856

Bvt. Maj. Gen. David E. Twiggs, assigned March 18, 1857, assumed command May 18, 1857

Col. Henry Wilson, Seventh Infantry, March 24, 1858, temporary command

Bvt. Maj. Gen. David E. Twiggs, June 1, 1858

Lt. Col. Washington Seawell, Eighth Infantry, December 7, 1859

Bvt. Col. Robert E. Lee, Lieutenant Colonel, Second Cavalry, assigned February 6, 1860, assumed command February 20, 1860

Bvt. Maj. Gen. David E. Twiggs, assigned November 7, 1860, assumed command November 27, 1860

Col. Carlos A. Waite, Fifth Infantry, assigned January 28, 1861, assumed command February 19, 1861

Department of Texas abandoned April 22, 1861

Merged with Western Department, July 3, 1861

Maj. Gen. John C. Frémont, July 25, 1861

Headquarters, St. Louis, Missouri, July 25, 1861

Maj. Gen. David Hunter, U.S. Volunteers, November 2, 1861

Merged with Department of the Gulf, February 23, 1862

Maj. Gen. Benjamin F. Butler, U.S. Volunteers, March 20, 1862

Headquarters, New Orleans, May 1, 1862

Maj. Gen. Nathaniel P. Banks, U.S. Volunteers, December 17, 1862

Merged with Division of West Mississippi, May 7, 1864

Maj. Gen. Stephen A. Hurlbut, U.S. Volunteers, September 23, 1864

Department of the Gulf, re-established, February 10, 1865

Maj. Gen. Nathaniel P. Banks, U.S. Volunteers, March 18, 1865

Merged with Division of the Southwest, May 17, 1865

Headquarters, New Orleans, May 29, 1865

Maj. Gen. Philip H. Sheridan, May 29, 1865

(District of Texas)

Bvt. Maj. Gen. Gordon Granger, June 13, 1865

Department of Texas re-established, June 27, 1865

Maj. Gen. Horatio G. Wright, U.S. Volunteers, assigned June 27, 1865, assumed command August 6, 1865

Headquarters, Galveston, August 6, 1865

Merged into Department of the Gulf (Florida, Texas, Louisiana), August 1866

Headquarters, New Orleans, August 6, 1865

Maj. Gen. Philip H. Sheridan, as of August 6, 1865

(District of Texas)

Maj. Gen. Horatio G. Wright, U.S. Volunteers, August 21, 1865

Bvt. Maj. Gen. George W. Getty, September 24, 1866

Bvt. Maj. Gen. Samuel P. Heintzelman, October 24, 1866

Bvt. Maj. Gen. Charles Griffin, November 28, 1866

Merged into Fifth Military District (Louisiana, Texas), March 11, 1867

Maj. Gen. Philip H. Sheridan, March 11, 1867

(District of Texas)

Bvt. Maj. Gen. Charles Griffin, March 11, 1867, appointed Colonel, Thirty-fifth Infantry, September 6, 1867

Bvt. Maj. Gen. Joseph A. Mower, Colonel, Thirty-ninth Infantry, September 16, 1867

Bvt. Maj. Gen. Joseph J. Reynolds, September 16, 1867

Maj. Gen. Winfield S. Hancock, November 29, 1867

Bvt. Maj. Gen. Joseph J. Reynolds, Colonel, Twenty-sixth Infantry, March 18, 1868

Bvt. Maj. Gen. Robert C. Buchanan, Colonel, First Infantry, March 25, 1868

Fifth Military District (Texas), July 28, 1868

Headquarters, Austin, August 10, 1868

Bvt. Maj. Gen. Joseph J. Reynolds, Colonel, Twenty-sixth Infantry, August 10, 1868

Bvt. Maj. Gen. Edward R. S. Canby, December 22, 1868

Bvt. Maj. Gen. Joseph J. Reynolds, Colonel, Twenty-sixth Infantry, April 8, 1869

Department of Texas, March 31, 1870

Headquarters, Austin, April 16, 1870

Bvt. Maj. Gen. Joseph J. Reynolds, Colonel, Third Cavalry, April 16, 1870

Headquarters, San Antonio, November 1, 1870

Brig. Gen. Christopher C. Auger, assigned November 1, 1871, assumed command January 29, 1872

Brig. Gen. Edward O. C. Ord, assigned March 11, 1875, assumed command April 11, 1875

Col. David S. Stanley, Twenty-second Infantry, December 9, 1880

Brig. Gen. Christopher C. Auger, January 3, 1881

Col. Benjamin H. Grierson, Tenth Cavalry, September 22, 1883

Brig. Gen. Christopher C. Auger, October 26, 1883

Brig. Gen. Ranald S. Mackenzie, November 1, 1883

Maj. Gen. John M. Schofield, December 19, 1883

Brig. Gen. David S. Stanley, May 8, 1884

Brig. Gen. Frank Wheaton, May 4, 1892

Brig. Gen. Zenas R. Bliss, assigned April 30, 1895, assumed command May 18, 1895

Brig. Gen. William M. Graham, June 17, 1897

Merged With Department of the Gulf, March 11, 1898 (all southern states)

Headquarters, Atlanta, March 11, 1898

Brig. Gen. A. C. M. Pennington, U.S. Volunteers, March 11, 1898

(District of Texas)

Brig. Gen. William M. Graham, March 12, 1898

Department of Texas re-established, June 6, 1899

Headquarters, San Antonio, June 24, 1899

Col. Chambers McKibbin, Twelfth Infantry, June 24, 1899, through 1900

---

*"Report of the Adjutant General of the Army," in the annual *Report of the Secretary of War*, 1848-1900; Raphael P. Thian, *Notes Illustrating the Military Geography of the United States, 1813–1880* (Washington, D.C.: Government Printing Office, 1881).

Headquarters building, Fort Brown. Originally named Fort Texas during the Mexican War when the Seventh Infantry constructed its earthworks in March 1846, Fort Brown was the longest continually serving nineteenth-century post in Texas. The fort ended a hundred years of army service at the close of World War II. *Photograph courtesy Lawrence T. Jones III, Austin.*

PART III

U.S. ARMY SITES IN TEXAS, 1836–1900*

Alamo. 1846–1847, 1849–1861, 1865–1877. The Spanish mission San Antonio de Valero, at its third or 1724 site, was leased by the departmental quartermaster at San Antonio for $150 a month from 1850 to 1856 and used for storage. After the Civil War the Army again leased the Alamo as a storehouse until the San Antonio Depot was completed in 1877.

Camp Las Animas. 1854. A temporary site ten miles west of present Agua Nueva in Jim Hogg County, recorded as being established on a rancho fifty-four miles north and west of Fort Brown from May 20 to September 30, 1854, by Lt. Julius P. Garesché and Company K, Fourth Artillery.

Artesian Well (Pope's Camp, Pope's Well). 1855–1858. Two of a series of wells attempted to add water points to the Llano Estacado by Capt. John Pope, Corps of Topographical Engineers, during the period 1855–1858. Two were attempted near the Loving County, Texas–New Mexico border, thirty miles below the junction of Delaware Creek and the Pecos River, one in 1855 and one in 1857–1858. Neither well was successful.

Austin (Austin Arsenal, Camp Austin, Camp Maxwell, Post of Austin, Camp Sanders; see Camp Maxwell, Camp Sanders). 1845–1846, 1848–1852, 1865–1875. At a site on the east bank of the Colorado River on the west edge of Austin the post was first occupied by Bvt. Maj.

Benjamin L. Beall and Company I, Second Dragoons, from October 10, 1845, to June 1846 during the Mexican War. Reoccupied November 20, 1848, by Capt. John H. King and Companies F and I, First Infantry, Austin served as a supply depot in the antebellum and post-Civil War eras and was the headquarters for the District of Texas and Department of Texas from August 10, 1868, to November 1, 1870. It was abandoned by two companies of Tenth Infantry in November 1875.

Camp Bailey. 1875. The temporary San Antonio camp of two companies of the Tenth Infantry (the site of present Fort Sam Houston), when the companies arrived from Austin in November 1875.

Camp Bainbridge (see Fort Terrett).

Camp Barranca. 1860–1861. A camp established on the Rio Grande between Edinburg and Fort Brown by Capt. George Stoneman and Company E, Second Cavalry, and abandoned March 20, 1861.

Barrel Springs. 1868. A mail station twenty-two miles northwest of Fort Davis protected by a guard force from the post from 1868 through the 1870s.

Camp Belknap. 1846. The first camp of this name was a temporary Mexican War camp for volunteer forces, occupied August to September 1846, five miles above the mouth of the Rio Grande on the Texas side.

Fort Belknap (Camp Belknap). 1851–1859, 1867. Established June 24, 1851, by Capt. Carter L. Stevenson and one company of Fifth Artillery on the north bank of the Salt Fork of the Brazos River in present Young County. The site was named November 1, 1851, for Col. William G. Belknap, Fifth Infantry, and briefly reoccupied and abandoned in September 1867.

Camp Bexar (see also San Antonio). 1845–1846. Established on October 20, 1845, six miles south of the town, Camp Bexar was the first U.S. Army camp at San Antonio, commanded by Maj. T. T. Fauntleroy with

Companies A and G, Second Dragoons. The camp was active until October 1846.

Camp Blake. 1854. Field camp of Lt. Samuel H. Reynolds and Company K, First Infantry, on the upper Devils River, April 2 to September 30, 1854.

Camp Blanco. 1849. Temporary field camp apparently on the Blanco River of Capt. Washington I. Newton and Company G, Second Dragoons in the period July–August 1849.

Fort Bliss (Post Opposite El Paso, Camp Concordia; see Camp Concordia). 1846, 1847, 1849–1851, 1853–1861, 1862 to present. At this upper Rio Grande site of army expeditions in 1846 and 1847, Capt. Jefferson Van Horne, with the headquarters and Companies A, B, C, and E, Third Infantry, established a post at the rancho of Benjamin F. Coons on September 14, 1849. Abandoned in 1851, the Eighth Infantry re-established Post at El Paso in December 1853 at nearby Magoffinsville. Named Fort Bliss on March 8, 1854, in honor of Bvt. Lt. Col. William W. S. Bliss, President Zachary Taylor's son-in-law and Mexican War adjutant, who died August 5, 1853, the post was occupied by Union volunteer forces during the Civil War. Floodwaters forced the relocation of the post and the army leased Concordia Rancho, which the Thirty-fifth Infantry occupied in March 1868. After moving the post to downtown rented buildings called "Garrison Town," in 1878–1880, the army moved back to the banks of the Rio Grande near Hart's Mill in 1880. The sixth and present site of the post was established in October 1893 by the Eighteenth Infantry, on city-donated land on La Noria Mesa, four miles north of the Rio Grande.

Camp Boveda. 1863. Temporary headquarters of XIII Corps during the Civil War on Los Olmos Creek, twenty miles south of present Kingsville.

Camp at Brazos Agency. 1859. During the Brazos Indian Agency troubles of March–May 1859, an infantry company occupied the agency headquarters, three miles east of present Graham in Young County, to protect the agent and the Indians from a group of local citizens. The camp was initially occupied in May 1859 by Capt. John H. King and Company I, First Infantry. The Indians were removed to the Indian Territory in 1859.

Brazos Santiago. 1846–1861, 1863–1865, 1866–1874. Established as a supply depot for Brig. Gen. Zachary Taylor's Army of Occupation on the eastern end of Brazos Island, across the Laguna Madre from Point Isabel, the post was the most important logistics site of the Mexican War. It was first occupied in March 1846; a formal post was established in June 1846 and commanded by Capt. Giles Porter with Company A, First Artillery. A hurricane on October 7–8, 1867, destroyed many of the government buildings and a subsequent storm, on September 3–5, 1874, ended its use by the Quartermaster Department.

Fort Brown (Fort Texas, Fort Taylor, Brownsville Barracks). 1846–1861, 1863–1864, 1865–1906, 1913–1946. Established at present Brownsville by Brig. Gen. Zachary Taylor and his Army of Occupation in the Mexican War, this long-serving fort was a key post in controlling the Rio Grande. Called Fort Texas when first occupied by the Seventh Infantry on March 27, 1846, the name was changed to honor Maj. Jacob Brown, Seventh Infantry, who died of wounds while in command of the post during the Mexican War siege on May 9, 1846. The original fort was a six-bastioned earthen field work with a ditch, one of the few formal defensive works the army built in Texas. After a legal dispute that lasted three decades, the government finally purchased the site from the heirs of Maria Josefa Cavazos in April 1895. The post was deactivated in 1945.

Brownsville National Military Cemetery. Established in February 1868 by the Cemeterial Branch of the Quartermaster's Department on twenty-five acres of Fort Brown. Martin Schmidt became the first civilian superintendent in February 1872 when the cemetery held 2,687 graves of Union dead from White Ranch, Brazos Santiago, Redmond's Ranch, Ringgold Barracks, Victoria, Roma, and Corpus Christi, of which 1,409 were unknown.

Camp Buchanan. 1855. A camp of Capt. Andrew J. Linsay and Company H, Mounted Rifles, near San Antonio in November 1855.

Post at Buffalo Springs (Camp Tucker). 1867–1868. Established in present Clay County on April 18, 1867, by Capt. Benjamin T. Hutchins and Companies A and E, Sixth Cavalry, the camp was originally named for Capt. Henry Tucker, Sixth Cavalry, who died October 20, 1866. The post was abandoned November 20, 1867.

Camp Buffalo Springs. 1849. A temporary camp in August 1849 of Capt. James B. Bomford and Companies F and H, Eighth Infantry, on the banks of the Trinity River, two hundred miles north of Austin.

Camp Bugle (see Camp Drum).

Camp Burbank. 1854–1855. An expedition camp of December 1854 to April 1855 on Limpia Creek, above Fort Davis, for Maj. John S. Simpson and Companies C, G, and A, Mounted Rifles; Company F, Eighth Infantry; and 246 Texas Mounted Volunteers. It was named for Lt. John G. Burbank, Eighth Infantry, who died September 10, 1847, of wounds received at Molino del Rey.

Camp Burwell. 1855. A temporary camp of Capt. Daniel Ruggles and Companies D, F, and H, Fifth Infantry, at Eagle Pass established November 29, 1855. Probably named for Lt. William T. Burwell, Fifth Infantry, killed at Molino del Rey on September 8, 1847.

Camp Cabell. 1898. A Spanish-American War camp at Dallas of the Second Texas Volunteer Infantry Regiment, which was named in honor of CSA Brig. Gen. William L. Cabell, four-time mayor of Dallas.

Camp California Springs (see Camp Hudson).

Camp Capron. 1900. The temporary San Antonio camp of the Thirty-third U.S. Volunteer Infantry Regiment as it prepared to embark for the Philippine Islands. Named for Allyn K. Capron, the popular regular army officer and First U.S. Volunteer "Rough Rider" Cavalry company commander, who was killed at the Battle of Las Guásimas, Cuba, on June 24, 1898.

Camp Casa Blanca (Camp Merrill). 1850. A temporary field camp on what was then called Casa Blanca Creek, in present Jim Wells County, near the Nueces River crossing of the Corpus Christi-San Antonio road, twenty-five miles northwest of Corpus Christi. Near the site of the old Spanish fort of Lipantitlán, the camp was first established in February 1850 by Capt. Samuel M. Plummer with Companies H and K, First Infantry. The Army and the Texas Rangers used the camp intermittently as a sub-post of Fort Merrill.

Camp Cass (see Camp at Eagle Spring).

Castroville Military Station. 1849. Temporary camp on the Medina River at the town of Castroville for Company A, Eighth Infantry, in 1849.

Camp Cazneau. 1850. Temporary First Infantry camp on Onion Creek near Austin, established in March 1850.

Camp on the Chacon. 1854. Established on Chacon Creek, twenty-six miles east of Fort Duncan, on May 20, 1854, by Capt. William E. Prince and Companies D and E, First Infantry. The camp was abandoned in late July.

Centralia Station. 1868–1884. A mail station halfway between the Pecos and Concho Rivers in Reagan County that was often occupied by army detachments to protect the El Paso mail.

Camp Los Ceritos. 1855. Established forty miles northwest of Laredo on May 13, 1855, by Company H, Fifth Infantry, this camp was abandoned June 15, 1855.

Camp Chadbourne. 1849. A temporary camp established in May 1849 near Fredericksburg by Companies D, H, I, and K, Eighth Infantry, and named for Lt. Theodore L. Chadbourne, Eighth Infantry, who was killed in the Battle of Resaca de la Palma in 1846.

Fort Chadbourne. 1852–1861, 1867–1868. Established on Oak Creek, a tributary of the Colorado River in Coke County, on October 28, 1852, by Capt. John Beardsley and Companies A and K, Eighth Infantry. Named for Lt. Theodore L. Chadbourne, Eighth Infantry, who was killed in the Battle of Resaca de la Palma. The Texas chief quartermaster leased the post from Samuel A. Maverick on September 20, 1856, on a twenty-year contract for $25 per month.

Camp Charlotte. 1868–1869, 1874–1889. A stockaded outpost at the junction of Kiowa Creek and the Middle Concho River, in current Irion County, fifty-five miles west of its parent post Fort Concho. The camp was established to help protect the Trans-Pecos mail route.

Camp Cibolo Creek. 1850. Temporary camp near San Antonio of Company B, Eighth Infantry.

Fort Clark (Fort Riley). 1852–1861, 1866–1946. Originally called Fort Riley when established on Las Moras Creek, at present Brackettville, on June 20, 1852, by Maj. Joseph H. La Motte and Companies C and E, First Infantry. The post was named on July 16, 1852, for Maj. John B. Clark, First Infantry, who died in 1847 during the Mexican War. The land was leased on a twenty-year contract for $50 per month from Samuel A. Maverick on July 30, 1852; the government purchased the post from Mary A. Maverick on December 11, 1883.

Post on the Clear Fork of the Brazos (see Fort Phantom Hill).

Camp Colorado. 1856–1861, 1869. First established six miles north of the Colorado River on Mulewater Creek in Coleman County, on August 2, 1856, by Capt. Earl Van Dorn and Companies A and F, Second Cavalry. In 1857 the post moved twenty three miles north to Jim Ned Creek, ten miles northwest of present Coleman.

Camp Conception. 1846. Temporary two-company Second Dragoon camp in the period March-October 1846, probably near present Kingsville.

Camp Concho. 1858. A temporary scouting camp and sub-post of Fort Chadbourne, established on the south bank of the North Concho River, just above the junction of Vineyards Creek, now Grape Creek, ten miles northwest of San Angelo in Tom Green County

Fort Concho (Camp Hatch, Camp Kelly). 1867–1889. The post was established December 4, 1867, at the junction of the Main and North Concho River in present San Angelo by Capt. George G. Huntt and Companies M and H, Fourth Cavalry. First named for Maj. John P. Hatch, Fourth Cavalry, the name changed to honor Capt. Michael J. Kelly, Fourth Cavalry, who died August 13, 1867, and the name changed again on February 6, 1868. The site was leased from the Adams & Wickes freighting company for $200 per month and the post was abandoned on June 20, 1889.

Camp Concordia (see also Fort Bliss). 1868–1877. An 1867 Rio Grande flood at El Paso forced the two companies of Thirty-fifth Infantry at Fort Bliss to move the post and lease nearby Concordia Rancho, which they occupied in March 1868. On March 11, 1869, the camp was renamed Fort Bliss, which remained active until January 1877, when the post was temporarily abolished.

Conner's Station. 1848–1849. A camp on Richland Creek, in present Navarro County west of Corsicana, established by Capt. Henry H. Sibley and Company I, Second Dragoons, and active from December 1848 to March 1849.

Camp Conquista. 1856. Temporary camp in Karnes County south of San Antonio at the Conquista Creek junction of the San Antonio River; it was established by Capt. John G. Walker and one company of Mounted Rifles.

Camp Cooper. 1856–1861. A site established by Companies A, E, F, and K, Second Cavalry, on the Clear Fork of the Brazos on the Comanche Indian Reservation in current Throckmorton County, twenty miles north of Albany. Some army records indicate that Maj. William J. Hardee founded the post on January 2, 1856, others attest that Col. Albert S. Johnston officially established the post the following day. It was named for the Adjutant General of the Army, Col. Samuel Cooper, who had helped select the officers for the newly formed Second Cavalry Regiment. The post was abandoned on February 21, 1861.

Camp Corpus Christi (Fort Marcy). 1845–1846, 1849–1856, 1862, 1865–1866, 1869. The first Mexican War camp in Texas was established on the beach at Corpus Christi on August 15, 1845, by Brig. Gen. Zachary Taylor's Army of Occupation. Taylor's troops built a series of gun platforms, sometimes dubbed Fort Marcy, after Secretary of War William L. Marcy, as well as a supply depot. Corpus Christi became a supply depot in 1850, and was the departmental headquarters from November 11, 1852, to October 1, 1855.

Post at Corsicana. 1870. The county courthouse in the town of Corsicana was briefly occupied in May 1870 by Capt. A. R. Chafee and Company I, Sixth Cavalry.

Camp Crawford. (see Fort McIntosh).

Fort Crockett (see also Camp Hawley). 1897–1900, 1911, 1917–1953. Established on the eastern end of Galveston Island on the site of a former Confederate battery, construction began for this coastal fortification in 1898, and was first occupied by a detachment from Battery G, First Artillery. The Confederates had named the battery for Davy Crockett and the U.S. Army retained the name.

Fort Croghan (Post on Hamilton Creek, Camp Croghan, Camp Hamilton). 1849–1853. A post established above McCulloch's Station on Hamilton Creek, a tributary of the Colorado River three miles south of present Burnet, in Burnet County on March 18, 1849, by Bvt. 2d Lt. Charles H. Tyler and Company A, Second Dragoons. First named for the creek, the site moved to present Burnet and became Camp Croghan after the Inspector General of the Army, Col. George Croghan, a national hero in the War of 1812, who died of cholera in January 1849. The army leased the site on March 22, 1852, from Peter Kerr on a ten-year contract for $60 per month.

Camp Davant. 1856. A temporary camp near Bandera Pass in Bandera County established by Lt. John H. Edson and one company of Mounted Rifles in the summer of 1856. The site was named for 2d Lt. William M. Davant, Mounted Rifles, who drowned in the Rio Grande on October 1, 1855.

Fort Davis (Painted Comanche Camp). 1854–1861, 1867–1891. Established on October 7, 1854, at a pictograph site called Painted Comanche Camp near Limpia Creek in the Davis Mountains by Lt. Col. Washington Seawell with the headquarters and Companies A, C, D, F, G, and H, Eighth Infantry. Named for Secretary of War Jefferson Davis, the post was leased from John James on October 16, 1856, on a twenty-year contract for $25 per month. The government renewed the lease for $75 per month in 1867, purchased part of the post in 1883, and abandoned the fort on July 3, 1891.

Post at Davis' Landing (see Fort Ringgold).

Camp Del Rio (Camp San Felipe). 1876–1896, 1913–1921. At the site of a well-used antebellum military campsite in present Val Verde County, the post was established on San Felipe Creek, a tributary of the Rio Grande, on September 6, 1876, by Capt. J. M. Kelly and Company E, Tenth Cavalry. Leased on a twenty-year contract in 1869 for $19 per month from John Twohig, part of the site, named Camp Del Rio in March 1881, was deeded to the federal government from the state of Texas in 1882.

Camp Detention (see Fort Terrett).

Camp Dolores. 1854. Temporary camp occupied by Companies C, D, and G, Eighth Infantry. Probably located in Webb County at the mouth of Dolores Creek, eighteen miles south of Laredo.

Camp Drum (Camp Bugle). 1851–1852. Camp Drum was a temporary field camp on the Rio Grande, fifty miles south of Laredo, established December 13, 1851, by Company K, Fourth Artillery, near the village of Carrizo, a few miles from present Zapata in Zapata County. At the same time the Second Dragoons established a camp at the site called Camp Bugle.

Fort Duncan (Rio Grande Station, Camp Eagle Pass). 1849–1861, 1868–1883, 1886, 1893–1927. This post on the Rio Grande near Paso del Águila, or Eagle Pass, in Maverick County, was established by Capt. Sidney Burbank and Companies A, B, and F, First Infantry, on March 27, 1849. The post was named for Col. James Duncan, the Fourth Artillery Mexican War hero who died on July 3, 1849. Leased on a seventeen-year contract for $130 per month from John Twohig on June 5, 1860, the army continued to lease from Twohig for $75 per month after the Civil War, and purchased the site on March 31, 1894.

Camp Eagle Pass (see Fort Duncan).

Camp at Eagle Spring (Camp Cass). 1854. Temporary camp ninety miles below El Paso on the north side of the Eagle Mountains, at the last water hole on the military road before entering Quitman Canyon from the south, eighteen miles southeast of present Sierra Blanca. Established as Camp Cass by Companies B and E, Eighth Infantry, in 1854, and occupied by Maj. Charles F. Ruff and a company of Mounted Rifles in 1855, the site, sometimes called Ojos del Águila, was used throughout the nineteenth century. In the late 1870s Eagle Spring was routinely occupied by detachments of the Tenth Cavalry as a sub-post of Fort Davis.

Camp at Edinburg. 1853, 1860, 1866. A temporary camp established at present day Hidalgo in Hidalgo County, from May 20 to August 26, 1853, by Lt. George W. Howland and Company C, Mounted Rifles, and in April 1860 by Companies I and H, Second Cavalry. The site was briefly occupied after the Civil War.

Camp Elizabeth. 1874–1886. Serving as a sub-post of Fort Concho, the site was established at an old Texas Ranger camp on the North Concho River, apparently near old Camp Concho, forty-nine miles northwest of San Angelo in present Sterling County near Sterling City.

Fort Elliott (Cantonment North Fork of the Red River, Cantonment on the Sweetwater). 1875–1890. The site was established first on the North Fork of the Red River on February 3, 1875, as an advance supply point under Maj. James Biddle and Companies B, C, E, and K, Sixth Cavalry, and Companies C, D, E, and I, Fifth Infantry. The post was then moved eleven miles north to Sweetwater Creek in present Wheeler County, a few miles southeast of Mobeetie, and reestablished June 5, 1875, by Maj. Henry C. Bankhead and Companies B and E, Fourth Cavalry, and Companies E and H, Nineteenth Infantry. Named on February 21, 1876, for Maj. Joel H. Elliott, Seventh Cavalry, who died after Custer's attack on Black Kettle's camp on the Washita River in November 1868, the fort was leased from the state of Texas and the Houston and Great Northern Railroad Company for a dollar a year and abandoned on October 20, 1890.

Fort Ewell. 1852–1854. A post established on the San Antonio-Laredo Road crossing on the south bank of the Nueces River in present La Salle County, ten miles west of Cotulla, on May 18, 1852, by Lt. Col. William Wing Loring and three companies of Mounted Rifles. The fort was named for Lt. Thomas Ewell, Mounted Rifles, who was killed at Cerro Gordo on April 18, 1847, and the post was abandoned in October 1854.

Camp at Faver's Ranch. 1880. Temporary scouting camp in the Chinati Mountains near the Big Bend established September 19, 1880, by Lt. Col. William R. Shafter with Companies G and H, First Infantry, and a detachment of Seminole-Negro scouts.

Camp Florilla. 1848–1849. A camp on the Medina River, west of San Antonio, established by Capt. George A. H. Blake and Company A, Second Dragoons. It was active from December 1848 to April 1849 and was probably named for Florilla Tyler, the popular French wife of Lt. Charles H. Tyler of Company C, Second Dragoons.

Camp Ford. 1863–1865. A camp occupied by six thousand U.S. Army prisoners of war established in 1863 by the Confederate government near Tyler.

Galveston National Military Cemetery. Established in 1867 by the Cemeterial Branch of the Quartermaster's Department on two and a half acres between Broadway and Avenue K, the cemetery contained 321 Union graves from Galveston, Port Lavaca, Green Lake, and Victoria when the site was removed from the federal system after a title dispute in 1869.

Post of Galveston (see also Fort Crockett, Camp Hawley, Fort Nelson, Fort Point, Fort San Jacinto, Fort Travis). 1846, 1862, 1863, 1865–1870. Galveston was intermittently occupied as an arsenal depot during the Mexican War; by Companies D, G, and I, Forty-second Massachusetts Infantry, on December 25, 1862; and by the 114th Ohio Infantry on June 5, 1865.

Camp Gardenier. 1854. Located on the West Prong of the Nueces River, forty miles northwest of Fort Clark on a military trail to Fort Terrett in present Edwards County, this camp was occupied from May 19 to July 31, 1854, by Capt. Joseph B. Plummer and Company C, First Infantry, and briefly reoccupied in July 1856 by the same company commanded by Lt. Seth M. Barton. It was named for Capt. John R. B. Gardenier, First Infantry, who died June 26, 1850.

Fort Gates (Post on the Leon). 1849–1852. A post established on the north bank of the Leon River in Coryell County on October 26, 1849, by Capt. William R. Montgomery with Companies D and I, Eighth

Infantry. Named for Capt. Collinson R. Gates, Eighth Infantry, who died June 28, 1849, the fort was abandoned in March 1852.

Fort Graham (Camp Thornton). 1849–1853. The post was first established at Towash Village by Capt. Ripley A. Arnold and Companies F and I, Second Dragoons, on March 27, 1849, and named for Capt. Seth Thornton, Second Dragoons, who commanded the first skirmish of the Mexican War and was killed at San Antonio, Mexico, on August 19, 1847. In April 1849 the camp was moved six miles north on the east bank of the Brazos River, now Lake Whitney in present Hill County, six miles northwest of Whitney, near a former Anadarko Indian site called José Maria Village. The post was renamed, probably for Lt. Col. William M. Graham, Eleventh Infantry, who was killed September 8, 1847, at the Battle of Molino del Rey. The fort closed November 9, 1853.

Camp Grierson. 1878–1882. A camp at Grierson's Springs in Reagan County intermittently occupied as a sub-post of Fort Concho. Established by Lt. Mason Maxon, Tenth Cavalry, and named for his wife's uncle, Col. Benjamin H. Grierson, Tenth Cavalry. The site was last occupied by the regular army in September 1882.

Fort Griffin (Camp Wilson). 1867–1881. A fort established July 31, 1867, on the Clear Fork of the Brazos in present Shackelford County by Lt. Col. Samuel D. Sturgis and Companies F, I, K, and L, Sixth Cavalry. First named for Lt. Henry H. Wilson, Sixth Cavalry, who died December 24, 1866, the name of the post was changed on February 6, 1868, to honor the Fifth Military District Commander, Col. Charles Griffin, Thirty-fifth Infantry, who died September 15, 1867. The post was abandoned on May 31, 1881.

Camp Groce (Camp Liendo). 1865. A small Confederate POW camp established in 1862 three miles east of Hempstead on the Liendo Plantation of Leonard W. Groce and occupied in August 1865 by Custer's Cavalry Division.

Camp Guadalupe River. 1848. A camp of Companies A, E, G, I, and K,

Eighth Infantry, located just north of Victoria when the regiment deployed to Texas in 1848.

Camp Hamilton (see Fort Croghan**).**

Post on Hamilton Creek (see Fort Croghan).

Fort Hancock (Camp Rice). 1881–1895. Lt. Samuel L. Woodward with Company K, Tenth Cavalry, established Camp Rice, six miles north of Fort Quitman on the Rio Grande in present Hudspeth County, on April 15, 1881, as an outpost of Fort Davis. It was moved to the Southern Pacific Railroad on July 9, 1882, and moved again in August to the Rio Grande, fifty miles below El Paso. Named on May 14, 1886, for Maj. Gen. Winfield Scott Hancock, who died February 9, 1886, the government purchased the site in 1884 and abandoned it on November 1, 1895.

Camp Harney. 1853. Established on the lower Rio Grande opposite Guerrero, Mexico, February 27 to August 15, 1853, by Lt. Gordon Granger and Company F, Mounted Rifles, the camp was named for Col. William S. Harney, Second Dragoons, who was in temporary command of the Department of Texas.

Camp Hatch (see Fort Concho).

Camp Hawley (see also Fort Crockett). 1898. Established on the eastern end of Galveston Island next to Fort Crockett in July 1898, this site was the temporary camp of the First U.S. Volunteer Infantry (Texas Immunes) during the Spanish American War.

Camp Houston (see Fort Martin Scott).

Camp Hudson (Camp California Springs, Camp on the San Pedro). 1854, 1857–1861, 1867–1868, 1871–1877. Camp California Springs was a field camp established a few hundred yards south of the second crossing of the Devils River on the San Antonio-El Paso military road by Company K, First Infantry, on March 31, 1854. A few months afterward, in July 1854, Companies A and H, Eighth Infantry, had a temporary encampment at the same site, which they called Camp on the San Pedro, the common name in the 1850s for the Devils River. Camp Hudson, located in present Val Verde County, twenty miles north of Comstock, was established as a post on June 7, 1857, by Lt. Theodore Fink and one company of Eighth Infantry. It was named for Lt. Walter W. Hudson, First Infantry, who died of wounds on April 19, 1850, the first regular army officer killed in the Texas Indian wars. Leased on July 1, 1859, from John James on a twenty-year contract for $50 per month, the post was intermittently occupied after the Civil War until January 1877.

Indianola Depot (Powder Horn). 1850–1861, 1862, 1863, 1865–1866, 1868. At Powder Horn Inlet on the west side of Matagorda Bay, Indianola became the major sea port for quartermaster and subsidence supplies destined for the logistical center of San Antonio. The U.S. Army leased a wharf and warehouse from William Cook from 1850 to 1861, paying $140 per month by 1860. Although the army had ceased its depot operation at Indianola in the post-Civil War years, it was used as a port of entry for troops until the devastating hurricane in September 1875.

Fort Inge (Post On the Leona). 1849–1855, 1856–1861, 1866–1869. A fort established by Capt. Seth Eastman, First Infantry, March 13, 1849, on the Leona River, one mile south of present Uvalde. The post was named on December 28, 1849, for Lt. Zebulon M. P. Inge, Second Dragoons, who was killed at the Battle of Resaca de la Palma on May 9, 1846. The site was leased from David Murphee on December 16, 1852, on a five-year contract for $50 per month, and renewed for twenty years with George T. Howard on April 13, 1860. The army abandoned the post on March 19, 1869.

Camp Inge. 1846, 1848–1849. The first camp so named was a three-company Second Dragoon frontier camp existing in July 1846, twenty miles west of the Nueces River near Corpus Christi. A second camp of the same name was established at Ross's Station on the Bosque River south-

west of present Waco in McLennan County by Capt. Ripley A. Arnold
and Company F, Second Dragoons, and existed from December 8, 1848,
to February 1849. The last camp of that name was established at San
Antonio by Capt. William J. Hardee with Company C, Second
Dragoons, and was active in March-April 1849. All camps were named
for Lt. Zebulon M. P. Inge, Second Dragoons, who was killed in the
horse charge at the Battle of Resaca de la Palma.

Camp Irwin (Camp Placedo). 1846. Established as a temporary Mexican
War camp on Placedo Creek northwest of Port Lavaca in October 1846;
named for Port Lavaca quartermaster Capt. James R. Irwin.

Point Isabel (see Fort Polk).

Camp Ives. 1859–1861. A sub-post four miles north of Camp Verde on
Turtle Creek in Kerr County, established October 2, 1859, by Lt. Wesley
Owens and Company I, Second Cavalry. Probably named for Owens'
West Point classmate Lt. Brayton C. Ives, First Infantry, who died at
Fort Clark on June 27, 1857.

Camp Jackson. 1854. Established in October 1854 by Companies A and
H, First Infantry, at Rodeo, twenty miles from Fort Duncan and Eagle
Pass. The camp was abandoned December 8, 1854.

Fort Jacksboro (see Fort Richardson).

Jefferson Depot. 1865–1870. A quartermaster and subsistence depot
established in 1865 in the northeast Texas town of Jefferson. The depot
received supplies from New Orleans via the Red River and Cypress
Bayou and sent them by contract wagon on to Forts Richardson and
Griffin. The depot discontinued operations on May 31, 1870.

Camp J. E. Johnston. 1852. According to the post returns this camp,
named for Lt. Col. Joseph E. Johnston, Corps of Topographical
Engineers, was established on the North Branch of the Concho River
about ten miles northwest of present San Angelo by Col. John Garland

and five companies of Eighth Infantry, and was active from March 15 to November 18, 1852. However, other army records indicate there was an additional camp of this name on the Middle Concho River four miles west of present Arden in Irion County, which became the site of a Butterfield Stage stop called Johnson's Station.

Camp Kelly (see Fort Concho).

Camp Kirby. 1857. Temporary camp of the Second Cavalry in 1857 on Agua Dulce Creek, forty miles northwest of Corpus Christi.

Fort Lancaster. 1855–1861, 1867–1868, 1871. A post established on the left bank of Live Oak Creek, a tributary of the Pecos River in present Crockett County, on August 20, 1855, by Capt. Stephen D. Carpenter and Companies H and K, First Infantry. Named for Carpenter's West Point classmate Lt. Job R. H. Lancaster, First Infantry, who was killed by lightning July 5, 1841, during the Second Seminole War in Florida.

Camp Langtry. 1870–1888. Intermittently used as a temporary scouting camp near the Rio Grande, fifteen miles above the mouth of the Pecos River in Val Verde County, the site was leased from Cesario Torres of Fort Stockton for eight dollars a month in the 1880s.

Camp Laredo. 1860. A camp of Capt. Arthur T. Lee and Companies C, D, and F, Eighth Infantry, near Laredo in January 1860.

Camp Las Laxas. 1854. The camp of Company G, Eighth Infantry, on the Rio Grande thirty miles above Ringgold Barracks from May 31 to August 29, 1854.

Port Lavaca. 1846–1847, 1849–1851. As a transfer point to off-load supplies destined for San Antonio, the Army used this port in Calhoun County to provide logistics for the Mexican War buildup from June 1846 to March 1847. Before all supply operations in this sector shifted to Indianola in 1852, the Quartermaster Department leased buildings on Lavaca Bay in 1851.

Camp Lawson. 1857–1860. An intermittently used camp for the Second Cavalry and Eighth Infantry at the Leona River crossing of the lower Presidio Road from San Antonio to Presidio de San Juan Bautista in present Frio County. It was established as an official post on October 27, 1859, by Capt. Arthur T. Lee and Company C, Eighth Infantry. The camp probably was named for Surgeon General Thomas Lawson.

Post on the Leon (see Fort Gates).

Post on the Leona (see Fort Inge).

Camp Liendo (see Camp Groce).

Camp Limpia. 1853, 1855. On Limpia Creek fifteen miles north of Fort Davis, this site was occupied by Companies B, E, I, and K, Eighth Infantry, in December 1853, and by Companies A and G, Eighth Infantry, from February 22 to March 1, 1855.

Camp Llano Estacado. 1859. Temporary scouting camp of Company H, Eighth Infantry, on the upper Pecos River in 1859.

Fort Lincoln (Camp Seco, Camp on the Seco River). 1849–1852. The site was first occupied as Camp on the Seco River, a temporary field camp on Seco Creek two miles north of D'Hanis in Medina County, in January-February 1849 by Capt. Sidney Burbank and Companies A and B, First Infantry. It was established as a post, Camp Seco, on July 7, 1849, by Lt. James Longstreet and Companies E and G, Eighth Infantry, and named for Capt. George Lincoln, Eighth Infantry, who was killed at Buena Vista on February 23, 1847. The post was abandoned July 20, 1852.

Camp Live Oak Creek. 1854, 1857. The first camp of this name was established by a detachment of First Infantry somewhere on Live Oak Creek in Crockett County from April 13 to October 20, 1854. The second site with this name was on the same creek, one mile from Fort Lancaster, as a camp of Company G, Eighth Infantry, in 1857.

Camp Lopeño. 1856. Field camp established April 30, 1856, forty-three miles above Ringgold Barracks in Zapata County by Lt. Benjamin Wingate and Company K, Fifth Infantry.

Camp Lugubre (see Fort Terrett).

Camp Lugubrious (see Fort Terrett).

McCulloch's Station (see Fort Croghan). 1848–1849. On Hamilton Creek, a tributary of the Colorado River three miles south of present Burnet, in Burnet County, Capt. Hamilton W. Merrill and Company B, Second Dragoons, established this temporary camp from December 4, 1848, to April 1849.

Fort McIntosh (Camp Crawford). 1849–1858, 1860–1861, 1865–1946. Originally called Camp Crawford for Secretary of War George W. Crawford when established at Laredo on March 3, 1849, by Lt. Egbert L. Vielé and Company G, First Infantry. Named on December 28, 1849, for Lt. Col. James S. McIntosh, Fifth Infantry, who died of wounds received at the Battle of Molino del Rey on September 26, 1847, the post was one of the few in Texas to have a formal field fortification, a star fort earthwork built by the Fifth Infantry in 1853 under the supervision of Maj. Richard Delafield. Leased from Don Dolores Garcia on November 16, 1863, on a ten-year option for $62 per month, the site moved in 1859 under a new $50-per-month twenty-year lease with the city signed in 1860. In September 1874 the city of Laredo deeded ownership of the post to the federal government, and the post closed May 31, 1946.

Fort McKavett (Camp San Saba). 1852–1859, 1868–1883. A fort established in present Menard County as a regimental camp near the head of the San Saba River on March 14, 1852, by Lt. Col. Thomas Staniford with the headquarters and Companies B, D, E, F, and H, Eighth Infantry. It was named for Capt. Henry McKavett, Eighth Infantry, who was killed September 21, 1846, in the Battle of Monterrey. The post closed on June 30, 1883.

Fort Marcy (see Camp Corpus Christi).

Marshall, Texas. 1866, 1868. This temporary post in the town of Marshall in Harrison County was occupied for one month beginning January 20, 1866, by Maj. M. W. Desmond and a detachment of Nineteenth Pennsylvania Cavalry, Eighteenth Illinois Infantry, and Eightieth U.S. Colored Troops. The final regular army garrison of Marshall, Capt. Thomas M. K. Smith and Company B, Twenty-sixth Infantry, occupied the town from February 1 to December 30, 1868.

Fort Mason. 1851–1859, 1860–1861, 1866–1869. Established July 6, 1851, near Comanche Creek of the Llano River in present Mason County by Capt. Hamilton W. Merrill and Companies A and B, Second Dragoons. This post was named for Lt. George T. Mason, Second Dragoons, who was killed in the first skirmish of the Mexican War at La Rosia on April 25, 1846. The post was leased on a twenty-year $50-per-month contract on June 1, 1860, from Richard A. Howard, and a $10-per-month contract with Gustav Schlescher; the army abandoned the post on March 23, 1869.

Camp Maxwell. 1848. A Second Dragoon regimental headquarters camp at Austin in November and December 1848.

Camp Melbourne (see Camp Melvin).

Camp Melvin (Camp Melbourne). 1868–1870, 1875–1876, 1881. An outpost on the western border of present Crockett County, two miles east of Sheffield, thirty-five miles above its parent post of Fort Lancaster, Camp Melvin was established at Connelley's Crossing, Fennelly's Crossing, or what came to be called Pontoon Bridge Crossing of the Pecos River in August 1868 by Lt. Robert Wesley and Company A, Forty-first Infantry. When Fort Lancaster closed in 1871, Camp Melvin became a sub-post of Fort Stockton.

Camp Merrill (see Camp Casa Blanca).

Fort Merrill. 1850–1855. Established on the south bank of the Nueces River six miles southeast of present George West in Live Oak County, March 1, 1850, by Capt. Samuel M. Plummer and Companies H and K, First Infantry. It was named for Capt. Moses E. Merrill, Fifth Infantry, who was killed September 8, 1847, at Molino del Rey. The post was abandoned December 1, 1855.

Cantonment at Meyer's Springs. 1870s, 1880–1881. Sometimes called Mayer's Springs, this site was a patrol camp used by the Seminole-Negro scouts in the late 1870s in Terrell County near the Rio Grande in the Meyers Canyon-Lozier Canyon junction. From September 3, 1880, to January 1881 it was the temporary camp of Capt. Robert G. Heiner and Company A, First Infantry.

Fort Montgomery. 1864. This fort was an earthwork of several connected redoubts constructed by U.S. XIII Corps on the Rio Grande a mile and a half above Fort Brown.

Camp Las Moras. 1854. On Las Moras Creek near Fort Clark, this was a camp of Companies C and A, Seventh Infantry, as they escorted the U.S. Boundary Survey.

El Muerto. A military campsite and mail station at Deadman's Hole thirty miles west of Fort Davis, used by many military units in the nineteenth century, and established as an outpost of Fort Davis in 1868.

Nacogdoches. 1836, 1867, 1869. This town near the Louisiana border was first occupied by the army in the aftermath of the Texas Revolution as a temporary post of observation by Lt. Col. William Whistler with three companies of First Dragoons and six companies of Seventh Infantry, for a total force of 341 soldiers from July 27 to December 17, 1836. During Reconstruction it was temporarily occupied by two companies of Twenty-sixth Infantry in 1867 and by a company of the Sixth Cavalry in 1869.

Fort Nelson. 1863. An artillery post constructed on Virginia Point at the site of Confederate Fort Hébert after the Union capture of Galveston in 1862.

Camp Neville Springs. 1880–1891. Located on Government Springs Road, 1.5 miles east of the campground of what is now Big Bend National Park, the springs served as a temporary patrol camp and outpost for scouts from Fort Clark, Camp Peña Colorado, and Fort Davis.

Cantonment North Fork of the Red River (see Fort Elliott).

Camp Nowlin. 1859. A temporary outpost of the Brazos Indian Reservation, probably located in Archer County on the Little Wichita River.

Camp Olmos. 1846. A temporary camp of Companies A and G, Second Dragoons, on Los Olmos Creek twenty miles southwest of present Kingsville, from December 1845 to March 1846.

Camp Page. 1847. A Second Dragoons regimental camp at the mouth of the Rio Grande that was active in January and February 1847.

Painted Comanche Camp (see Fort Davis).

Camp Palo Blanco. 1855. A temporary camp near what was then called the Palos Blancos Mountains, near the Devils River in Val Verde County, occupied by Capt. Daniel Ruggles and Company A, Fifth Infantry, on August 30, 1855.

Camp Patterson. 1846. Named for Volunteer Maj. Gen. Robert Patterson, Taylor's commander of the volunteers assembling on the Rio Grande, this camp was occupied from August to December 1846 on the Texas side of the river, nine miles below Matamoros.

Camp Pecan. 1850, 1856. A temporary camp near the upper Colorado River, probably near the Pecan Creek-Llano River junction in Llano County, established July 20, 1850, by Company A, Second Dragoons. Lt.

Joseph H. McArthur and Company H, Second Cavalry, reoccupied the camp for one month beginning July 30, 1856.

Camp at the Mouth of the Rio Pecos. 1880–1881. During a First Infantry expedition to the Big Bend in 1880 Capt. Fregus Walker and Companies E and I, First Infantry, established this camp to guard the quartermaster wagon crossing of the Pecos near its intersection with the Rio Grande. The camp remained active until February 1881.

Camp on the La Peña. 1854. A field site established May 21 to September 1854 forty-three miles southeast of Fort Duncan on La Peña Creek by Companies A and H, First Infantry, commanded by Capt. James N. Caldwell.

Camp Peña Blanco (see Cantonment at Peña Colorado).

Cantonment at Peña Colorado (Camp Peña Blanco, Camp Rainbow Cliffs). 1879–1893. Camp Peña Blanco, an 1878 scouting camp of the Tenth Cavalry, was first established as a post, Camp Rainbow Cliffs, at Peña Colorado Creek, four miles southwest of present Marathon on the Southern Pacific Railroad, on August 27, 1879, by Lt. H. B. Quimby and Company F, Twenty-fifth Infantry. The post was named Cantonment at Peña Colorado on March 15, 1880, and was leased for $50 per month from Myer and Solomon Halff; it was abandoned in January 1893.

Camp Pendencia. 1859. A field camp and sub-post of Fort Duncan on the Rio Grande opposite Presidio del Rio Grande and the old mission San Juan Bautista at present Guerrero, Mexico. This site, active in the mid-1850s, was officially established as a military post by Capt. Charles D. Jordan on October 25, 1859, with Companies C and D, Eighth Infantry.

Fort Phantom Hill (Post on Clear Fork of the Brazos). 1851–1854, 1857, 1871–1880. Established fifteen miles north of present Abilene on November 14, 1851, by Maj. John J. Abercrombie and Companies C and

G, Fifth Infantry, the official name remained Post on Clear Fork of the Brazos, but locally it was called "Phantom Hill" for the hill on which it was built. Although closed as a major post on April 6, 1854, the site was briefly used by Lt. Henry C. Wood and Company D, First Infantry, in February 1857 and was intermittently occupied as a sub-post of Fort Griffin after the Civil War.

Camp Phelps. 1852. A one-month border camp on the Rio Grande twenty miles below Ringgold Barracks established on January 28, 1852, by Lt. James Holmes and Company K, Fourth Artillery.

Camp El Pico. 1855. A field camp on the Rio Grande ten miles north of Laredo, occupied June 15 to September 30, 1855, by Company H, Fifth Infantry.

Camp Pindido. 1856. A camp of Company F, Eighth Infantry, forty miles east of Fort Davis occupied in April 1856.

Pine Spring. A Butterfield stage stop at the south end of the present Guadalupe Mountains National Park, occupied by the Tenth Cavalry as a sub-post of Fort Davis in the late 1870s.

Camp Pitt. 1848. Temporary camp of December 21–26, 1848, established by Capt. Collinson R. Gates and Companies A, E, and G, Eight Infantry. It was twelve miles northwest of Port Lavaca, probably on Chocolate Bayou.

Camp Placedo (see Camp Irwin).

Fort Point (see Fort San Jacinto).

Fort Polk. 1846–1850, 1865–1871. Established at Point Isabel as a supply depot for Brig. Gen. Zachary Taylor's Army of Occupation, the post was first occupied March 26, 1846, by Capt. John Munroe with Company G, Fourth Artillery, and Company A, First Infantry. After the Civil War

Point Isabel was a sub-post of Fort Brown. It was named May 12, 1846, for President James K. Polk and closed as a major post on February 9, 1850.

Pope's Camp (see Artesian Well).

Pope's Well (see Artesian Well).

Presidio, Texas. 1873–1883. This site of Presidio del Norte on the Rio Grande in present Presidio County and its civilian defensive work of Fort Leaton often played host to army patrols in the 1850s. In December 1873 Capt. David D. Van Valzah and Company D, Twenty-fifth Infantry, occupied the town for four weeks during a period of border troubles. From September 1880 to February 1881, Presidio became a sub-post of Fort Davis and the winter camp of a battalion of First Infantry commanded by Capt. Thomas M. Tolman.

Camp Prisontown. A Confederate prisoner-of-war camp two miles from Camp Verde that held Union troops captured in operations on the Texas coast.

Preston Supply Depot. 1851–1853. A quartermaster supply point at Preston Bend on the Red River in present Grayson County that was used to furnish troops in the Indian Territory.

Fort Quitman. 1858–1861, 1862–1863, 1868–1877, 1882. A post established September 28, 1858, on the Rio Grande seventy-five miles below El Paso, one mile north of the where the El Paso-San Antonio Military Road struck the Rio Grande in present Hudspeth County. The fort was founded by Capt. Arthur T. Lee with Companies C and H, Eighth Infantry, and was named for Congressman and Mexican War hero Maj. Gen. John A. Quitman, who died July 17, 1858. It was re-established January 1, 1868, by Company F, Ninth Cavalry. The site was abandoned as a major post on January 5, 1877, but intermittently continued as a sub-post of Fort Davis until 1882.

Camp Rainbow Cliffs (see Cantonment at Peña Colorado).

Red River Camp. 1856. A temporary camp on the Red River to the north of Camp Cooper occupied by Companies B and C, First Infantry, on September 26, 1856.

Camp at Redmond's Ranche. 1853, 1866. A temporary camp on the Rio Grande at Carrizo, near modern Zapata, a trading center owned by Englishman Henry Redmond. The camp was established midway between Ringgold Barracks and Fort McIntosh on March 3, 1853, by Lt. Gordon Granger and Company F, Mounted Rifles. It was occupied briefly after the Civil War.

Camp Relief. 1855. A camp on Limpia Creek near Fort Davis, occupied in February 1855 by Maj. John S. Simonson's expedition to the Trans-Pecos with Companies A, C, and G, Mounted Rifles; Company F, Eighth Infantry; and Companies B, C, and E, Texas Mounted Volunteers.

Camp Rice (see Fort Hancock).

Fort Richardson (Fort Jacksboro). 1866–1867, 1867–1878. Established at Jacksboro on Lost Creek, a tributary of the Trinity River, and first known as Fort Jacksboro when it was occupied on July 4, 1866, by Capt. G. C. Cram and Company I, Sixth Cavalry. The post was named on February 6, 1868, for Volunteers Maj. Gen Israel B. Richardson, who died November 3, 1862, of wounds received at Antietam on September 17, 1862. The post was abandoned May 23, 1878.

Camp Ricketts. 1851–1852, 1853. Capt. Joseph A. Haskins and Companies D and F, First Artillery, established this border camp on the Rio Grande near Edinburg in Hidalgo County in December 1851. Abandoned on April 2, 1852, the camp was temporarily occupied by Company C, Mounted Rifles, who returned again in the period May 20 to August 26, 1853.

Fort Riley (see Fort Clark).

Fort Ringgold (Post at Davis' Landing, Camp Ringgold, Ringgold Barracks). 1846–1847, 1848–1859, 1859–1861, 1865–1906, 1913–1917, 1941–1944. Davis' Landing, now Rio Grande City, was a wood stop at the terminus of steamer navigation on the Rio Grande opposite Camargo, Mexico, and was used extensively in Mexican War. At the close of the war Capt. Joseph H. La Motte and Companies C and G, First Infantry, established Post of Davis' Landing on October 26, 1848. The site was named Camp Ringgold in October 1848, Ringgold Barracks on July 16, 1849, and Fort Ringgold on December 30, 1878, to honor the American tactical innovator of highly mobile or "flying" field artillery, Capt. Samuel Ringgold, Third Artillery, who died May 11, 1846, of wounds received at the Battle of Palo Alto on May 8, 1846. The army leased the post on a five-year contract for $50 per month from Henry Clay Davis on October 20, 1853; the government took ownership of the property on March 30, 1878, by having the land condemned from Davis and other disputed title claimants.

Camp on Rio Grande. 1860. The name for two temporary one-company Second Cavalry camps on the Rio Grande in 1860, one established between Ringgold Barracks and Edinburg by Capt. Nathan G. Evans and Company H, and one established by Lt. Manning M. Kimmel and Company G just above Brownsville.

Rio Grande Station (see Fort Duncan).

Post of Roma. 1851, 1852, 1865. This sub-post of Ringgold Barracks was established on the banks of the Rio Grande at the town of Roma on December 5, 1851, as a Second Dragoon quartermaster site commanded by Lt. Daniel Huston. In the period January 19 to March 18, 1852, Roma was the post of Capt. William E. Prince and Company E, First Infantry. From July to December 1865 Roma was occupied by Col. William W. Woodward and the Third Brigade, Second Division, of XXV Corps.

Camp Rosario. 1860–1861. A camp established on the Rio Grande below

Edinburg in Hidalgo County by Capt. Albert G. Brackett and Company I, Second Cavalry, from June 1860 to March 20, 1861.

Ross's Station. (see Camp Inge).

Camp Sabinal. 1856. A temporary Second Cavalry camp from July 12 to October 3, 1856, on the San Antonio-El Paso military road crossing of the Sabinal River in present Uvalde County. The camp initially was established by Capt. Albert G. Brackett and Company I, Second Cavalry.

Camp on Sabinal River. 1846. A temporary outpost commanded by Bvt. Maj. Benjamin L. Beall and two companies of Second Dragoons in September and October 1846.

St. Joseph's Island Depot. 1845–1846. At the southeast corner of Corpus Christi Bay, this island was the original landing site of Brig. Gen. Zachary Taylor's Army of Occupation on July 27, 1845, and served as a supply depot from that date to March 1846, when the army's line of communication was shifted by sea to Brazos Santiago.

Camp Salado. 1849. Temporary camp of the Third Infantry Regiment established near San Antonio from April to June 1849.

Camp Salinena (Rancho Las Salinia). 1854, 1856. A temporary field camp thirty miles north of Ringgold Barracks occupied May 17 to July 30, 1854, by Company C, Eighth Infantry, and reoccupied April 21–30, 1856, by Company E, Fifth Infantry.

Camp Salintas. 1855. A temporary camp on Woll's Road between Fort Duncan at Eagle Pass and Fort Inge at Uvalde, established December 14, 1855, by Companies C, J, and K, Fifth Infantry.

Camp Salt Lake. 1854. This sub-post of Fort Brown was occupied by Lt. Robert V. W. Howard and Company M, Fourth Artillery, and Company A, Seventh Infantry, from May 27 to November 30, 1854. It was eighty-five miles northwest of Fort Brown, about six miles northwest of present

Raymondville in Willacy County. The camp served as a field supply depot to support patrols of the Mounted Rifles Regiment.

Fort Sam Houston (see Post of San Antonio).

Post of San Antonio (Alamo, Camp Bexar, Camp Worth, Camp Terrett, Camp Salado, Camp Sheridan, San Antonio Barracks, San Antonio Arsenal, San Antonio Depot, Fort Sam Houston; see also Alamo, Camp Bailey, Camp Bexar, Camp Worth, Camp Terrett, Camp Sheridan, Camp Salado). 1845–1846, 1848 to present. The U.S. Army presence in San Antonio began as Camp Bexar, a Second Dragoons camp established on October 20, 1845, six miles south of town. San Antonio was the site of various camps and served as the departmental headquarters because of its central strategic location and remained the preeminent military site in nineteenth-century Texas. San Antonio Arsenal, an ordnance depot, was established in 1858 and deeded to the government in 1859. Construction of the Quartermaster Department's San Antonio Depot, often called the Quadrangle, began in June 1876 on city-donated land around Government Hill and was completed in July 1877 with the addition of an upper story for departmental headquarters in 1879–1880. After the purchase of additional lands in 1882, 1883 and 1887 the post began an expansion project in 1885 for barracks and quarters, which was completed in 1890. On September 11, 1890, the Post of San Antonio and the San Antonio Depot became Fort Sam Houston in honor of the military commander of the Texas Revolution.

San Antonio National Military Cemetery. A military cemetery established on November 15, 1867, by the Cemeterial Branch of the Quartermaster's Department on 1.09 acres on Sulphur Springs Road at Powder House Hill, one mile east of the city, on property donated by the city and mayor W. C. A. Thielepape on November 15, 1867, with an additional 1.89 acres donated April 14, 1871, and 1.75 acres on April 10, 1884. By 1871 the cemetery held 281 Union dead, including forty-one unknowns, from the Medina River, Salado Creek, Austin, and the local city cemeteries. The first civilian superintendent, Thomas A.

Fitzpatrick, a former sergeant of the Eighteenth Pennsylvania Cavalry, was appointed in 1875.

Camp San Antonio Wells. 1854. A field camp in present Jim Hogg County, forty-five miles north of Ringgold Barracks, occupied May 16 to August 30, 1854, by Lt. Horace Haldeman and Company F, Eighth Infantry.

Camp Sanders (see also Austin). 1865. A camp of the Sixth Cavalry half a mile west of Austin when the regiment arrived in Texas after the Civil War. The site was established November 29, 1865, and named for Volunteer Brig. Gen. William P. Sanders, Captain, Sixth Cavalry, who was killed at the siege of Knoxville in 1863.

San Diego, Texas. 1878–1882. A Jim Wells County sub-post of Fort McIntosh established April 16, 1878, by Capt. Andrew P. Caraher and Company F, Eighth Cavalry. The camp was abandoned April 26, 1882.

Presido of San Elizario. 1849–1851, 1862–1863. Located at an eighteenth-century Spanish military site on the Rio Grande twenty-five miles below El Paso, the post was established September 15, 1849, by Capt. William S. Henry and Companies I and K, Third Infantry, as a sub-post of El Paso.

Camp San Felipe (see Camp Del Rio).

Fort San Jacinto (Fort Point). 1898–1900, 1911–1946. Constructed on the site of Confederate Fort Point, and initially called by the same name, this Endicott Board formal coastal fortification was on the northeastern end of Galveston Island. Construction of its batteries began in 1898 and the fort was first occupied April 20, 1898, by Capt. Clermont L. Best with Battery G, First Artillery. Named in February 1899 for the famous battle of the Texas Revolution, construction of the battery was completed in 1901.

Camp on the Rio San Pedro. 1855. A field camp on the Devils River, often called the San Pedro in the 1850s, in present Val Verde County, established April 30, 1855, by Company I, Fifth Infantry, while escorting the Pacific Railroad Survey.

Camp on the San Pedro (see Camp Hudson).

Camp San Saba (see Fort McKavett).

Camp Santa Rosa. 1879. A scouting camp established in the summer of 1879 by Company B, Tenth Cavalry, at a water hole thirty miles north of Fort Stockton near the Pecos River in present Pecos County.

Camp J. M. Scott. 1854. A field camp established as a sub-post on Las Moras Creek, twenty-eight miles north of Fort Duncan at Eagle Pass, from May 23 to December 8, 1854, by Companies B and G, First Infantry. It was named for Capt. John M. Scott, First Infantry, who died October 26, 1850.

Fort Martin Scott (Camp Houston, Post at Fredericksburg). 1848–1851, 1866. Originally called Camp Houston when established near Fredericksburg by Capt. Seth Eastman and Company D, First Infantry, on December 5, 1848, the post was named December 28, 1849, for Lt. Col. Martin Scott, Fifth Infantry, who was killed on September 8, 1847, at the Battle of Molino del Rey. Capt. Eugene B. Beaumont and Company A, Fourth Cavalry, occupied the post from October 18 to December 28, 1866.

Camp Seco (see Fort Lincoln).

Camp on the Seco River (see Fort Lincoln).

Seven Springs. 1878. A scouting camp twenty miles north of Fort Davis occupied June through September 1878 by Company H, Twenty-fifth Infantry. The camp subsequently became an intermittent outpost of Fort Davis during the late 1870s.

Camp Shafter. 1873. An temporary outpost of Fort Duncan established twenty-six miles east on Comanche Creek in present Zavala County, on May 28, 1873, by Capt. William O'Connell and Company M, Fourth Cavalry. The camp was named for Lt. Col. William R. Shafter in command of Fort Duncan.

Camp Sheridan. (see also San Antonio). 1866. The San Antonio base camp of the Fourth Cavalry Regiment when it arrived in Texas in 1866.

Camp Stewart. 1856. A temporary camp on Hondo Creek near Quihi in Medina County, established by Capt. John B. Magruder and three companies of Mounted Rifles and First Artillery.

Fort Stockton. 1859–1861, 1867–1886. Established as a camp on March 23, 1859, at Comanche Spring in current Pecos County by Lt. Walter Jones and one company of First Infantry. Many sources claim it was named for Mexican War naval hero Commodore Robert F. Stockton, but he did not die until 1866. It was probably named for Lt. Edward D. Stockton, First Infantry, who died March 13, 1857. The post was abandoned June 27, 1886.

Camp E. B. Strong. 1855. A temporary camp established October 17, 1855, at Woll's Crossing of the Nueces River in present Uvalde County, by Company D, Mounted Rifles, and Companies C, G, and K, Fifth Infantry. The camp was named for Lt. Erastus B. Strong, Fifth Infantry, who was killed at the Battle of Molino del Rey, September 8, 1847.

Cantonment on the Sweetwater (see Fort Elliott).

Fort Taylor (see Fort Brown).

Fort Terrett (Camp Detention, Camp Lugubre, Camp Lugubrious, Camp Bainbridge, Post on the Rio Llano). 1852–1854. Located twenty-five miles west of modern Junction, this post on the North Fork of the Llano River was first called Camp Detention when established by Lt. Col. Henry Bainbridge and the headquarters and Companies A, H, I, and K of the First Infantry on February 5, 1852. The fort was named on October 16, 1852, for Lt. John C. Terrett, First Infantry, who was killed in the Battle of Monterrey, and the post was abandoned February 26, 1854.

Camp Terrett (see also San Antonio). 1849. The original temporary camp of Capt. John H. King and Companies F and I, First Infantry, when they arrived in San Antonio February 26, 1849. It was probably named for Lt. John C. Terrett, First Infantry, who was killed in the Battle of Monterrey.

Fort Texas (see Fort Brown).

Camp Thornton (see Fort Graham).

Fort Travis. 1899–1900, 1911–1946. Construction of four batteries of this Endicott Board formal coastal fortification began in 1898 at Bolivar Point, as part of the Galveston Bay defenses. Initially manned on October 25, 1899, by the Coastal Artillery, it was taken over in August 1900 by a detachment of First Artillery from Fort San Jacinto. The fort was named for Alamo defender Lt. Col. William B. Travis.

Camp Trinidad. 1865–1868. Located near Lake Trinidad and recorded as being thirty-seven miles south of San Patricio and six miles west of modern Kingsville, this Fourth Cavalry field camp was established in March 1865 and used until 1868.

Camp Tucker (see Post at Buffalo Springs).

Camp Twiggs. 1846. A Second Dragoons four-company camp near the Palo Alto battlefield that was occupied from May to August 1846.

Camp Uphazy. 1854. A camp near San Antonio occupied by Company B, First Infantry, from February 28 to March 18, 1854.

Camp Van Camp. 1859. There were at least three temporary camps so named, all in honor of Lt. Cornelius Van Camp, Second Cavalry, who was killed at the Battle of Wichita Village in 1858. The first was established in present Pecos County, thirteen miles northeast of Fort Stockton, from April 30 to July 30, 1859, by Companies E and J, Second Cavalry, and Company D, First Infantry. The second was described in the returns as being six miles west of Antelope Hills in present Shackelford County and was occupied by Capt. Albert G. Brackett and Company I, Second Cavalry, from July 16 to August 15, 1859. The third was a temporary camp occupied at Horsehead Crossing of the Pecos River, twelve miles southwest of present Crane in Crane County, established April 30 to August 29, 1859, by Lt. Henry C. Wood and one company of First Infantry. Some sources list an additional camp of this name on the Brazos River in Young County.

Camp Verde (Camp Prisontown). 1856–1861, 1866–1869. A site in current Kerr County established on the north bank of Verde Creek, north of Bandera Pass, July 8, 1856, by Capt. Innis N. Palmer and Company D, Second Cavalry. This camp housed the Army's "Camel Experiment" until the outbreak of the Civil War. It was abandoned April 1, 1861.

Camp Near Victoria. 1848. Established one mile from the town on the Guadalupe River, this camp was occupied only in December 1848 to allow five companies of the Eighth Infantry to escape a cholera epidemic at Port Lavaca.

Camp on Big Wichita. 1855. The field camp of an expedition that departed Fort Chadbourne on February 1, 1855, consisting of Companies D and G, Second Dragoons, and Companies A, D, and F, Texas Mounted Volunteers. The expedition abandoned the camp on February 17, 1855, and returned to Fort Chadbourne.

Camp Wichita. 1870. A temporary camp on the East Fork of the Little Wichita River ten miles above Buffalo Springs in Clay County. It was established in September 1870 by Maj. Robert M. Morris and Companies A, D, and G, Sixth Cavalry, and Company K, Eleventh Infantry.

Camp Wilcox. 1858. A temporary camp established on the East Fork of the Trinity River by Companies A and I, Seventh Infantry, on February 28, 1858.

Camp Wilson (see Fort Griffin).

Camp Witherell. 1861. A name given to the camp of the regulars awaiting transport at Brazos Santiago during the federal exodus at the start of the Civil War. It was so named after the drowning death on March 21, 1861, of Lt. James B. Witherell, Second Cavalry.

Camp Wolf Canyon. 1854. A field camp of Companies C, E, F, and G, Eighth Infantry, in November 1854 in the vicinity of Fort Davis.

Camp G. W. F. Wood. 1857, 1860–1861. A post established May 20, 1857, on the headwaters of the Nueces River in present Real County by Capt. George W. Wallace and Lt. Edwin D. Phillips and Company G, First Infantry. Although the First Infantry abandoned the camp on October 29, 1857, it was subsequently occupied January 21, 1860, by Lt. John B. Hood and Company K, Second Cavalry. The site was named for Capt. George W. F. Wood, First Infantry, who died November 8, 1854.

Camp Worth. 1849, 1854. A two-company camp of Eighth Infantry established at San Antonio in the period January 20 to September 30, 1849. A second camp at the same location was briefly occupied in February 1854 by Maj. Joseph H. La Motte and Company H, Fifth Infantry.

Fort Worth. 1849–1853. Established on the West Fork of the Trinity River on June 6, 1849, by Capt. Ripley A. Arnold and Company F, Second Dragoons, the post was named for Departmental Commander Bvt. Maj. Gen. William Jenkins Worth, Colonel, Eighth Infantry, who died May 7, 1849. The army abandoned the fort on September 17, 1853.

*Sources for post and camp histories are the annual *Report of the Secretary of War*, 1836–1900; National Archives and Records Service Microfilm no. M617, "Returns From United States Military Posts 1800–1916," Microfilm no. M661, "Historical Information Relating To Military Posts and Other Installations ca. 1700–1900," Records of the United States Army Adjutant General's Office, 1780–1917, Record Group (RG) 94; Headquarters of the Military Division of the Missouri, *Outline Descriptions of the Posts in the Military Division of the Missouri, Commanded by Lieutenant General P. H. Sherdian* (Chicago: Headquarters, Military Division of the Missouri, 1876. Reprint. Bellevue, Nebr.: The Old Army Press, 1969); Inspector General's Office, *Outline Descriptions of the Posts and Stations of Troops in the Geographic Divisions and Departments of the United States* (Washington, D.C.: Government Printing Office, 1872); Office of the Judge Advocate General, *United States Military Reservations, National Cemeteries and Military Parks: Title, Jurisdiction, Etc.* (Washington, D.C.: Government Printing Office, 1910); Quartermaster General's Office, *Outline Description of U.S. Military Posts and Stations in the Year 1871* (Washington, D.C.: Government Printing Office, 1872); Robert W. Frazer, *Forts of the West* (Norman: University of Oklahoma Press, 1965); Herbert M. Hart, *Tour Guide to Old Western Forts* (Fort Collins, Colo.: Old Army Press, 1980); National Park Service, *Soldier and Brave: Historic Places Associated with Indian Affairs and the Indian Wars in the Trans-Mississippi West,* The National Survey of Historic Sites and Buildings, vol. 12, ed. Robert G. Ferris, (Washington, D.C.: United States Department of the Interior, National Park Service, 1971); Robert B. Roberts, *Encyclopedia of Historic Forts: The Military, Pioneer, and Trading Posts of the United States* (New York: Macmillan Publishing Company, 1988); Ron Tyler, Douglas E. Barnett, Roy R. Barkley, Penelope C. Anderson, and Mark F. Odintz (eds.), *The New Handbook of Texas* (6 vols.; Austin: Texas State Historical Association, 1996), I, 923–949, II, 1086–1123; Walter Prescott Webb (ed.), *The Handbook of Texas* (3 vols.; Austin: Texas State Historical Association, 1952), I, 277–286, 619–635, III, 137–140, 304–309; Robert Wooster, *History of Fort Davis, Texas* (Southwest Cultural Resources Center, Professional Paper No. 34. Santa Fe: Southwest Region, National Park Service, Department of the Interior, 1990), 185–186, 223, 230, 332, 304.

Post Guard House and guard detail, Fort Clark, ca. 1870s. This building became the post hospital in the 1880s. The First Infantry Regiment established Fort Clark in 1852 and leased this site near present Brackettville for fifty dollars per month from Samuel A. Maverick. The army purchased the post from Mary Maverick in 1883. *Photograph courtesy Lawrence T. Jones III, Austin.*

POST GARRISONS, 1848–1900*

Snapshot of major military garrisons in Texas for October-November of each year as reported by the Adjutant General of the Army.*

1836
Total U.S. Army troops in Texas: 341
Nacogdoches (July-December): First Dragoons; Seventh Infantry (nine companies); Lt. Col. W. Whistler

1845
Total U.S. Army troops in Texas: 4,079
Departmental commander: Brig. Gen. Z. Taylor
Military headquarters: Corpus Christi
Corpus Christi (July 31–December), Taylor's Army of Occupation: Second Dragoons; Third, Fourth, Fifth, Seventh, and Eighth Infantry; Second and Third Artillery (sixty companies)
Austin (November): Second Dragoons (one company); Capt. B. L. Beall
Camp Bexar at San Antonio (October): Second Dragoons (two companies); Maj. T. T. Fauntleroy

1846
Total U.S. Army troops in Texas: 4,400
Departmental commander: Brig. Gen. Z. Taylor
Military headquarters: Corpus Christi

Corpus Christi (January–March 8); Brig. Gen. Z. Taylor

Taylor's Army of Occupation: Second Dragoons; Third, Fourth, Fifth, Seventh, and Eighth Infantry; Second and Third Artillery (sixty companies)

Fort Texas or Fort Brown opposite Matamoros (March 27–August 22)

Taylor's Army of Occupation: Second Dragoons; Third, Fourth, Fifth, Seventh, and Eighth Infantry; Second and Third Artillery (sixty companies)

San Antonio (August–September): Brig. Gen. J. E. Wool

Wool's Center Division: First and Second Dragoons; Sixth Infantry; Texas Volunteer Artillery; Arkansas Horse; Kentucky Foot; Illinois Infantry (forty-seven companies): 3,400 total

Austin (to May): Second Dragoons (two companies); Capt. B. L. Beall

Camp on the Sabinal (September): Second Dragoons (two companies); Capt. B. L. Beall

El Paso (December 27): Doniphan's Expedition: Col. A. Doniphan, First Missouri Mounted Infantry

Depots: Port Lavaca, Brazos Santiago, Point Isabel (detachments)

1847

Total U.S. Army troops in Texas: 1,000

Fort Brown (detachment)

Fort Polk (detachment)

Depots: Brazos Santiago, Point Isabel (detachment)

1848

Total U.S. Army troops in Texas: 1,560

Departmental commander: Maj. Gen. D. E. Twiggs (November 1, 1848)

Military headquarters: Galveston (November 1, 1848)

Departmental commander: Col. W. J. Worth (December 26, 1848)

Military headquarters: San Antonio (December 26, 1848)

Fort Polk: Fourth Artillery (one company); Lt. H. M. Whiting

Fort Brown: First Infantry (three companies); Capt. S. M. Plummer

Davis' Landing, Rio Grande: Fourth Artillery; First Infantry (three companies); Capt. J. H. La Motte

Post on Median River: Second Dragoons (one company); Capt. G. A. H. Blake

McCulloch's Station, Colorado River: Second Dragoons (one company); Capt. H. W. Merrill

Ross' Station, Bosque River: Second Dragoons (one company); Capt. R. A. Arnold

Richland Creek: Second Dragoons (one company); Capt. H. H. Sibley

Fredericksburg: First Infantry (one company); Capt. S. Eastman

Austin: First Infantry (four companies); Capt. J. R. B. Gardenier

Rio Grande Frontier: Second Dragoons (two companies); Capt. W. J. Hardee

El Paso: Orders issued for establishment

1849

Total U.S. Army troops in Texas: 1,488

Departmental commander: Col. G. M. Brooke

Military headquarters: San Antonio

San Antonio: Eighth Infantry (two companies); Maj. P. Morrison

Fort Polk: Fourth Artillery (one company); Maj. G. Porter

Fort Brown: First Infantry (three companies); Lt. Col. H. Wilson

Ringgold Barracks: Fourth Artillery; First Infantry (two companies); Capt. J. H. La Motte

Laredo: First Infantry (two companies); Capt. J. H. King

Eagle Pass: First Infantry (four companies); Capt. J. M. Scott

Post on the Leona River: Second Dragoons; Eighth Infantry (two companies); Capt. W. J. Hardee

Camp on the Rio Seco: Second Dragoons; Eighth Infantry (two companies); Lt. J. Longstreet

Fredericksburg: Second Dragoons; Eighth Infantry (two companies); Capt. H. W. Merrill

Post on Hamilton Creek: Second Dragoons (one company); Capt. G. A. H. Blake

Post on the Leon River: Eighth Infantry (two companies); Capt. W. R. Montgomery

Fort Graham: Second Dragoons; Eighth Infantry (two companies); Capt. J. V. Bomford

Fort Worth (Trinity River): Second Dragoons, Eighth Infantry (two companies); Capt. R. A. Arnold

El Paso: Third Infantry (six companies); Capt. J. Van Horne

1850

Total U.S. Army troops in Texas: 1,868

Departmental commander: Col. G. M. Brooke

Military headquarters: San Antonio

San Antonio: Eighth Infantry (two companies); Col J. Garland

Fort Polk: Quartermaster staff

Fort Brown: Fourth Artillery (two companies); Maj. G. Porter

Corpus Christi: Fifth Infantry (two companies); Maj. J. J. Abercrombie

Ringgold Barracks: First Infantry (two companies); Capt. J. H. La Motte

Fort McIntosh (Laredo): First Infantry (two companies); Capt. S. Burbank

Fort Duncan (Eagle Pass): First Infantry (four companies); Maj. T. Morris

Fort Inge (Leona River): Second Dragoons; Eighth Infantry (two companies); Capt. W. J. Hardee

Fort Lincoln (Seco Creek): Second Dragoons; Eighth Infantry (two companies); Maj. P. Morrison

Fort Martin Scott (Fredericksburg): Second Dragoons; Eighth Infantry (two companies); Lt. Col. T. Staniford

Fort Croghan (Hamilton Creek): Second Dragoons; Eighth Infantry (two companies); Capt. A. T. Lee

Fort Gates (Leon River): Eighth Infantry (two companies); Capt. R. B. Screven

Fort Graham: Second Dragoons; Eighth Infantry (two companies); Capt. J. V. Bomford

Fort Worth (Trinity River): Second Dragoons, Eighth Infantry (two companies); Capt. R. A. Arnold

Fort Merrill: First Infantry (two companies); Capt. S. M. Plummer

Austin: Headquarters, Second Dragoons; Col W. S. Harney

El Paso: Third Infantry (two companies); Capt. J. Van Horne

1851

Total U.S. Army troops in Texas: 2,819

Departmental commander: Col. P. F. Smith

Military headquarters: San Antonio

San Antonio: Eighth Infantry (one company); Capt. I. V. D. Reeve

Fort Brown: First and Fourth Artillery (four companies); Capt. G. Nauman

Corpus Christi: Seventh Infantry (two companies); Capt. G. R. Paul

Ringgold Barracks: First Infantry (two companies); Capt. J. H. La Motte

Fort McIntosh: First Infantry (two companies); Capt. S. Burbank

Fort Duncan: First Infantry (three companies); Lt. Col. H. Bambridge

Fort Inge: Second Dragoons (one company); Capt. W. J. Hardee

Fort Lincoln: Second Dragoons; Eighth Infantry (two companies); Capt. W. I. Newton

Fort Martin Scott: Eighth Infantry (two companies); Lt. Col. T. Staniford

Fort Croghan: Eighth Infantry (two companies); Capt. J. Sprague

Fort Gates: Eighth Infantry (two companies); Lt. Col. C. A. Waite

Fort Graham: Second Dragoons (two companies); Capt. H. H. Sibley

Fort Worth: Eighth Infantry (two companies); Capt. J. V. Bomford

Fort Merrill: First Infantry (two companies); Capt. R. S. Granger

Austin: Eighth Infantry (one company); Capt. L. Smith

Fort Mason: Second Dragoons (two companies); Capt. H. W. Merrill

Camp Belknap: Fifth Infantry (five companies); Col. G. Loomis

Post on Clear Fork of the Brazos (Fort Phantom Hill): Fifth Infantry (five companies); Maj. J. J. Abercrombie

1852

Total U.S. Army troops in Texas: 3,016

Departmental commander: Col. P. F. Smith

Military headquarters: Corpus Christi (November 11, 1852)

Fort Brown: Fourth Artillery (two companies); Lt. H. M. Whiting

Ringgold Barracks: Seventh Infantry (two companies); Capt. G. R. Paul

Fort McIntosh: First Infantry (two companies); Capt. G. W. Wallace

Fort Duncan: First Infantry (two companies); Maj. T. Morris

Fort Inge: Mounted Rifles (one company); Capt. A. J. Lindsay

Fort Graham: Second Dragoons (two companies); Capt. W. J. Hardee

Fort Worth: Second Dragoons (one company); Capt. H. W. Merrill

Fort Croghan: Second Dragoons (one company); Capt. H. H. Sibley

Fort Merrill: Mounted Rifles (detachment); Lt. W. E. Jones

Fort Mason: Second Dragoons (two companies); Capt. C. A. May

Fort Belknap: Fifth Infantry (five companies); Col. G. Loomis

Fort Ewell: Mounted Rifles (two companies); Lt. Col. W. W. Loring

Fort Clark: First Infantry (two companies); Capt. W. E. Prince

Fort Terrett: First Infantry (four companies); Lt. Col. H. Bainbridge

Fort McKavett: Eighth Infantry (five companies); Maj. P. Morrison

Post on Clear Fork of the Brazos (Fort Phantom Hill): Fifth Infantry (five companies); Lt. Col. C. A. Waite

Camp Johnston (Concho River): Eighth Infantry (five companies); Col. J. Garland

Fort Chadbourne: Eighth Infantry (two companies); Capt. J. Beardsley

In the field: Mounted Rifles (five companies)

1853

Total U.S. Army troops in Texas: 3,294

Departmental commander: Col. P. F. Smith

Military headquarters: Corpus Christi

Fort Brown: Fourth Artillery; Seventh Infantry (five companies); Maj. G. Porter

Ringgold Barracks: Fourth Artillery; Eighth Infantry (five companies); Lt. Col. W. Seawell

Fort McIntosh: First Infantry (two companies); Capt. G. W. Wallace

Fort Duncan: First Infantry (five companies); Maj. T. Morris

Fort Inge: Mounted Rifles (two companies); Maj. G. B. Crittenden

San Antonio: Quartermaster staff

Fort Graham: Second Dragoons (one company); Lt. R. Anderson

Fort Merrill: Mounted Rifles (two companies); Capt. T. Duncan

Fort Mason: Second Dragoons (two companies); Capt. C. A. May

Fort Belknap: Second Dragoons; Fifth Infantry (two companies); Capt. H. W. Merrill

Fort Ewell: Mounted Rifles (two companies); Lt. G. W. Howland

Fort Clark: First Infantry (two companies); Capt. J. H. King

Fort Terrett: Second Dragoons; First Infantry (two companies); Capt. R. S. Granger

Fort McKavett: Eighth Infantry (one company); Capt. J. V. Bomford

Post on Clear Fork of the Brazos (Fort Phantom Hill): Second Dragoons; Fifth Infantry (two companies); Capt. H. H. Sibley

Fort Chadbourne: Second Dragoons; Eighth Infantry (two companies); Lt. J. M. Hawes

El Paso, en route: Eighth Infantry (four companies); Maj. E. B. Alexander

In the field: Mounted Rifles (two companies)

1854

Total U.S. Army troops in Texas: 2,886

Departmental commander: Col. P. F. Smith

Military headquarters: Corpus Christi

Fort Brown: Fourth Artillery (three companies); Maj. G. Porter

Ringgold Barracks: Mounted Rifles; Fourth Artillery; Fifth Infantry (eight companies); Col. G. Loomis

Fort McIntosh: Mounted Rifles; First Artillery; Fifth Infantry (ten companies); Lt. Col. W. W. Loring

Fort Duncan: First Artillery; First Infantry (seven companies); Col. J. Plympton

Fort Inge: Mounted Rifles (two companies); Maj. J. S. Simonson

San Antonio: Quartermaster staff

Fort Merrill: Mounted Rifles (two companies); Capt. A. Porter

Fort Belknap: Second Dragoons; Seventh Infantry (three companies); Maj. E. Steen

Fort Ewell: Mounted Rifles (two companies); Lt. G. W. Howland

Fort Clark: First Infantry (two companies); Capt. J. H. King

Fort McKavett: Second Dragoons (one company); Capt. W. I. Newton

Fort Chadbourne: Second Dragoons (two companies); Capt. P. Calhoun

Fort Davis: Eighth Infantry (six companies); Lt. Col. W. Seawell

Camp on San Pedro River (Devils River): First Infantry (one company); Capt. R. S. Granger

Camp Live Oak Creek (Camp Lancaster): First Infantry (one company); Capt. B. H. Arthur

Fort Bliss: Eighth Infantry (four companies); Maj. E. B. Alexander

Escort to Boundary Commission: First and Seventh Infantry (detachments); Lt. E. K. Smith

1855

Total U.S. Army troops in Texas: 3,652

Departmental commander: Col. P. F. Smith

Military headquarters: San Antonio (October 1, 1855)

Fort Brown: Fourth Artillery (three companies); Maj. G. Porter

Ringgold Barracks: Mounted Rifles; Fourth Artillery; Fifth Infantry (seven companies); Maj. J. H. La Motte

Fort McIntosh: Mounted Rifles; First Artillery; Fifth Infantry (ten companies); Lt. Col. W. W. Loring

Fort Duncan: Mounted Rifles; First Artillery; First Infantry (four companies); Capt. S. Burbank

Fort Inge: Mounted Rifles (two companies); Lt. W. B. Lane

Fort Merrill: Mounted Rifles (one company); Lt. L. S. Baker

Fort Belknap: First and Seventh Infantry (four companies); Capt. G. R. Paul

Fort Clark: Mounted Rifles (one company); Maj. J. S. Simonson

Fort McKavett: First Infantry (two companies); Lt. Col. H. Bambridge

Fort Chadbourne: First Infantry (two companies); Capt. S. Eastman

Fort Davis: Eighth Infantry (six companies); Lt. Col. W. Seawell

Fort Lancaster: First Infantry (two companies); Capt. S. D. Carpenter

Camp at Eagle Spring: Mounted Rifles (one company); Capt. C. F. Ruff

Fort Bliss: First Artillery; Eighth Infantry (four companies); Capt. J. B. Magruder

Escort to Pacific railroad survey: Fifth Infantry (one company); Capt. C. L. Stevenson

En route to department: Second Cavalry (ten companies); Col. A. S. Johnston

1856

Total U.S. Army troops in Texas: 4,047

Departmental commander: Col. A. S. Johnston

Military headquarters: San Antonio

Fort Brown: Fourth Artillery (three companies); Maj. G. Porter

Ringgold Barracks: Mounted Rifles; Fourth Artillery; Fifth Infantry (seven companies); Lt. Col. C. A. Waite

Fort McIntosh: Mounted Rifles; First Artillery; Fifth Infantry (seven companies); Capt. R. B. Marcy

Fort Duncan: Mounted Rifles; First Artillery; First Infantry (five companies); Capt. A. Porter

Camp on the Leona (Fort Inge): Mounted Rifles (headquarters detachment); Lt. Col. W. W. Loring

Fort Belknap: First, Seventh Infantry (four companies); Capt. G. R. Paul

Fort Clark: Mounted Rifles; First Artillery (three companies); Capt. J. B. Magruder

Fort McKavett: First Infantry (two companies); Lt. Col. H. Bainbridge

Fort Chadbourne: First Infantry (two companies); Capt. S. Eastman

Fort Davis: Eighth Infantry (six companies); Lt. Col. W. Seawell

Fort Lancaster: First Infantry (two companies); Capt. R. S. Granger

Fort Mason: Second Cavalry (six companies); Maj. G. H. Thomas

Camp Cooper: Second Cavalry (four companies); Lt. Col. R. E. Lee

Camp Conquista (San Antonio River): Mounted Rifles (one company); Capt. J. G. Walker

Camp Stewart (Quihi): Mounted Rifles (one company); Capt. T. G. Rhett

Camp Davant (Bandera Pass): Mounted Rifles (one company); Lt. J. H. Edson

Fort Bliss: Eighth Infantry (two companies); Maj. T. H. Holmes

1857

Total U.S. Army troops in Texas: 2,351

Departmental commander: Brig. Gen. D. E. Twiggs

Military headquarters: San Antonio

Fort Brown: First Artillery (two companies); Maj. F. Taylor

Ringgold Barracks: First Artillery (one company); Capt. S. Jones

Fort McIntosh: Second Cavalry (one company); Capt. A. G. Brackett

Fort Duncan: First Infantry (one company); Maj. S. Burbank

Fort Inge: Second Cavalry (one company); Capt. E. K. Smith

Fort Belknap: Seventh Infantry (two companies); Capt. G. R. Paul

Fort Clark: Second Cavalry (two companies); Capt. J. Oakes

Fort McKavett: First Infantry (two companies); Lt. S. B. Holabird

Fort Chadbourne: First Infantry (two companies); Capt. J. H. King

Fort Davis: Eighth Infantry (five companies); Lt. Col. W. Seawell

Fort Lancaster: First Infantry (two companies); Capt. R. S. Granger

Fort Mason: Second Cavalry (two companies); Maj. G. H. Thomas

Camp Cooper: Second Cavalry; First Infantry (four companies); Lt. Col. R. E. Lee

Camp Verde (Bandera Pass): Second Cavalry (one company); Capt. I. N. Palmer

Camp G. W. F. Wood (Nueces River): First Infantry (one company); Lt. E. D. Phillips

Camp Colorado: Second Cavalry (one company); Capt. E. Van Dorn

Camp Hudson (Devils River): Eighth Infantry (one company); Lt. T. Fink

Fort Bliss: Mounted Rifles; Eighth Infantry (three companies); Capt. I. V. D. Reeve

1858

Total U.S. Army troops in Texas: 2,472

Departmental commander: Brig. Gen. D. E. Twiggs

Military headquarters: San Antonio

San Antonio Barracks: First Artillery (one company); Capt. B. H. Hill

Fort Brown: First Artillery (one company); Maj. F. Taylor

Ringgold Barracks: First Artillery (one company); Lt. J. E. Slaughter

Fort McIntosh: First Infantry (detachment); Lt. G. A. Williams

Fort Duncan: First Infantry (two companies); Maj. S. Burbank

Fort Inge: First Infantry (detachment); Lt. H. Biggs

Fort Belknap: Second Cavalry; First Infantry (one company); Capt. R. W. Johnson

Near Fort Belknap, field camp: Second Cavalry (nine companies); Maj. G. H. Thomas

Fort Clark: First Infantry (two companies); Lt. J. A. Mower

Fort McKavett: First Infantry (one company); Capt. J. B. Plummer

Fort Chadbourne: First Infantry (two companies); Capt. J. H. King

Fort Davis: Eighth Infantry (four companies); Lt. Col. W. Seawell

Fort Lancaster: First Infantry (two companies); Capt. S. D. Carpenter

Fort Mason: First Infantry (detachment); Lt. W. E. Burnet

Camp Verde: First Artillery (detachment); Lt. W. M. Graham

Camp Colorado: First Infantry (detachment); Lt. J. H. Holman

Camp Hudson: Eighth Infantry (two companies); Capt. L. Smith

Fort Quitman: Eighth Infantry (two companies); Capt. J. V. Bomford

Artesian Well (Pope's Well, Delaware Creek and Pecos River): Second Cavalry; Eighth Infantry (detachments); Capt. J. Pope

Fort Bliss: Mounted Rifles; Eighth Infantry (two companies); Maj. T. H. Holmes

1859

Total U.S. Army troops in Texas: 2,493

Departmental commander: Brig. Gen. D. E. Twiggs

Military headquarters: San Antonio

San Antonio Barracks: First Infantry (one company); Lt. J. H. Holman

Fort Inge: Eighth Infantry (one company); Capt. R. P. Maclay

Fort Clark: First Artillery (three companies); Capt. S. K. Dawson

Fort Chadbourne: First Infantry (one company); Capt. G. W. Wallace

Fort Davis: Eighth Infantry (one company); Lt. Col. W. Seawell

Fort Lancaster: First Infantry (one company); Capt. R. S. Granger

Camp Verde: First Infantry (one company); Maj. S. P. Heintzelman

Camp Colorado: Second Cavalry (one company); Capt. C. J. Whiting

Camp Hudson: Eighth Infantry (one company); Lt. Z. R. Bliss

Fort Quitman: Eighth Infantry (one company); Capt. J. V. Bomford

Camp Cooper: Second Cavalry; First Infantry (four companies); Maj. G. H. Thomas

Brazos Agency: First Infantry (two companies); Capt. J. B. Plummer

Camp Van Camp (Horsehead Crossing of the Pecos River): First Infantry (one company); Lt. H. C. Wood

Fort Stockton: First Infantry (one company); Lt. W. Jones

Fort Bliss: Mounted Rifles; Third Infantry (two companies); Capt. W. I. Elliott

Wichita Expedition, Camp Radziminski, Indian Territory: Second Cavalry (four companies); Capt. E. K. Smith

Pecos Expedition: Second Cavalry (two companies); Capt. G. Stoneman

Echol's Exploring Party (Trans–Pecos): Eighth Infantry (two companies); Lt. E. L. Hartz

1860

Total U.S. Army troops in Texas: 3,009

Departmental commander: Lt. Col. R. E. Lee

Military headquarters: San Antonio

San Antonio Barracks: First Infantry (one company); Capt. J. H. King

Fort Brown: First and Second Artillery (three companies); Capt. H. J. Hunt

Ringgold Barracks: Eighth Infantry (two companies); Capt. A. T. Lee

Fort McIntosh: Eighth Infantry (one company); Lt. E. D. Blake

Fort Duncan: First Artillery (one company); Lt. H. W. Closson

Fort Inge: Second Cavalry (one company); Capt. J. Oakes

Fort Clark: First Artillery (one company); Capt. W. H. French

Fort Chadbourne: First Infantry (one company); Lt. Col. G. Morris

Fort Davis: Eighth Infantry (two companies); Lt. Col. W. Seawell

Fort Lancaster: First Infantry (one company); Capt. R. S. Granger

Fort Mason: Second Cavalry (two companies); Maj. E. Van Dorn

Camp Verde: First Infantry (one company); Maj. S. P. Heintzelman

Camp Colorado: Second Cavalry (one company); Capt. E. K. Smith

Camp Hudson: Eighth Infantry (one company); Capt. L. Smith

Fort Quitman: Eighth Infantry (detachment); Lt. J. G. Taylor

Camp Cooper: Second Cavalry (one company); Maj. G. H. Thomas

Camp Wood: Second Cavalry (one company); Lt. J. B. Hood

Fort Stockton: First Infantry (one company); Capt. S. D. Carpenter

Camp Rosario (Rio Grande, below Edinburg): Second Cavalry (one company); Capt. A. G. Brackett

Camp Barranca (Rio Grande, above Fort Brown): Second Cavalry (one company); Capt. G. Stoneman

Camp on Rio Grande (above Fort Brown): Second Cavalry (one company); Lt. M. M. Kimmel

Camp on Rio Grande (near Ringgold Barracks): Second Cavalry (one company); Capt. N. G. Evans

Echol's exploring party (Trans–Pecos): First and Eighth Infantry (detachments); Lt. J. H. Holman

On Pecos River: Third Infantry (three companies); Col. B. L. E. Bonneville

Fort Bliss: Eighth Infantry (one company); Capt. T. G. Pitcher

Note: Indian Territory posts of Fort Cobb, Fort Arbuckle, and Fort Washita were also part of the Department of Texas

1861

Departmental commander: Brig. Gen. D. E. Twiggs

Military headquarters: San Antonio

Federal property surrendered to State of Texas, Gen. Order No. 5, Headquarters, Department of Texas, February 18, 1861. Surrender ordered March 1, 1861.

Post, date surrendered or abandoned, units (companies)

San Antonio Barracks, February 16, First Infantry (one company)

Fort Brown, March 20, First, Second Artillery (two companies)

Ringgold Barracks, March 7, Eighth Infantry (two companies)

Fort McIntosh, March 12, Eighth Infantry (one company)

Fort Duncan, March 20, First Artillery (three companies)

Fort Inge, March 19, Second Cavalry (one company)

Fort Clark, March 19, First Artillery (one company)

Fort Chadbourne, March 23, First Infantry (one company)

Fort Davis, April 22, April 13, Eighth Infantry (one company)

Fort Lancaster, March 19, First Infantry (one company)

Fort Mason, March 29, Second Cavalry (two companies)

Camp Verde, February 21, Second Cavalry (one company)

Camp Colorado, February 26, Second Cavalry (one company)

Camp Hudson, March 17, Eighth Infantry (one company)

Fort Quitman, April 5, Eighth Infantry (one company)

Camp Cooper, February 21, Second Cavalry, First Infantry (two companies)

Camp Wood, March 15, Second Cavalry (one company)

Fort Stockton, April 10, Eighth Infantry (one company)

Fort Bliss, March 13, Eighth Infantry (three companies)

Camp Rosario, March 20, Second Cavalry (one company)

Camp Barranca, March 20, Second Cavalry (one company)

Note: All escaped Texas but Eighth Infantry, Companies B, E, H, I, K, and F coming from West Texas, which were captured at San Lucas Spring, west of the Medina River on May 9, 1861; the majority soon were paroled.

1862

Galveston (October–January 1863): Commodre W. B. Renshaw, USN

Corpus Christi: Naval Squadron

Sabine City: Naval Squadron

Indianola: Naval Squadron

El Paso (December): First California Infantry (three companies)

1863

Dana's XIII Corps of Army of the Gulf were at:

Matagorda Island (November 1863–March 1864)

Mouth of Rio Grande (November 1863 to 1865)

Brownsville (November 1863–July 1864)

Indianola (December 1863–March 1864)

Mustang Island (December 1863–March 1864)

Brazos Santiago (November 1863 to 1865)

Laredo (March–April)

El Paso: Fifth California Infantry (two companies)

Fort Quitman (August): California column (detachment)

Fort Quitman (September): California column (detachment)

1864

Brazos Santiago: Second Texas Union Cavalry; Sixty-second Infantry (twenty companies)

El Paso: Fifth California Infantry (three companies)

1865

Total U.S. Army troops in Texas: 39,000

Houston, Galveston, Harrisburg, Liberty, Brenham, and Millican: Mower's Division of Granger's XIII Corps

Marshall and Tyler: Herron's Division of XIII Corps

Indianola, Green Lake, and Victoria: Stanley's IV Corps

Austin and Hempstead: Custer's Cavalry Division

San Antonio: Merritt's Cavalry Division

Corpus Christi, Roma, and Ringgold Barracks: Weitzel's XXV Corps

Brownsville: Steele's Division of XIII Corps

Fort Bliss: Fifth Infantry Regiment (two companies)

En route to Texas: Fourth and Sixth Cavalry

1866

Total U.S. Army troops in Texas: 8,500

District of Texas commander: Bvt. Maj. Gen. C. Griffin

Military headquarters: Galveston (August 6, 1865)

As of October 20, based on "Stations of Troops in District of Texas on the Twentieth Day of October," Maj. E. H. Sachops, A.A.A.G to Adjutant General, NARS RG 94, District of Texas, Letters Received, 1866, Headquarters, District of Texas, Galveston:

Galveston: Seventeenth and Thirty-eighth Infantry (ten companies)

Houston: Seventeenth Infantry (two companies)

Richmond: Seventeenth Infantry (one company)

Brenham: Seventeenth Infantry (one company)

Matagorda: Seventeenth Infantry (one company)

Millican: Seventeenth Infantry (one company)

Victoria: Seventeenth Infantry (one company)

Clinton: Fourth Cavalry (one company)

La Grange: Fourth Cavalry (one company)

Tyler: Sixth Cavalry (one company)

Sherman: Sixth Cavalry (one company)

Austin: Sixth Cavalry (four companies)

Jacksboro: Sixth Cavalry (two companies)

Sterling: Sixth Cavalry (one company)

Waco: Sixth Cavalry (one company)

Weatherford: Sixth Cavalry (one company)

Indianola: Thirty-eighth Infantry (nine companies)

Corpus Christi: Nineteenth Infantry (two companies)

Rancho Santa Maria: Nineteenth Infantry (one company)

Rancho Cortinas: Nineteenth Infantry (one company)

Rancho Blanco: Nineteenth Infantry (one company)

Rancho Las Penitas: Nineteenth Infantry (one company)

Edinburg: Nineteenth Infantry (one company)

Fort Brown and Brownsville: Fourth Cavalry; First Artillery; Nineteenth, 114th, and 117th Infantry (sixteen companies)

White Ranch: 114th Infantry (one company)

Ringgold Barracks: 114th Infantry (five companies)

Roma: 114th Infantry (one company)

Redmond's Ranch: 114th Infantry (one company)

Fort McIntosh: 114th Infantry (two companies)

San Antonio: Seventeenth Infantry (three companies)

Camp Sheridan (San Antonio): Fourth Cavalry (six companies)

Fort Martin Scott: Fourth Cavalry (one company)

Fort Inge: Fourth Cavalry (one company)

Fort Bliss: 125th Infantry (two companies)

Additional frontier assignments in November and December 1866:

Camp Verde, November 30: Fourth Cavalry (three companies)

Fort Clark, December 10: Fourth Cavalry (one company)

Fort Mason, December 24: Fourth Cavalry (two companies)

1867

Total U.S. Army troops in Texas: 4,733

Departmental commander: Maj. Gen. W. S. Hancock

Military headquarters: Galveston

Galveston: Seventeenth Infantry (three companies); Lt. G. H. Cram

Houston: Seventeenth Infantry (two companies); Lt. W. M. Van Horne

Hempstead: Seventeenth Infantry (two companies); Capt. G. Lancaster

Brenham: Seventeenth Infantry (one company); Capt. E. Collins

Round Top: Seventeenth Infantry (one company); Lt. H. S. Howe

Centerville: Twenty-sixth Infantry (one company); Capt. J. H. Bradford

Woodville: Seventeenth Infantry (one company); Capt. L. H. Sanger

Victoria: Thirty-fifth Infantry (one company); Capt. S. H. Lathrop

Goliad: Thirty-fifth Infantry (one company); Lt. J. D. Vernay

Refugio: Thirty-fifth Infantry (one company); Lt. J. R. Fitch

Lockhart: Twenty-sixth Infantry (one company); Lt. H. C. Peterson

Seguin: Thirty-fifth Infantry (one company); Capt. G. W. Smith

Mount Pleasant: Sixth Cavalry (two companies); Maj. S. H. Starr

Nacogdoches: Twenty-sixth Infantry (two companies); Capt. T. M. K.
    Smith

Tyler: Twenty-sixth Infantry (four companies); Maj. L. C. Bootes

Sherman: Sixth Cavalry (one company); Lt. T. M. Tolman

Austin: Sixth Cavalry (one company); Col. J. Oakes

Waco: Twenty-sixth Infantry (one company); Capt. J. J. Emerson

Weatherford: Thirty-fifth Infantry (one company); Capt. C. Steelhammer

Lampasas: Twenty-sixth Infantry (one company); Capt. A. W. Evans

Green Lake: Thirty-fifth Infantry (one company); Lt. A. B. Bonnaffon

Fort Belknap: Sixth Cavalry (one company); Lt. G. Schreyer

Camp Wilson (Fort Griffin): Sixth Cavalry (three companies); Lt. Col. S. D. Sturgis

Fort Chadbourne: Fourth Cavalry (five companies); Capt. G. G. Huntt

Fort Mason: Fourth Cavalry (one company); Capt. J. A. Thompson

Camp Verde: Fourth Cavalry (two companies); Maj. J. P. Hatch

San Antonio: Thirty-fifth Infantry (two companies); Maj. J. S. Mason

Fort Inge: Fourth Cavalry (one company); Lt. N. J. McCafferty

Fort Clark: Fourth Cavalry (one company); Lt. B. L. Fletcher

Fort McIntosh: Forty-first Infantry (one company); Capt. J. C. Conner

Ringgold Barracks: Forty-first Infantry (three companies); Col. R. S. Mackenzie

Fort Brown: Ninth Cavalry; First Artillery; Forty-first Infantry (six companies); Col J. J. Reynolds

Brazos Santiago: Forty-first Infantry (one company); Lt. G. E. Albee

Camp Tucker (Post at Buffalo Springs): Sixth Cavalry (four companies); Capt. B. T. Hutchins

Camp Hudson: Ninth Cavalry (two companies); Capt. J. M. Bacon

Fort Stockton: Ninth Cavalry (four companies); Col. E. Hatch

Fort Davis: Ninth Cavalry (four companies); Lt. Col. W. Merritt

Camp Concordia (El Paso): Thirty-fifth Infantry (two companies); Capt. E. C. Mason

1868

Total U.S. Army troops in Texas: 5,675

District commander: Col. J. J. Reynolds

Military headquarters: Austin (August 10, 1868)

Galveston: Seventeenth Infantry (two companies); Capt. G. H. Cram

Brenham: Seventeenth Infantry (one company); Capt. E. Collins

Pilot Grove: Sixth Cavalry (one company); Lt. J. H. Sands

Sulphur Springs: Sixth Cavalry (one company); Capt. T. M. Tolman

Woodland: Twenty-sixth Infantry (one company); Capt. T. M. K. Smith

Marshall: Fifteenth Infantry (nine companies); Col. D. L. Shepherd

Jefferson: Fifteenth Infantry (one company); Capt. J. Custis

Austin: Fourth, Sixth Cavalry; Seventeenth Infantry (four companies);
Maj. E. Gay

Dallas: Seventeenth Infantry (one company); Lt. H. Norton

Belton: Seventeenth Infantry (one company); Capt. G. Lancaster

Indianola: Thirty-fifth Infantry (one company); Capt. F. W. Bailey

Point Isabel: Twenty-sixth Infantry (one company); Lt. C. F. Roe

San Ygnacio: Twenty-sixth Infantry (one company); Lt. E. O. Gibson

Lake Trinidad: Fourth Cavalry (one company); Capt. N. J. McCafferty

Fort Richardson: Sixth Cavalry; Seventeenth Infantry (six companies);
Maj. S. H. Starr

Fort Griffin: Sixth Cavalry; Seventeenth Infantry (four companies); Lt.
Col. S. B. Hayman

Fort Concho: Fourth Cavalry; Seventeenth and Thirty-fifth Infantry
(four companies); Maj. G. A. Gordon

Fort McKavett: Fourth Cavalry; Thirty-fifth Infantry (four companies);
Capt. E. B. Beaumont

Fort Mason: Thirty-fifth Infantry (one company); Capt. P. E. Halcomb

Camp Verde: Thirty-fifth Infantry (one company); Capt. H. A. Ellis

San Antonio: Thirty-fifth Infantry (two companies); Maj. J. S. Mason

Fort Inge: Forty-first Infantry (one company); Capt. D. M. Sells

Fort Clark: Ninth Cavalry; Forty-first Infantry (four companies); Maj.
A. P. Morrow

Fort Duncan: Ninth Cavalry; Forty-first Infantry (three companies); Lt.
Col. W. R. Shafter

Fort McIntosh: Fourth Cavalry (one company); Lt. A. F. Bayard

Ringgold Barracks: Twenty-sixth Infantry (three companies); Capt. J. H.
Bradford

Fort Brown: Fourth and First Cavalry; Twenty-sixth Infantry (five companies); Lt. Col. A. McD. McCook

Fort Stockton: Ninth Cavalry; Forty-first Infantry (six companies); Capt.
G. H. Gamble

Fort Davis: Ninth Cavalry; Forty-first Infantry (five companies); Lt. Col.
W. Merritt

Fort Quitman: Ninth Cavalry; Forty-first Infantry (three companies);
Capt. G. A. Purrington

Camp Concordia (El Paso): Thirty-fifth Infantry (two companies); Capt. E. C. Mason

1869

Total U.S. Army troops in Texas: 4,612

District commander: Col. J. J. Reynolds

Military headquarters: Austin

Austin: Fourth Cavalry; Eleventh Infantry (three companies); Col. L. P. Graham

Galveston: Tenth and Eleventh Infantry (two companies); Col. A. C. Gillem

Nacogdoches: Sixth Cavalry (one company); Lt. E. C. Hentig

Brenham: Eleventh Infantry (one company); Capt. J. Biddle

Bryan: Eleventh Infantry (one company); Capt. T. H. Norton

Columbus: Eleventh Infantry (one company); Capt. C. A. Wikoff

Helena: Fourth Cavalry; Tenth Infantry (two companies); Capt. G. H. Crosman

Livingston: Sixth Cavalry (one company); Capt. S. M. Whitside

Greenville: Sixth Cavalry; Eleventh Infantry (three companies); Lt. Col. C. J. Whiting

Tyler: Sixth Cavalry (two companies); Maj. R. M. Morris

Jefferson: Fourth and Sixth Cavalry; Eleventh Infantry (seven companies); Maj. L. Bissell

Waco: Sixth Cavalry (one company); Capt. J. B. Johnson

Lampasas: Fourth Cavalry (one company); Capt. E. B. Beaumont

Corpus Christi: Fourth Cavalry; Tenth Infantry (two companies); Maj. J. K. Mizner

Fort Richardson: Sixth Cavalry; Thirty-eighth Infantry (five companies); Col. J. Oakes

Fort Griffin: Fourth Cavalry; Twenty-fourth Infantry (three companies); Capt. J. Lee

Fort Concho: Ninth Cavalry; Forty-first Infantry (three companies); Capt. G. H. Gamble

Fort McKavett: Ninth Cavalry; Forty-first Infantry (four companies); Col. R. S. Mackenzie

San Antonio: Fourth Cavalry; Tenth Infantry (two companies); Lt. Col. J. H. Carleton

Fort Clark: Ninth Cavalry; Forty-first Infantry (two companies); Capt. J. M. Bacon

Fort Duncan: Ninth Cavalry; Forty-first Infantry (two companies); Capt. G. B. Hoge

Fort McIntosh: Fourth Cavalry; Tenth Infantry (two companies); Maj. T. M. Anderson

Ringgold Barracks: Tenth Infantry (two companies); Capt. J. B. Parke

Fort Brown: Fourth Cavalry; Tenth Infantry (four companies); Col. H. B. Clitz

Fort Stockton: Ninth Cavalry; Forty-first Infantry (four companies); Maj. T. F. Wade

Fort Davis: Ninth Cavalry; Forty-first Infantry (four companies); Lt. Col. W. Merritt

Fort Quitman: Ninth Cavalry; Forty-first Infantry (three companies); Maj. A. P. Morrow

Fort Bliss: Twenty-fourth Infantry (one company); Maj. H. C. Merriman

1870

Total U.S. Army troops in Texas: 4,842

Departmental commander: Col. J. J. Reynolds

Military headquarters: San Antonio (November 1, 1870)

San Antonio: Fourth Cavalry; Tenth Infantry (two companies); Col. L. P. Graham

Jefferson: Eleventh Infantry (two companies); Maj. L. Bissell

Waco: Eleventh Infantry (two companies); Maj. N. A. M. Dudley

Austin: Tenth Infantry (one company); Maj. J. K. Mizner

Fort Richardson: Fourth and Sixth Cavalry; Eleventh Infantry (twelve companies); Col. J. Oakes

Fort Griffin: Fourth and Sixth Cavalry; Eleventh Infantry (six companies); Lt. Col. C. J. Whiting

Fort Concho: Ninth Cavalry; Eleventh Infantry (eight companies); Col. A. C. Gillem

Fort McKavett: Ninth Cavalry; Twenty-fourth and Twenty-fifth Infantry (six companies); Lt. Col. W. R. Shafter

Fort Clark: Ninth Cavalry; Twenty-fourth and Twenty-fifth Infantry (six companies); Lt. Col. E. W. Hinks

Fort Duncan: Ninth Cavalry; Twenty-fourth and Twenty-fifth Infantry (four companies); Maj. Z. R. Bliss

Fort McIntosh: Fourth Cavalry; Tenth Infantry (two companies); Maj. T. M. Anderson

Ringgold Barracks: Fourth Cavalry; Tenth Infantry (four companies); Lt. Col. A. McD. McCook

Fort Brown: Fourth Cavalry; Tenth Infantry (five companies); Col. H. B. Clitz

Fort Stockton: Ninth Cavalry; Twenty-fourth and Twenty-fifth Infantry (four companies); Maj. T. F. Wade

Fort Davis: Ninth Cavalry; Twenty-fourth and Twenty-fifth Infantry (seven companies); Col. E. Hatch

Fort Quitman: Ninth Cavalry; Twenty-fourth and Twenty-fifth Infantry (four companies); Maj. A. P. Morrow

Fort Bliss: Twenty-fourth Infantry (one company); Capt. F. M. Crandall

1871

Total U.S. Army troops in Texas: 3,853

Departmental commander: Col. J. J. Reynolds

Military headquarters: San Antonio

San Antonio: Fourth Cavalry; Tenth Infantry (two companies); Lt. Col. J. H. Carleton

Austin: Tenth Infantry (one company); Capt. E. E. Sellers

Fort Richardson: Fourth Cavalry; Eleventh Infantry (eleven companies); Col. R. S. Mackenzie

Fort Griffin: Fourth and Sixth Cavalry; Eleventh Infantry (seven companies); Col. W. H. Wood

Fort Concho: Fourth and Ninth Cavalry; Eleventh Infantry (six companies); Maj. J. P. Hatch

Fort McKavett: Ninth Cavalry; Twenty-fourth Infantry (eight companies); Col. A. Doubleday

Fort Clark: Ninth Cavalry; Twenty-fifth Infantry (six companies); Col. G. L. Andrews

Fort Duncan: Ninth Cavalry; Twenty-fourth and Twenty-fifth Infantry (four companies); Maj. Z. R. Bliss

Fort McIntosh: Tenth Infantry (one company); Lt. C. E. Jewett

Ringgold Barracks: Tenth Infantry (three companies); Maj. T. M. Anderson

Fort Brown: Tenth Infantry (four companies); Lt. Col. A. McD. McCook

Fort Stockton: Ninth Cavalry; Twenty-fourth and Twenty-fifth Infantry (four companies); Maj. T. F. Wade

Fort Davis: Ninth Cavalry; Twenty-fourth and Twenty-fifth Infantry (three companies); Lt. Col. W. R. Shafter

Fort Quitman: Ninth Cavalry; Twenty-fourth Infantry (two companies); Maj. A. P. Morrow

Fort Bliss: Ninth Cavalry; Twenty-fifth Infantry (two companies); Capt. C. Bentzoni

1872

Total U.S. Army troops in Texas: 3,944

Departmental commander: Brig. Gen. C. C. Auger

Military headquarters: San Antonio

San Antonio: Tenth, Twenty-fifth Infantry (two companies); Capt. N. Prime

Austin: Tenth Infantry (one company); Capt. E. E. Sellers

Fort Richardson: Fourth Cavalry; Eleventh Infantry (ten companies); Col. R. S. Mackenzie

Fort Griffin: Fourth Cavalry; Eleventh Infantry (five companies); Col. W. H. Wood

Fort Concho: Fourth Cavalry; Eleventh Infantry (six companies); Maj. J. P. Hatch

Fort McKavett: Ninth Cavalry; Twenty-fourth Infantry (seven companies); Col. A. Doubleday

Fort Clark: Ninth Cavalry; Twenty-fourth Infantry (seven companies); Lt. Col. W. Merritt

Fort Duncan: Ninth Cavalry; Twenty-fourth Infantry (three companies); Maj. H. C. Merriam

Fort McIntosh: Ninth Cavalry; Twenty-fourth Infantry (two companies); Capt. C. N. W. Cunningham

Ringgold Barracks: Ninth Cavalry; Tenth Infantry (two companies); Maj. T. M. Anderson

Fort Brown: Fourth Cavalry; Tenth Infantry (six companies); Lt. Col. A. McD. McCook

Fort Stockton: Ninth Cavalry; Twenty-fifth Infantry (three companies); Maj. Z. R. Bliss

Fort Davis: Ninth Cavalry; Twenty-fifth Infantry (three companies); Col. G. L. Andrews

Fort Quitman: Twenty-fifth Infantry (two companies); Capt. D. D. Van Valzah

Fort Bliss: Twenty-fifth Infantry (one company); Capt. F. M. Coxe

1873

Total U.S. Army troops in Texas: 4,450

Departmental commander: Brig. Gen. C. C. Auger

Military headquarters: San Antonio

Austin: Tenth Infantry (one company); Capt. E. E. Sellers

Fort Richardson: Tenth Cavalry; Eleventh Infantry (seven companies); Col W. H. Wood

Fort Griffin: Tenth Cavalry; Eleventh Infantry (five companies); Lt. Col. G. P. Buell

Fort Concho: Ninth and Tenth Cavalry; Eleventh Infantry (six companies); Lt. Col. W. Merritt

Fort McKavett: Ninth Cavalry; Tenth Infantry (seven companies); Col. H. B. Clitz

Fort Clark: Fourth and Ninth Cavalry; Tenth and Twenty-fifth Infantry (fourteen companies); Col. R. S. Mackenzie

Fort Duncan: Fourth Cavalry; Twenty-fourth Infantry (four companies); Lt. Col. W. R. Shafter

Fort McIntosh: Twenty-fourth Infantry (one company); Capt. C. C. Hood

Ringgold Barracks: Ninth Cavalry; Twenty-fourth Infantry (eight companies); Col. E. Hatch

Fort Brown: Twenty-fourth Infantry (five companies); Maj. H. C. Merriman

Fort Stockton: Ninth Cavalry; Twenty-fifth Infantry (four companies); Capt. E. G. Bush

Fort Davis: Ninth Cavalry; Twenty-fifth Infantry (four companies); Maj. Z. R. Bliss

Fort Quitman: Twenty-fifth Infantry (one company); Capt. C. Bentzoni

Fort Bliss: Twenty-fifth Infantry (one company); Capt. F. M. Coxe

1874

Total U.S. Army troops in Texas: 4,271

Departmental commander: Brig. Gen. C. C. Auger

Military headquarters: San Antonio

Austin: Tenth Infantry (one company); Capt. E. E. Sellers

Fort Richardson: Tenth Cavalry; Eleventh Infantry (seven companies); Col W. H. Wood

Fort Griffin: Tenth Cavalry; Eleventh Infantry (six companies); Lt. Col. G. P. Buell

Fort Concho: Tenth Cavalry; Tenth and Eleventh Infantry (eight companies); Maj. H. Douglas

Fort McKavett: Fourth Cavalry; Tenth Infantry (six companies); Col. H. B. Clitz

Fort Clark: Fourth Cavalry; Tenth Infantry (eleven companies); Col. R. S. Mackenzie

Fort Duncan: Fourth Cavalry; Twenty-fourth and Twenty-fifth Infantry (four companies); Capt. J. W. French

Fort McIntosh: Twenty-fourth Infantry (one company); Capt. C. C. Hood

Ringgold Barracks: Ninth Cavalry; Twenty-fourth Infantry (eight companies); Col. E. Hatch

Fort Brown: Twenty-fourth Infantry (five companies); Capt. H. Corbin

Fort Stockton: Ninth Cavalry; Tenth and Twenty-fifth Infantry (four companies); Capt. E. G. Bush

Fort Davis: Ninth Cavalry; Twenty-fifth Infantry (four companies); Col. G. L. Andrews

Fort Quitman: Twenty-fifth Infantry (one company); Capt. C. Bentzoni

Fort Bliss: Twenty-fifth Infantry (one company); Capt. F. M. Coxe

1875

Total U.S. Army troops in Texas: 3,728

Departmental commander: Brig. Gen. E. O. C. Ord

Military headquarters: San Antonio

San Antonio: Tenth Infantry (one company); Capt. E. E. Sellers

Cantonment North Fork of the Red River (Fort Elliott, Department of the Missouri): Fourth Cavalry; Nineteenth Infantry (six companies); Maj. H. C. Bankhead

Fort Richardson: Eleventh Infantry (three companies); Col W. H. Wood

Fort Griffin: Tenth Cavalry; Eleventh Infantry (five companies); Capt. C. L. Choisy

Fort Concho: Ninth and Tenth Cavalry; Tenth and Eleventh Infantry (nine companies); Col. B. H. Grierson

Fort McKavett: Tenth Cavalry; Tenth Infantry (seven companies); Col. H. B. Clitz

Fort Clark: Ninth Cavalry; Tenth Infantry (eight companies); Col. E. Hatch

Fort Duncan: Ninth Cavalry; Twenty-fourth Infantry (three companies); Lt. Col. W. R. Shafter

Fort McIntosh: Twenty-fourth Infantry (one company); Capt. F. M. Crandall

Ringgold Barracks: Ninth Cavalry; Twenty-fourth Infantry (five companies); Maj. T. F. Wade

Fort Brown: Ninth Cavalry; Twenty-fourth Infantry (seven companies); Col. J. H. Potter

Fort Stockton: Tenth Cavalry; Twenty-fifth Infantry (four companies); Lt. Col. M. M. Blunt

Fort Davis: Tenth Cavalry; Twenty-fifth Infantry (six companies); Col. G. L. Andrews

Fort Quitman: Twenty-fifth Infantry (one company); Capt. C. Bentzoni

Fort Bliss: Twenty-fifth Infantry (one company); Maj. Z. R. Bliss

En route within department: Eighth Cavalry (six companies); Maj. A. J. Alexander

1876

Total U.S. Army troops in Texas: 3,106

Departmental commander: Brig. Gen. E. O. C. Ord

Military headquarters: San Antonio

San Antonio: Tenth Infantry (one company); Capt. E. E. Sellers

Fort Elliott: Nineteenth Infantry (six companies); Capt. C. W. Hotsenpiller

Fort Richardson: Tenth Cavalry (one company); Capt. T. A. Baldwin

Fort Griffin: Tenth Cavalry (three companies); Capt. P. L. Lee

Fort Concho: Tenth Cavalry; Tenth Infantry (five companies); Col. B. H. Grierson

Fort McKavett: Tenth Cavalry; Tenth Infantry (seven companies); Col. H. B. Clitz

Fort Clark: Eighth Cavalry; Tenth Infantry (four companies); Maj. W. R. Price

Fort Duncan: Eighth Cavalry; Tenth and Twenty-fourth Infantry (four companies); Lt. Col W. R. Shafter

Fort McIntosh: Twenty-fourth Infantry (two companies); Maj. G. W. Schofield

Ringgold Barracks: Eighth Cavalry; Twenty-fourth Infantry (eight companies); Maj. A. J. Alexander

Fort Brown: Eighth Cavalry; Twenty-fourth Infantry (seven companies); Lt. Col. T. C. Devin

Fort Stockton: Tenth Cavalry; Twenty-fifth Infantry (four companies); Capt. D. D. Van Valzah

Camp San Felipe (Camp Del Rio): Tenth Cavalry (one company); Capt. J. M. Kelly

Fort Davis: Tenth Cavalry; Twenty-fifth Infantry (six companies); Maj. Z. R. Bliss

Fort Quitman: Twenty-fifth Infantry (one company); Capt. C. Bentzoni

Fort Bliss: Twenty-fifth Infantry (one company); Capt. J. Paulus

1877

Total U.S. Army troops in Texas: 3,300

Departmental commander: Brig. Gen. E. O. C. Ord

Military headquarters: San Antonio

San Antonio: Tenth Infantry (one company); Capt. R. P. Wilson

Fort Elliott: Fourth Cavalry; Nineteenth Infantry (four companies); Lt. Col. J. P. Hatch

Fort Richardson: Tenth Cavalry (one company); Lt. Col. J. W. Davidson

Fort Griffin: Tenth Cavalry (one company); Capt. P. L. Lee

Fort Concho: Tenth Cavalry; Twenty-fifth Infantry (five companies); Capt. N. Nolan

Fort McKavett: Tenth Cavalry; Tenth Infantry (six companies); Maj. T. M. Anderson

Fort Clark: Eighth and Tenth Cavalry; Tenth, Twenty-fourth, and Twenty-fifth Infantry (fourteen companies); Lt. Col. W. R. Shafter

Fort Duncan: Tenth Cavalry; Twenty-fourth Infantry (three companies); Maj. G. W. Schofield

Fort McIntosh: Tenth Infantry (one company); Capt. E. E. Sellers

Ringgold Barracks: Eighth Cavalry; Twenty-fourth Infantry (seven companies); Maj. W. R. Price

Fort Brown: Eighth Cavalry; Twenty-fourth Infantry (seven companies); Lt. Col. N. B. Sweitzer

San Felipe (Camp Del Rio): Tenth Cavalry (one company); Capt. J. M. Kelly

Fort Stockton: Twenty-fifth Infantry (three companies); Lt. Col. M. M. Blunt

Fort Davis: Tenth Cavalry; Tenth Infantry (four companies); Col. G. L. Andrews

1878

Total U.S. Army troops in Texas: 4,132

Departmental commander: Brig. Gen. E. O. C. Ord

Military headquarters: San Antonio

Note: Fort Bliss and Fort Elliott were in the Department of the Missouri until 1887 and 1890, respectively.

San Antonio: Second Artillery; Twentieth Infantry (five companies); Maj. J. McMillan

Fort Elliott: Fourth Cavalry; Nineteenth Infantry (four companies); Lt. Col. J. P. Hatch

Fort Griffin: Tenth Cavalry (one company); Capt. S. H. Lincoln

Fort Concho: Tenth Cavalry; Twenty-fifth Infantry (six companies); Col. B. H. Grierson

Fort McKavett: Tenth Infantry (five companies); Col. H. B. Clitz

Fort Clark: Fourth, Eighth Cavalry; Tenth and Twentieth Infantry (sixteen companies); Col. R. S. Mackenzie

Fort Duncan: Fourth Cavalry; Twenty-fourth Infantry (four companies); Lt. Col. W. R. Shafter

Fort McIntosh: Eighth Cavalry; Tenth and Twenty-fourth Infantry (five companies); Maj. W. R. Price

Ringgold Barracks: Eighth Cavalry; Twenty-fourth Infantry (six companies); Lt. Col. N. B. Sweitzer

Fort Brown: Eighth Cavalry; Twentieth Infantry (nine companies); Col. G. Sykes

San Diego: Eighth Cavalry (one company); Capt. A. B. Kauffman

San Felipe (Camp Del Rio): Tenth Cavalry; Twenty-fifth Infantry (two companies); Capt. C. Bentzoni

Fort Stockton: Tenth Cavalry; Twenty-fifth Infantry (five companies); Maj. N. B. McLaughlen

Fort Davis: Tenth Cavalry; Twenty-fifth Infantry (six companies); Col. G. L. Andrews

Fort Bliss, vicinity: Ninth Cavalry; Fifteenth Infantry, (five companies); Maj. N. W. Osborne

1879

Total U.S. Army troops in Texas: 4,319

Departmental commander: Brig. Gen. E. O. C. Ord

Military headquarters: San Antonio

San Antonio: Second Artillery; Twentieth Infantry (three companies); Capt. J. H. Patterson

Fort Elliott: Fourth and Tenth Cavalry; Nineteenth Infantry (five companies); Capt. N. Nolan

Fort Griffin: Twenty-second Infantry (one company); Capt. J. B. Irvine

Fort Concho: Tenth Cavalry; Twenty-fifth Infantry (seven companies); Maj. A. Mills

Fort McKavett: Twenty-second Infantry (five companies); Col. D. S. Stanley

Fort Clark: Fourth and Eighth Cavalry; Second Artillery; Twentieth Infantry (fourteen companies); Col. R. S. Mackenzie

Fort Duncan: Fourth Cavalry; Twenty-fourth Infantry (four companies); Lt. Col. J. E. Yard

Fort McIntosh: Eighth Cavalry; Twenty-fourth Infantry (four companies); Capt. J. C. Gilmore

Fort Ringgold: Eighth Cavalry; Twenty-fourth Infantry (six companies); Maj. D. R. Clendenin

Fort Brown: Eighth Cavalry; Twentieth Infantry (nine companies); Maj. C. R. Layton

San Diego: Eighth Cavalry (one company); Capt. A. B. Kauffman

San Felipe (Camp Del Rio): Fourth Cavalry; Twenty-fifth Infantry (two companies); Capt. C. Bentzoni

Fort Stockton: Tenth Cavalry; Twenty-fifth Infantry (five companies); Lt. Col. M. M. Blunt

Fort Davis: Tenth Cavalry; Twenty-fifth Infantry (six companies); Capt. C. D. Viele

Camp Peña Colorado: Twenty-fourth Infantry (one company); Lt. H. B. Quinby

Fort Bliss, vicinity: Ninth Cavalry; Fifteenth Infantry, (three companies); Maj. N. W. Osborne

1880

Total U.S. Army troops: 3,860

Departmental commander: Brig. Gen. E. O. C. Ord

Military headquarters: San Antonio

San Antonio: First, Twenty-second Infantry (two companies); Capt. C. J. Dickey

Fort Elliott: Fourth Cavalry; Twenty-third Infantry (three companies); Lt. Col. J. P. Hatch

Fort Griffin: Twenty-second Infantry (one company); Capt. J. B. Irvine

Fort Concho: Tenth Cavalry; Twenty-fourth Infantry (nine companies); Col. B. H. Grierson

Fort McKavett: Twenty-second Infantry (four companies); Maj. A. L. Hough

Fort Clark: Fourth, Eighth Cavalry; Second Artillery; Twentieth Infantry (fourteen companies); Col. D. S. Stanley

Fort Duncan: Eighth Cavalry; Twentieth Infantry (two companies); Capt. J. S. McNaught

Fort McIntosh: Eighth Cavalry; Twenty-fourth Infantry (four companies); Maj. S. S. Sumner

Fort Ringgold: Eighth Cavalry; Twenty-first Infantry (four companies); Maj. D. R. Clendenin

Fort Brown: Eighth Cavalry; Second Artillery; Twentieth, Twenty-second Infantry (fourteen companies); Col. E. Otis

San Diego: Eighth Cavalry (one company); Capt. A. B. Kauffman

Corpus Christi: Second Artillery (one company); Capt. E. B. Williston

Camp San Felipe (Camp Del Rio): Eighth Cavalry (one company); Capt. S. B. M. Young

Fort Stockton: Tenth Cavalry; Twenty-fourth Infantry (three companies); Maj. R. F. O'Beirne

Fort Davis: Tenth Cavalry; Twenty-fourth Infantry (six companies); Lt. Col. J. E. Yard

Camp Peña Colorado: Twenty-fifth Infantry (one company); Lt. C. J. Crane

Fort Bliss: Ninth Cavalry; Fifteenth Infantry (three companies); Maj. N. W. Osborne

1881

Total U.S. Army troops in Texas: 3,630

Departmental commander: Brig. Gen. C. C. Auger

Military headquarters: San Antonio

San Antonio: Sixteenth, Twenty-second Infantry (two companies); Capt. C. J. Dickey

Fort Elliott: Fourth Cavalry; Twenty-fourth Infantry (two companies); Maj. H. E. Noyes

Fort Concho: Tenth Cavalry; Sixteenth Infantry (ten companies); Col. B. H. Grierson

Fort McKavett: Sixteenth Infantry (five companies); Col. G. Pennypacker

Fort Clark: Eighth Cavalry; Twenty-second Infantry (thirteen companies); Col. D. S. Stanley

Fort Duncan: Eighth Cavalry; Twenty-second Infantry (three companies); Lt. Col. A. J. Dallas

Fort McIntosh: Eighth Cavalry; Twentieth and Twenty-second Infantry (five companies); Maj. S. S. Sumner

Fort Ringgold: Eighth Cavalry; Second Artillery; Twentieth Infantry (four companies); Maj. C. R. Layton

Fort Brown: Eighth Cavalry; Twentieth Infantry (seven companies); Col. E. Otis

Fort Stockton: Tenth Cavalry; First Infantry (four companies); Lt. Col. T. F. Wade

Fort Davis: Tenth Cavalry; First Infantry (twelve companies); Col. W. R. Shafter

Camp Peña Colorado: First Infantry (one company); Capt. K. Bates

Fort Bliss: Ninth Cavalry; Fifteenth Infantry (three companies); Capt. H. R. Brinkerhoff

1882

Total U.S. Army troops in Texas: 3,193

Departmental commander: Brig. Gen. C. C. Auger

Military headquarters: San Antonio

San Antonio: Twenty-second Infantry (three companies); Capt. C. J. Dickey

Fort Elliott: Fourth Cavalry; Twenty-fourth Infantry (four companies); Maj. R. F. O'Beirne

Fort Concho: Tenth Cavalry; Sixteenth Infantry (eight companies); Lt. Col. A. L. Hough

Fort McKavett: Sixteenth Infantry (one company); Maj. H. Jewett

Fort Clark: Eighth Cavalry; Twenty-second Infantry (twelve companies); Col. D. S. Stanley

Fort Duncan: Eighth Cavalry; Twenty-second Infantry (three companies); Lt. Col. A. J. Dallas

Fort McIntosh: Eighth Cavalry; Sixteenth and Nineteenth Infantry (three companies); Maj. S. S. Sumner

Fort Ringgold: Eighth Cavalry; Nineteenth Infantry (four companies); Maj. R. H. Offley

Fort Brown: Eighth Cavalry; Nineteenth Infantry (seven companies); Col. C. H. Smith

Fort Stockton: Tenth Cavalry (two companies); Lt. Col. T. F. Wade

Fort Davis: Tenth Cavalry; Sixteenth Infantry (ten companies); Col. B. H. Grierson

Camp Peña Colorado: Tenth Cavalry (one company); Capt. C. D. Viele

Fort Bliss: Twenty-third Infantry (two companies); Capt. O. W. Pollock

1883

Total U.S. Army troops in Texas: 2,842

Departmental commander: Brig. Gen. C. C. Auger

Military headquarters: San Antonio

San Antonio: Eighth Cavalry; Third Artillery; Sixteenth Infantry (four companies); Col. E. Otis

Fort Elliott: Fourth Cavalry; Twenty-fourth Infantry (four companies); Maj. R. F. O'Beirne

Fort Concho: Tenth Cavalry; Sixteenth Infantry (six companies); Col. M. M. Blunt

Fort Clark: Eighth Cavalry; Nineteenth Infantry (twelve companies); Col. C. H. Smith

Fort McIntosh: Eighth Cavalry; Sixteenth Infantry (three companies); Capt. H. A. Theaker

Fort Ringgold: Eighth Cavalry; Nineteenth Infantry (four companies); Maj. R. H. Offley

Fort Brown: Eighth Cavalry; Nineteenth Infantry (two companies); Capt. J. H. Bradford

Fort Stockton: Tenth Cavalry; Sixteenth Infantry (three companies); Lt. Col. T. F. Wade

Fort Davis: Tenth Cavalry; Sixteenth Infantry (ten companies); Col. B. H. Grierson

Camp Peña Colorado: Tenth Cavalry (one company); Lt. W. R. Harmon

Fort Bliss: Twenty-third Infantry (two companies); Maj. J. S. Fletcher

1884

Total U.S. Army troopsin Texas: 2,858

Departmental commander: Brig. Gen. D. S. Stanley

Military headquarters: San Antonio

San Antonio: Eighth Cavalry; Third Artillery; Sixteenth Infantry (four companies); Col. E. Otis

Fort Elliott: Fourth Cavalry; Twentieth and Twenty-fourth Infantry (four companies); Maj. C. C. Rawn

Fort Concho: Tenth Cavalry; Sixteenth Infantry (six companies); Col. M. M. Blunt

Fort Clark: Eighth Cavalry; Nineteenth Infantry (eleven companies); Lt. Col. Z. R. Bliss

Fort McIntosh: Eighth Cavalry; Sixteenth Infantry (three companies); Capt. H. A. Theaker

Fort Ringgold: Eighth Cavalry; Nineteenth Infantry (four companies); Maj. R. H. Offley

Fort Brown: Eighth Cavalry; Nineteenth Infantry (two companies); Capt. J. H. Bradford

Camp Del Rio: Eighth Cavalry (one company); Capt. J. F. Randlett

Fort Stockton: Tenth Cavalry; Sixteenth Infantry (three companies); Lt. Col. T. F. Wade

Fort Davis: Tenth Cavalry; Sixteenth Infantry (eight companies); Col. B. H. Grierson

Camp Peña Colorado: Eighth Cavalry (one company); Lt. W. C. McFarland

Camp Rice (Fort Hancock): Tenth Cavalry (one company); Capt. T. A. Baldwin

Fort Bliss: Tenth Infantry (three companies); Maj. H. S. Hawkins

1885

Total U.S. Army troops in Texas: 2,623

Departmental commander: Brig. Gen. D. S. Stanley

Military headquarters: San Antonio

San Antonio: Eighth Cavalry; Third Artillery; Sixteenth Infantry (four companies); Col. E. Otis

Fort Elliott: Third Cavalry; Twenty-fourth Infantry (four companies); Maj. C. C. Rawn

Fort Concho: Third Cavalry; Sixteenth Infantry (six companies); Col. M. M. Blunt

Fort Clark: Eighth Cavalry; Nineteenth Infantry (eleven companies); Col. C. H. Smith

Fort McIntosh: Eighth Cavalry; Sixteenth Infantry (three companies); Maj. R. F. Bernard

Fort Ringgold: Eighth Cavalry; Nineteenth Infantry (four companies); Maj. W. L. Kellogg

Fort Brown: Eighth Cavalry; Nineteenth Infantry (three companies); Capt. J. H. Bradford

Camp Del Rio: Eighth Cavalry (one company); Capt. J. F. Randlett

Fort Stockton: Tenth Cavalry; Sixteenth Infantry (three companies); Maj. G. A. Purington

Fort Davis: Third Cavalry (three companies); Col. A. G. Brackett

Camp Peña Colorado: Third Cavalry (one company); Lt. G. K. Hunter

Camp Rice (Fort Hancock): Third Cavalry (one company); Maj. S. B. M. Young

Fort Bliss: Tenth Infantry (two companies); Maj. H. S. Hawkins

1886

Total U.S. Army troops in Texas: 2,775

Departmental commander: Brig. Gen. D. S. Stanley

Military headquarters: San Antonio

San Antonio: Eighth Cavalry; Third Artillery; Sixteenth Infantry (five companies); Col. E. Otis

Fort Elliott: Third Cavalry; Twenty-fourth Infantry (four companies); Maj. C. H. Carlton

Fort Concho: Third Cavalry; Sixteenth Infantry (six companies); Col. M. M. Blunt

Fort Clark: Third, Eighth Cavalry; Nineteenth Infantry (thirteen companies); Col. C. H. Smith

Fort McIntosh: Eighth Cavalry; Sixteenth Infantry (three companies); Maj. R. F. Bernard

Fort Ringgold: Eighth Cavalry; Nineteenth Infantry (three companies); Capt. E. H. Liscum

Fort Brown: Eighth Cavalry; Nineteenth Infantry (three companies); Maj. W. L. Kellogg

Camp Del Rio: Eighth Cavalry (one company); Capt. E. A. Godwin

Fort Davis: Third Cavalry, Sixteenth Infantry (four companies); Lt. Col. D. R. Clendenin

Camp Peña Colorado: Third Cavalry (one company); Capt. P. D. Vroom

Fort Hancock: Third Cavalry (one company); Maj. S. B. M. Young

Fort Bliss: Tenth Infantry (three companies); Capt. G. Barrett

1887

Total U.S. Army troops in Texas: 2,930

Departmental commander: Brig. Gen. D. S. Stanley

Military headquarters: San Antonio

San Antonio: Eighth Cavalry; Third Artillery; Sixteenth Infantry (nine companies); Col. E. Otis

Fort Elliott: Fifth Cavalry; Twenty-fourth Infantry (four companies); Maj. J. J. Upham

Fort Concho: Third Cavalry; Sixteenth Infantry (three companies); Maj. J. B. Parke

Fort Clark: Third and Eighth Cavalry; Nineteenth Infantry (thirteen companies); Col. C. H. Smith

Fort McIntosh: Eighth Cavalry; Sixteenth and Nineteenth Infantry (three companies); Maj. R. F. Bernard

Fort Ringgold: Sixteenth, Nineteenth Infantry (two companies); Maj. J. A. Wilcox

Fort Brown: Third Cavalry; Nineteenth Infantry (three companies); Maj. C. H. Carlton

Camp Del Rio: Eighth Cavalry (one company); Capt. H. W. Sprole

Fort Davis: Third Cavalry, Sixteenth Infantry (five companies); Lt. Col. D. R. Clendenin

Camp Peña Colorado: Third Cavalry (one company); Capt. J. B. Johnson

Fort Hancock: Third Cavalry (one company); Maj. S. B. M. Young

Fort Bliss: Sixteenth Infantry (two companies); Col. M. M. Blunt

1888

Total U.S. Army troops in Texas: 2,119

Departmental commander: Brig. Gen. D. S. Stanley

Military headquarters: San Antonio

San Antonio: Third Cavalry; Third Artillery; Nineteenth Infantry (eight companies); Col. C. H. Smith

Fort Elliott: Fifth Cavalry; Thirteenth Infantry (four companies); Maj. J. J. Upham

Fort Concho: Nineteenth Infantry (one company); Capt. G. F. Towle

Fort Clark: Third Cavalry; Nineteenth Infantry (nine companies); Col. A. G. Brackett

Fort McIntosh: Third Cavalry; Fifth Infantry (three companies); Maj. S. B. M. Young

Fort Ringgold: Third Cavalry; Fifth Infantry (three companies); Lt. Col. D. R. Clendenin

Fort Brown: Third Cavalry; Fifth Infantry (three companies); Maj. C. H. Carlton

Fort Davis: Fifth Infantry (two companies); Lt. Col. M. A. Cochrane
Camp Peña Colorado: Third Cavalry (one company); Lt. G. H. Morgan
Fort Hancock: Fifth Infantry (one company); Capt. T. H. Logan
Fort Bliss: Fifth Infantry (two companies); Capt. E. P. Ewers

1889

Total U.S. Army troops in Texas: 1,904
Departmental commander: Brig. Gen. D. S. Stanley
Military headquarters: San Antonio
San Antonio: Third Cavalry; Third Artillery; Nineteenth Infantry (nine companies); Col. C. H. Smith
Fort Elliott: Fifth Cavalry; Thirteenth Infantry (four companies); Maj. H. C. Cook
Fort Clark: Third Cavalry; Nineteenth Infantry (seven companies); Col. A. G. Brackett
Fort McIntosh: Third Cavalry; Fifth Infantry (three companies); Maj. S. B. M. Young
Fort Ringgold: Third Cavalry; Fifth Infantry (three companies); Maj. E. C. Woodruff
Fort Brown: Third Cavalry; Fifth Infantry (three companies); Capt. C. E. Hargous
Fort Davis: Fifth Infantry (two companies); Lt. Col. M. A. Cochrane
Camp Peña Colorado: Third Cavalry (one company); Lt. G. H. Morgan
Fort Hancock: Fifth Infantry (one company); Capt. T. H. Logan
Fort Bliss: Fifth Infantry (two companies); Col. N. W. Osborne

1890

Total U.S. Army troops in Texas: 2,450
Departmental commander: Brig. Gen. D. S. Stanley
Military headquarters: San Antonio
Fort Sam Houston (San Antonio): Third Cavalry; Second Artillery; Twenty-third Infantry (nine companies); Col. H. M. Black
Fort Elliott: Fifth Cavalry; Thirteenth Infantry (three companies); Maj. H. C. Cook
Fort Clark: Third Cavalry; Eighteenth Infantry (ten companies); Col. H. M. Lazelle

Fort McIntosh: Third Cavalry; Fifth Infantry (two companies); Col. A. G. Brackett

Fort Ringgold: Third Cavalry; Fifth Infantry (three companies); Maj. E. C. Woodruff

Fort Brown: Third Cavalry; Fifth Infantry (three companies); Lt. Col. J. J. Upham

Fort Davis: Fifth, Twenty-third Infantry (five companies); Maj. S. Overshine

Camp Peña Colorado: Third Cavalry (one company); Capt. O. Elting

Fort Hancock: Fifth Infantry (one company); Capt. T. H. Logan

Fort Bliss: Fifth Infantry (two companies); Col. N. W. Osborne

1891

Total U.S. Army troops in Texas: 1,701

Departmental commander: Brig. Gen. D. S. Stanley

Military headquarters: San Antonio

Fort Sam Houston: Third Cavalry; Third Artillery; Fifth and Twenty-third Infantry (eleven companies); Col. J. J. Coppinger

Fort Clark: Third Cavalry; Eighteenth Infantry (ten companies); Col. H. M. Lazelle

Fort McIntosh: Third Cavalry; Twenty-third Infantry (three companies); Col. A. P. Morrow

Fort Ringgold: Third Cavalry; Fifth Infantry (two companies); Capt. J. G. Bourke

Fort Brown: Third Cavalry (one company); Capt. J. B. Johnson

Camp Peña Colorado: Third Cavalry (one company); Lt. T. R. Rivers

Fort Hancock: Third Cavalry (one company); Capt. G. A. Dodd

Fort Bliss: Twenty-third Infantry (two companies); Maj. J. Henton

1892

Total U.S. Army troops in Texas: 1,743

Departmental commander: Brig. Gen. F. Wheaton

Military headquarters: San Antonio

Fort Sam Houston: Third Cavalry; Third Artillery; Fifth and Twenty-third Infantry (ten companies); Col. J. J. Coppinger

Fort Clark: Eighteenth Infantry (six companies); Col. H. M. Lazelle

Eagle Pass (Fort Duncan): Third Cavalry (one company); Maj. H. W. Wessells

Fort McIntosh: Third Cavalry; Eighteenth Infantry (three companies); Maj. G. A. Purington

Fort Ringgold: Third Cavalry; Eighteenth Infantry (three companies); Capt. G. A. Drew

Fort Brown: Third Cavalry (one company); Capt. J. B. Johnson

Camp Peña Colorado: Third Cavalry (one company); Capt. O. Elting

Fort Hancock: Third Cavalry (one company); Capt. G. A. Dodd

Fort Bliss: Twenty-third Infantry (two companies); Maj. J. Henton

1893

Total U.S. Army troops in Texas: 1,995

Departmental commander: Brig. Gen. F. Wheaton

Military headquarters: San Antonio

Fort Sam Houston: Fifth and Seventh Cavalry; Third Artillery; Fifth and Twenty-third Infantry (eleven companies); Col. J. J. Coppinger

Fort Clark: Third and Seventh Cavalry; Eighteenth Infantry (eight companies); Maj. T. E. Rose

Eagle Pass (Fort Duncan): Fifth Cavalry (one company); Capt. G. H. Paddock

Fort McIntosh: Fifth Cavalry; Eighteenth Infantry (three companies); Col. T. F. Wade

Fort Ringgold: Fifth Cavalry; Eighteenth Infantry (three companies); Maj. A. S. B. Keyes

Fort Brown: Fifth Cavalry (two companies); Maj. H. Wagner

Fort Hancock: Seventh Cavalry (one company); Capt. H. Jackson

Fort Bliss: Twenty-third Infantry (two companies); Maj. J. Henton

1894

Total U.S. Army troops in Texas: 2,053

Departmental commander: Brig. Gen. F. Wheaton

Military headquarters: San Antonio

Fort Sam Houston: Fifth and Seventh Cavalry; Third Artillery; Fifth and Eighteenth Infantry (nine companies); Col. T. F. Wade

Fort Clark: Fifth Cavalry; Twenty-third Infantry (eight companies); Col. J. J. Coppinger

Eagle Pass (Fort Duncan): Fifth Cavalry (one company); Capt. W. S. Edgerly

Fort McIntosh: Fifth Cavalry; Twenty-third Infantry (three companies); Capt. G. A. Goodale

Fort Ringgold: Fifth Cavalry; Twenty-third Infantry (three companies); Maj. A. S. B. Keyes

Fort Brown: Fifth Cavalry (two companies); Maj. H. Wagner

Fort Hancock: Seventh Cavalry (one company); Capt. H. Jackson

Fort Bliss: Eighteenth Infantry (four companies); Capt. W. H. McLaughlin

1895

Total U.S. Army troops in Texas: 2,211

Departmental commander: Brig. Gen. Z. R. Bliss

Military headquarters: San Antonio

Fort Sam Houston: Fifth and Seventh Cavalry; Third Artillery; Eighteenth Infantry (eleven companies); Col. T. F. Wade

Fort Clark: Fifth and Seventh Cavalry; Twenty-third Infantry (eight companies); Col. S. Overshine

Eagle Pass (Fort Duncan): Fifth Cavalry (one company); Capt. G. H. Paddock

Fort McIntosh: Fifth Cavalry; Twenty-third Infantry (three companies); Maj. W. Davis

Fort Ringgold: Fifth Cavalry; Twenty-third Infantry (three companies); Maj. D. W. Burke

Fort Brown: Fifth Cavalry (two companies); Maj. H. Wagner

Fort Hancock: Seventh Cavalry (one company); Capt. H. Jackson

Fort Bliss: Eighteenth Infantry (two companies); Col. D. Parker

1896

Total U.S. Army troops in Texas: 1,913

Departmental commander: Brig. Gen. Z. R. Bliss

Military headquarters: San Antonio

Fort Sam Houston: Fifth Cavalry; Third Artillery; Eighteenth Infantry (eleven companies); Col. T. F. Wade

Fort Clark: Fifth Cavalry; Twenty-third Infantry (six companies); Col. S. Overshine

Eagle Pass (Fort Duncan): Twenty-third Infantry (one company); Capt. L. Febiger

Fort McIntosh: Fifth Cavalry; Twenty-third Infantry (two companies); Maj. W. Davis

Fort Ringgold: Fifth Cavalry; Twenty-third Infantry (two companies); Maj. D. W. Burke

Fort Brown: Fifth Cavalry; Twenty-third Infantry (two companies); Maj. H. Wagner

Fort Bliss: Fifth Cavalry; Eighteenth Infantry (three companies); Col. D. D. Van Valzah

1897

Total U.S. Army troops in Texas: 1,581

Departmental commander: Brig. Gen. W. M. Graham

Military headquarters: San Antonio

Fort Sam Houston: Fifth Cavalry; First Artillery; Eighteenth Infantry (eleven companies); Col. L. H. Carpenter

Fort Clark: Fifth Cavalry; Twenty-third Infantry (six companies); Col. S. Overshine

Eagle Pass (Fort Duncan): Twenty-third Infantry (one company); Capt. L. Febiger

Fort McIntosh: Fifth Cavalry; Twenty-third Infantry (two companies); Maj. W. Davis

Fort Ringgold: Fifth Cavalry; Twenty-third Infantry (two companies); Maj. D. W. Burke

Fort Brown: Fifth Cavalry; Twenty-third Infantry (two companies); Maj. H. Wagner

Fort Bliss: Fifth Cavalry; Eighteenth Infantry (three companies); Col. D. D. Van Valzah

1898

Total U.S. Army troops in Texas: 4,398

Departmental commander: Brig. Gen. Z. R. Bliss

Military headquarters: San Antonio

March

Fort Sam Houston: Fifth Cavalry; First Artillery; Twenty-third Infantry (eleven companies); Col. L. H. Carpenter

Fort Clark: Fifth Cavalry; Twenty-third Infantry (six companies); Col. S. Overshine

Eagle Pass (Fort Duncan): Twenty-third Infantry (one company); Capt. L. Febiger

Fort McIntosh: Fifth Cavalry; Twenty-third Infantry (two companies); Maj. W. Davis

Fort Ringgold: Fifth Cavalry; Twenty-third Infantry (two companies); Maj. D. W. Burke

Fort Brown: Fifth Cavalry; Twenty-third Infantry (two companies); Maj. H. Wagner

Fort Bliss: Fifth Cavalry; Eighteenth Infantry (three companies); Col. D. D. Van Valzah

Spanish-American War deployments:

April 15: Fifth Cavalry ordered to South Carolina: Eighteenth and Twenty-third Infantry ordered to New Orleans

April 20: Fort Point (Galveston): First Artillery (one company); Capt. C. L. Best

April 23: First Artillery ordered to Chickamauga

May

San Antonio: Muster in First U.S. Volunteer Cavalry (Rough Riders)

Austin: Muster in of First Texas Volunteer Cavalry; First, Second, and Third Texas Volunteer Infantry

Galveston: Muster in of First U.S. Volunteer Infantry (Texas Immunes)

July

Fort Point (Galveston): First Artillery (one company); Fifth Infantry (one company)

Camp Hawley (Galveston): First U.S. Volunteer Infantry (Texas Immunes)

Houston: Muster in of Fourth Texas Volunteer Infantry

August

Fort Point (Galveston): Third Texas Volunteer Infantry (one company)

September

Fort Sam Houston: First Artillery (one company); Fourth Texas Volunteer Infantry (ten companies)

Corpus Christi: Third Texas Volunteer Infantry (one company)

Eagle Pass: Third Texas Volunteer Infantry (one company)

Fort Clark: Third Texas Volunteer Infantry (nine companies)

Fort McIntosh: First Texas Volunteer Cavalry (one company)
Fort Ringgold: First Texas Volunteer Cavalry (one company)
Fort Brown: First Texas Volunteer Cavalry (one company)
Fort Bliss: Third Texas Volunteer Infantry (one company)
October
Galveston: Muster out of First U.S. Volunteer Infantry
November
Dallas: Muster out of Second Texas Volunteer Infantry
San Antonio: Muster out of First Texas Volunteer Cavalry

1899
Total U.S. Army troops in Texas: 2,700
Departmental commander: Col. C. McKibbin
Military headquarters: San Antonio
February
Various posts: Muster out of Third Texas Volunteer Infantry
March
San Antonio: Muster out of Fourth Texas Volunteer Infantry
April
Galveston: Muster out of First Texas Volunteer Infantry
July
Fort Sam Houston: First Artillery; Twenty-fifth Infantry (two companies); Thirty-third U.S. Volunteer Infantry forming for deployment to Philippine Islands
Fort San Jacinto (Galveston): First Artillery (one company)
Sabine Pass: First Artillery (one company)
Fort Clark: Ninth Cavalry (one company)
Eagle Pass (Fort Duncan): Ninth Cavalry (one company)
Fort McIntosh: Twenty-fifth Infantry (one company)
Fort Ringgold: Ninth Cavalry (one company)
Fort Brown: Ninth Cavalry (one company)
Fort Bliss: Twenty-fifth Infantry (one company)

1900
Total U.S. Army troops in Texas: 1,200
Departmental commander: Col. C. McKibbin
Military headquarters: San Antonio

August

Fort Sam Houston: Twenty-fifth Infantry (two companies)

Fort San Jacinto (Galveston): First Artillery (detachment)

Fort Crockett (Galveston): First Artillery (detachment)

Fort Travis (Galveston): First Artillery (detachment)

Fort Clark: First Artillery (one company)

Eagle Pass (Fort Duncan): First Artillery (detachment)

Fort McIntosh: Tenth Cavalry (one company)

Fort Ringgold: Tenth Cavalry (one company)

Fort Brown: Tenth Cavalry (one company)

Fort Bliss: Twenty-fifth Infantry (one company)

* "Report of the Adjutant General of the Army," in the annual *Report of the Secretary of War*, 1836–1900; "Stations of Troops in District of Texas on the Twentieth Day of October," Maj. E. H. Sachops, A.A.A.G to Adjutant General, NARS RG 94, District of Texas, Letters Received, 1866 Headquarters, District of Texas, Galveston.

A staged frontier battle with the role of hostile Indians played by army scouts or soldiers dressed for the part. The army fought over two hundred combats in the Indian Wars of Texas; the majority of the actions were small unit skirmishes as the photograph depicts. *Photograph courtesy Lawrence T. Jones III, Austin.*

Summary of U.S. Army Combat Actions in the Indian Wars of Texas, 1849–1881*

July 12, 1849: Lt. Thomas D. Johns and a detachment of First Infantry from Laredo pursued Comanche raiders who had attacked a forage party twenty miles above Laredo. The Indians escaped into Mexico with stolen mules.

August 11, 1849: A Texas Mounted Volunteer detachment assigned to the army pursued Comanche raiders five miles north of Corpus Christi. Four Indians were killed; the army recovered a captive boy, horses, and mules.

August 24, 1849: Lt. Lewis Neill and a detachment of Company C, Second Dragoons, from Fort Inge pursued raiders who had stolen horses from the post stables the night of August 23. One Indian was killed and one wounded. The army recovered two horses and three mules.

November 21, 1849: A detachment of Company G, Second Dragoons, from Fort Lincoln skirmished with Comanches on the Rio Seco.

January 11, 1850: A mixed force of Second Dragoons and Texas Mounted Volunteers from Fort Lincoln and Fort Martin Scott pursued Indians who had raided Refugio and Castroville. The Indians fired the prairie and escaped with four hundred horses.

January 20, 1850: Company D, Eighth Infantry, from Fort Gates pursued Tonkawa raiders. The Indians abandoned equipment but escaped with stolen horses.

February 20, 1850: A detachment of Company E, Eighth Infantry, on wagon escort from Fort Inge to Fort Duncan was ambushed by Indians. One soldier was killed in action.

February 23, 1850: Lt. Egbert L. Vielé and a detachment of First Infantry from Fort McIntosh pursued Indians who had committed murder near Laredo. The Indians escaped in the brush after a three-day chase.

February 24, 1850: Lt. Walter W. Hudson and mounted Company G, First Infantry, from Fort McIntosh pursued and attacked Tonkawa who had raided the post stables. One Mexican boy captive was recovered, but the Indians escaped in the darkness. One Indian was wounded in action.

February 25, 1850: Lt. Walter W. Hudson and Company G, First Infantry, from Fort McIntosh attacked the camp of Tonkawa who had committed a murder near the post. The Indians escaped on foot after abandoning horses and equipment.

March 2–12, 1850: Capt. William J. Hardee and Company C, Second Dragoons, from Fort Inge were on a scout when they pursued Indians from Chacon Creek to the Rio Grande. The Indians escaped into Mexico.

March 3, 1850: A detachment of Company C, Second Dragoons, from Fort Inge were ambushed on the road while on wagon escort from Fort Duncan. One soldier was killed in action.

April 6, 1850: Lt. Walter W. Hudson and a detachment of Company G, First Infantry, from Fort McIntosh attacked a camp of Indians on the Nueces River who had stolen horses at Laredo.[1] Thirty horses were recovered but the Indians escaped.

April 7, 1850: Lt. Walter W. Hudson and a detachment of Company G, First Infantry, from Fort McIntosh pursued the Indians from the action of April 6. One soldier was killed in action, one officer (Lieutenant Hudson) died of wounds, four soldiers and four Indians were wounded in action. The army recovered three horses.

May 10, 1850: A sergeant and a detachment of Company G, First Infantry, from Fort McIntosh pursued Indians who had raided Laredo; the Indians escaped.

May 12, 1850: Lt. Samuel B. Holabird and Company G, First Infantry, from Fort McIntosh were on a scout when they were attacked while in camp near the Nueces River. The Indians escaped after a forty-mile pursuit.

May 13, 1850: Capt. John S. Ford and Ford Company, Texas Mounted Volunteers, assigned to the army at Fort McIntosh were on a scout to Nueces River when they attacked a Comanche war party near Arroyo San Boque. One Texas Mounted Volunteer was wounded in action, four Indians were killed and four wounded. The Volunteers recovered eleven horses and a mule.

May 14, 1850: Capt. John S. Ford and Ford Company, Texas Mounted Volunteers, assigned to the army at Fort McIntosh, continued pursuit of Comanches encountered on May 13. The Indians dispersed and escaped.

May 20, 1850: Lt. Charles G. Merchant with Company E, Eighth Infantry, and a detachment of Company C, Second Dragoons, from Fort Inge were on a scout of the Frio River when they attacked an Indian party and recovered forty horses. One officer (Lieutenant Merchant) was wounded in action.

June 12, 1850: Lt. Charles N. Underwood and a detachment of Companies H and K, First Infantry, from Fort Merrill were escorting the mail to Laredo when Indians attacked. Two soldiers were killed in action, one officer (Lieutenant Underwood) and five soldiers were wounded, one Indian was killed, and four Indians were wounded.

June 12, 1850: Lt. Andrew J. Walker and a detachment of Ford Company, Texas Mounted Volunteers, assigned to the army at Laredo, pursued an Indian party while on a scout. The Indians escaped.

June 15, 1850: Lt. Andrew J. Walker and a detachment of Ford Company, Texas Mounted Volunteers, assigned to the army at Laredo, pursued Comanche raiders. One Texas Mounted Volunteer was wounded, three Indians were killed, and three Indians were wounded. The Volunteers recovered horses.

June 21, 1850: Lt. Andrew J. Walker and a detachment of Ford Company, Texas Mounted Volunteers, assigned to the army at Laredo, pursued raiders who attempted to steal government horses. The Indians escaped into Mexico.

June 26, 1850: Lt. M. B. Highsmith and a detachment of Ford Company, Texas Mounted Volunteers, assigned to the army, were attacked in camp near San Antonio Viejo. One Indian was killed and the Indians captured ten horses and five mules.

June 28, 1850: Capt. John S. Ford and a detachment of Ford Company, Texas Mounted Volunteers, assigned to the army, were scouting near

San Antonio Viejo when they followed and attacked a party of Comanche. One Texas Mounted Volunteer was killed and one wounded. Three Indians were killed and four wounded; one of the wounded Indians was captured.

June 23–August 27, 1850: Capt. William J. Hardee's large-scale campaign staging out of Fort Inge into the Nueces River-Rio Grande area with ten companies of Second Dragoons and First Infantry and two companies of Texas Mounted Volunteers

The resulting actions were:

> **July 11**: Capt. James Oakes and Company G, Second Dragoons, were on a scout of the Nueces River when they pursued an Indian party. Two Indians were killed and the army captured twenty-one horses and one mule.
>
> **Mid-July**: Capt. William A. "Bigfoot" Wallace and Wallace Company, Texas Ranging Company, attached to the army, were on a scout of the Nueces River when they encountered an Indian party and were attacked. Three Rangers were wounded, seven Indians killed, and nine Indians wounded.
>
> **August 12**: Capt. James Oakes and Company G, Second Dragoons, encountered and attacked an Indian party while on a scout of the Nueces River. One officer (Captain Oakes) was wounded and three Indians were killed.
>
> **Mid-August**: Lt. Charles H. Tyler and a detachment of Company C, Second Dragoons, and detachment of Texas Mounted Volunteers from Fort Inge pursued an Indian party. Two Indians were killed and the army captured several horses.

August 1850: Company C, Second Dragoons, from Fort Inge attacked an Indian camp while on a scout of the Devils River. One Indian was killed and one wounded; the army captured forty horses.

September 1852: Lt. Daniel M. Frost and a detachment of Mounted Rifles on a scout pursued a party of Indians and captured horses and equipment.

March 1853: Near the lower Nueces River one night a party of Comanches stole three horses from Company F, Mounted Rifles. A detachment of eight soldiers pursued the Indians eighteen miles and attacked. One soldier was wounded, three Indians were killed, and the horses were recovered.

June 18, 1853: Company F, Mounted Rifles, caught a Comanche raiding party trying to cross the Rio Grande into Mexico one mile above San Ygnacio. Two soldiers were wounded and three Indians were killed; the army recovered thirty stolen horses and six mules.

May 9, 1854: Lt. George B. Crosby and an eleven-man detachment from Companies F and I, Mounted Rifles, from Fort Merrill were on a scout to Lake Trinidad when they encountered and attacked a party of Lipan Apache. Three soldiers were killed, one officer (Lieutenant Crosby) and two soldiers were wounded, three Indians were killed, and two Indians were wounded.

May 10, 1854: 1st Sgt. C. H. McNally and a detachment of Company D, Mounted Rifles, from Fort Merrill pursued Indians who had attacked a goverment wagon train near the post. After a twenty-five-mile chase the army recovered the plundered baggage and animals.

May 11, 1854: Cpl. William Wright and a twenty-man detachment of Company F, Mounted Rifles, attacked a band of Lipan Indians near Santa Gertrudis Creek near Corpus Christi. Six soldiers were wounded and four Indians were killed.

July 11, 1854: Capt. Michael E. Van Buren and Companies A and H, Mounted Rifles, from Fort Inge pursued and attacked a party of raiders near San Diego. One officer (Captain Van Buren) died of wounds, two soldiers were wounded, and five Indians were killed. The army recovered horses.

September 5, 1854: A detachment of Company D, Mounted Rifles, had a skirmish on the Rio Grande.

October 3, 1854: Capt. John G. Walker and Companies D and K, Mounted Rifles, and three citizen volunteers were escorting the department commander from El Paso when they pursued and attacked the camp of a band of Lipan Apache who had stolen cattle near Eagle Spring. One soldier was killed, one officer (Lt. Eugene A. Carr) and the citizen guide (José Policarpo "Polly" Rodríquez) were wounded, and seven Indians were killed.

October 11, 1854: Company F, First Infantry, had a skirmish on Live Oak Creek.

January 7, 1855: Company A and a detachment of Company G, Mounted Rifles, had a skirmish on the Pecos River.

July 22, 1855: Lt. Horace Randal and a detachment of Company I,

Mounted Rifles, from Fort Davis, attacked a party of Mescalero Apache who were raiding near Eagle Spring. Eight Indians were killed.

February 22, 1856: Capt. James Oakes and Company C, Second Cavalry, from Fort Mason, pursued and attacked a band of Wacos near the headwaters of the Nueces River. Two soldiers were wounded in action, one Indian was killed, and two Indians were wounded. The army captured all Indian horses and property.

March 8, 1856: Capt. Albert G. Brackett and a detachment of Company I, Second Cavalry, from Fort Mason, were on a scout near the Guadalupe River when they made a dismounted attack on a Lipan Apache camp. Three Indians were killed; the army recovered stolen horses, mules, and a bank draft for 1,000 British pounds sterling.

March 21, 1856: Cpl. William Fletcher and a detachment of Company F, First Artillery, from Fort McIntosh, pursued and attacked raiders on the Rio Grande and recovered three horses. Two Indians were wounded.

April 13, 1856: Capt. Thomas Claiborne Jr. with Companies B and D, Mounted Rifles and Company F, First Artillery, from Fort McIntosh and Fort Duncan, and Laredo Mayor Santos Benavidas and twenty-five citizens pursued Indian raiders three hundred miles and attacked a camp near the headwaters of the Nueces River. One Indian was killed and four Indians were taken prisoner. The army captured all Indian property and horses.

May 25, 1856: Capt. James Oakes and a detachment of Company C, Second Cavalry, from Fort Mason were on scout to the headwaters of the Concho River when they skirmished with a party of Comanche. One Indian was killed.

May 27, 1856: A detachment of Company H, Mounted Rifles, from Fort Clark had a skirmish on the Devils River.

July 1, 1856: While a part of Lt. Col. Robert E. Lee's expedition to the headwaters of the Brazos River, Capt. Earl Van Dorn and Company A, Second Cavalry, pursued and attacked a party of Comanche. Two Indians were killed and one taken prisoner. The army captured twelve horses.

July 26, 1856: Companies D and H, Eighth Infantry, from Fort Davis were on a scout to Muerto Creek when they skirmished with Indians and captured the Indians' horses.

August 30, 1856: While on an expedition out of Fort Clark to explore the

Pecos River area Capt. James Oakes with Company C, Second Cavalry; Company B, First Infantry; and Company I, First Artillery, encountered and attacked three small bands of Indians in one day. Four Indians were killed and four were wounded. The army captured horses and other property.

November 19, 1856: Lt. Walter H. Jenifer and a detachment of Company B, Second Cavalry, were on a scout from Fort Mason to the Llano River when they attacked a group of Comanches and captured some of the Indians' equipment.

November 26, 1856: Capt. William R. Bradfute with Company G, Second Cavalry, from Fort Mason were on a scout of the Concho River when they attacked a party of Comanche. One soldier was wounded, four Indians were killed, and two Indians were wounded. The army captured six horses.

December 18, 1856: Lt. James B. Witherell with Company C, Second Cavalry, and two officers from the Eighth Infantry skirmished with a party of Apache while on scout from Fort Clark to the Rio Grande.

December 21, 1856: Lt. James B. Witherell with Company C, Second Cavalry, and two officers from the Eighth Infantry while scouting from Fort Clark encountered and attacked a party of Apache on the Rio Grande. Two Indians were killed and two wounded; the army captured their horses and arms.

December 22, 1856: Capt. Richard W. Johnson and Company F, Second Cavalry, from Camp Colorado were on a scout to the Concho River when they dismounted and attacked a Comanche camp. Two soldiers were killed and two were wounded. Three Indians were killed and three were wounded. The army captured thirty-four horses and recovered a Mexican captive.

January 31, 1857: Detachments of Companies A and C, Eighth Infantry, from Fort Davis had a skirmish with Indians near Howard's Springs.

February 12, 1857: Lt. Robert C. Wood and Company B, Second Cavalry, from Fort Mason were on a scout of the North Fork of the Concho River when they pursued an Comanche trail for three days and attacked the party. One officer (Lieutenant Wood) was wounded, three Indians were killed, and two Indians were taken prisoner. The army captured all the Indians' horses and property.

February 13, 1857: 1st Sgt. Walter McDonald and a detachment of

Company D, Second Cavalry, from Camp Verde with guide José "Polly" Rodríquez and two citizen volunteers pursued Comanches who had stolen horses near Center Point. On Kickapoo Creek near the head of the South Concho River the command attacked the Indian camp. Two soldiers were killed in action and one died of wounds. Two Indians were killed and four Indians were wounded. The army recovered five horses and two mules.

April 4, 1857: Lt. Walter H. Jenifer and a detachment of Company B, Second Cavalry, from Fort Inge, were on a scout of the headwaters of the Nueces River when they attacked a Lipan Apache camp. Two Indians were killed and one wounded.

April 18, 1857: Lt. Robert C. Wood and a detachment of Company B, Second Cavalry, from Fort Inge, were on a scout to the headwaters of the Nueces River when they discovered a Lipan Apache camp. Since they were greatly outnumbered, the detachment was forced to withdraw and conduct a defense.

April 19, 1857: Lt. Robert C. Wood and a detachment of Company B, Second Cavalry, from Fort Inge, were on a scout to the headwaters of the Nueces River when they discovered a Lipan Apache camp. After initially being forced to withdraw and conduct a defense on April 18, they attacked the camp from an unexpected direction, which caused the Indians to flee. The army captured provisions and equipment.

June 30, 1857: Cpl. John Boyden and a detachment of Company B, Second Cavalry, from Fort Inge, were on a scout of the Frio River when they attacked a party of Comanche and captured horses and equipment.

July 2, 1857: Lt. Walter H. Jenifer and a detachment of Company B, Second Cavalry, were on a scout from Fort Inge to the Llano River when they attacked a party of Lipan Apache and captured horses and equipment.

July 20, 1857: Lt. John B. Hood and a detachment of Company G, Second Cavalry, while on a scout from Fort Mason to the Devils River, were lured into a Comanche ambush with a white parley flag. Hood attacked the Indian war party. One soldier was killed in action and one officer (Lieutenant Hood) and four soldiers were wounded. One soldier was listed as missing in action. Nine Indians were killed and ten Indians were wounded.

July 24, 1857: Sgt. Ernest Schroeder and a thirteen-man detachment of Eighth and First Infantry were on a mail escort from Fort Lancaster to Fort Davis when they conducted a defense after Indians attacked. Sergeant Schroeder and five Indians were killed in action.

July 24, 1857: Lt. Edward L. Hartz with a detachment of Companies C, D, F, and H, Eighth Infantry, from Fort Davis and a detachment of Companies H and K, First Infantry, from Fort Lancaster were conducting a ruse in the guise of a provision train between the posts. When Mescalero Apache attacked forty-five miles from Fort Lancaster the infantry concealed in the wagons killed three Apache and wounded three more.

July 25, 1857: Near Camp Hudson an army mail escort detachment was ambushed by Indians and conducted a defense.

August 10, 1857: Capt. Charles J. Whiting with a detachment of Companies C and K, Second Cavalry, from Fort Clark pursued Indian raiders to the Wichita Mountains in the Indian Territory and attacked the party. Two Indians were killed and three were wounded; the army captured thirty-three horses.

August 22, 1857: Sgt. William P. Leverett and a detachment of Company B, Second Cavalry, from Fort Inge attacked an Indian camp while on scout near the Llano River and captured horses and property.

September 24, 1857: Capt. Nathan G. Evans and Company H, Second Cavalry, from Camp Cooper attacked a party of Indians while on a scout near the headwaters of the Brazos River. Two Indian were killed; the army captured horses and equipment.

September 28, 1857: Sgt. Charles M. Patrick and a detachment of Company I, Second Cavalry, from Fort McIntosh pursued and attacked Indian horse raiders near Santa Catarina. One Indian was killed and four wounded. The army recovered twelve horses.

October 12, 1857: Lt. Wesley Owens and a detachment of Company I, Second Cavalry, from Fort McIntosh pursued and attacked Comanches who had been raiding Laredo and captured their horses and equipment.

October 30, 1857: Lt. Cornelius Van Camp and a detachment of Company D, Second Cavalry, from Camp Verde pursued Comanche raiders and attacked them on Verde Creek. Two Indians were wounded; the army captured all Indian property.

November 8, 1857: Lt. James B. Witherell and a detachment of Companies C and K, Second Cavalry, from Fort Clark pursued Comanches that had stolen mules November 2 from the Southern Overland Mail Company. Witherell attacked the Indians on the West Fork of the Nueces River. Witherell and three soldiers were wounded in action and one Indian was killed. The army recovered eighteen mules.

January 28, 1858: 1st Sgt. Walter McDonald and a detachment of Company D, Second Cavalry, from Camp Verde with citizen guide "Polly" Rodríquez pursued Comanche raiders and attacked them on the south branch of the Llano River. Three soldiers were wounded and two Indians were killed. The army recovered all stolen horses

June 16, 1858: Lt. William B. Hazen with detachments of Companies C, D, F, and H, Eighth Infantry, from Fort Davis attacked an Apache camp while on a scout of the Guadalupe Mountains. One Indian woman was taken prisoner. The army captured twenty-six horses and mules.

October 1, 1858: Known as the Wichita Expedition or Battle of Wichita Village. Capt. Earl Van Dorn and Companies A, F, H, and K, Second Cavalry, from Fort Belknap and a party of sixty Delaware, Caddo, Tonkawa, and Wichita Indian allies under Lawrence S. "Sul" Ross formed the Wichita Expedition to the Indian Territory. The expedition, operating out of Camp Radziminski, attacked a Penateka Comanche camp of 120 lodges on Rush Creek, Choctaw Nation. One officer (Lt. Cornelius Van Camp), two soldiers, and three Indian allies were killed in action and one soldier was listed as missing. One soldier and two Indian allies died of wounds received in the battle. One officer (Captain Van Dorn), nine soldiers, and two citizens (Ross and sutler J. F. Ward) were wounded. Approximately seventy Comanche were killed. The army captured three hundred horses.

February 13, 1859: Sgt. Maloney and a detachment of Company F, Eighth Infantry, from Fort Inge pursued and attacked Indian horse raiders. Three Indians were killed and the army recovered forty-nine horses.

May 2, 1859: Capt. Albert G. Brackett and Company I, Second Cavalry, from Fort Lancaster attacked a Comanche camp on the Rio Grande opposite Presidio de San Vicente while on an expedition to the Rio Grande. Two Indians were killed and the army captured enemy rations of horse meat.

May 13, 1859: Known as the Wichita Expedition, Fight on Crooked Creek. Capt. Earl Van Dorn and Companies A, F, H, and K, Second Cavalry, from Fort Belknap and a party of fifty-eight Indian scouts on the Wichita Expedition to the Indian Territory, operating out of Camp Radziminski, attacked a Kotsoteka Comanche camp of twenty lodges on Crooked Creek, Indian Territory. The command first captured the Indian horse herd and then attacked both mounted and dismounted. One soldier was killed and one died of wounds received in the battle. Two officers (Capt. Edmund Kirby Smith and Lt. Fitzhugh Lee), ten soldiers, and two Indian scouts were wounded. Fifty Comanche were killed and five wounded. The army captured thirty-six prisoners and one hundred horses.

May 20, 1859: Lt. William B. Hazen and Company F, Eighth Infantry, from Fort Inge and four citizen volunteers pursued and attacked Kickapoo horse raiders on the Nueces River. Four Indians were killed and one was wounded; the army recovered seven horses.

June 14, 1859: Lt. William B. Hazen and a detachment of Company F, Eighth Infantry, from Fort Davis pursued a party of Apache who had stolen horses from the post for 220 miles. Hazen found and attacked the Apache camp of fifteen lodges. One Indian was killed and one taken prisoner. The army recovered thirty horses and mules and captured all Indian property.

September 29, 1859: Lt. William B. Hazen and a detachment of Company F, Eighth Infantry, from Fort Inge pursued and attacked a party of Comanche horse raiders. One Indian was killed and one wounded. The army recovered 130 horses and one captive slave.

November 3, 1859: Lt. William B. Hazen and a detachment of Company F, Eighth Infantry, from Fort Inge with thirty citizen volunteers pursued a party of Comanche who had stolen horses and killed two citizens near Sabinal. Hazen attacked the Indians near the headwaters of the Llano River. One officer (Lieutenant Hazen) and three citizen volunteers were wounded in action. Seven Indians were killed and one was wounded. The army recovered thirty horses and captured eight firearms.

December 14, 1859: Cpl. Patrick Collins and a detachment of Company I, Second Cavalry, from Camp Verde with guide "Polly" Rodríquez and one citizen volunteer pursued and attacked dismounted a camp of Comanche raiders near the north branch of the Guadalupe River. One

Indian was killed and three were wounded. The army captured fifteen horses and some equipment.

January 16, 1860: Lt. Fitzhugh Lee and a detachment of Company B, Second Cavalry, from Camp Colorado pursued and attacked on Pecan Bayou a party of Comanche who had stolen horses near the post. Two Indians were killed and the army recovered twenty-four horses.

January 26, 1860: 1st Sgt. Robert N. Chapman with a detachment of Company A, Second Cavalry, from Fort Mason and three citizen volunteers were on a scout of Kickapoo Creek when they found and attacked dismounted a Comanche camp. Four soldiers and one citizen were wounded. Four Indians were killed and several were wounded. The army captured thirteen horses.

January 30, 1860: Sgt. Alex McK. Craig and a detachment of Company C, Second Cavalry, from Camp Lawson and seven citizen volunteers pursued Comanche raiders who had stolen horses on the Leona River. Craig attacked the raiders' camp on the Frio River. Two soldiers were wounded. Four Indians were killed and two Indians were wounded. The army recovered twenty-one horses.

February 13, 1860: Capt. Richard W. Johnson and a detachment of Companies A and F, Second Cavalry, from Fort Mason on a scout to the head of the Concho River found a Comanche camp, cut off their horse herd, and attacked dismounted. One soldier was wounded, one Indian was killed, and two Indians were wounded. The army captured fourteen horses.

May 7, 1860: Sgt. Thomas G. Dennin and a detachment of Company K, First Infantry, were was attacked by Indians while escorting government train near Howard's Springs. The Indians stole one horse, four mules, and four oxen. One citizen teamster was wounded and two Indians were killed.

August 28, 1860: Maj. George H. Thomas with a detachment of Company D and the regimental band, Second Cavalry, from Camp Cooper while on a scout to the Concho River pursued and attacked an Indian party near the Clear Fork of the Brazos River. One Indian made a dismounted stand with a lance and a bow and wounded one officer (Major Thomas) and five soldiers. This Indian was killed and the army captured twenty-eight horses.

August 28, 1860: Cpl. John Rutter and a detachment of Company B, Second Cavalry, from Camp Colorado pursued and attacked a party of Indians who had stolen horses near the post. One soldier was wounded and three Indians were killed. The army recovered all stolen horses and captured Indian equipment.

October 6, 1860: Capt. Samuel D. Sturgis with Companies A thru I, First Cavalry, and Indian scouts from the Indian Territory in a expedition along the Canadian River into Texas encountered and attacked a party of Indians. Three soldiers were killed and one was listed as missing in action. Three Indian scouts were killed and three soldiers were wounded; twenty-nine Indians were killed.

December 18, 1860: 1st Sgt. John W. Spangler with a detachment of Company H, Second Cavalry, from Camp Cooper joined with Lawrence S. "Sul" Ross and a Texas Ranging Company and a company of state volunteers from Fort Belknap on a scout to the Red River. On the Pease River they attacked a camp of Quahadis Comanches. Fourteen Indians were killed and three were taken prisoner. One of those captured, or rescued, was Cynthia Ann Parker, the mother of Quahadis warrior Quanah Parker; she was abducted from Fort Parker as a child in 1836. Additionally, the army captured forty-five horses. While many Texas histories credit this event to December 18, several official army reports record the Battle of Pease River as occurring on December 19, 1860.

Mid-February 1861: Lt. Abraham K. Arnold and a detachment of Company C, Second Cavalry, from Fort Inge pursued and attacked Comanche raiders who had stolen horses near the post. Some horses were recovered but the Indians escaped into Mexico.

* * *

December 24, 1866: A detachment of Company C, Fourth Cavalry, from Fort Clark had a skirmish with Indians on Mud Creek near the post.

January 19, 1867: A detachment of Company C, Fourth Cavalry, from Fort Clark had a skirmish with Indians on the Nueces River.

March 24, 1867: Capt. John A. Wilcox and a detachment of Company C, Fourth Cavalry, on a scout from Fort Clark, attacked a Comanche camp on the lower Pecos River. After burning the camp Wilcox had to defend against an Indian counterattack and conduct a fighting withdrawal. One soldier was listed as missing in action and one civilian guide (Serverino Patino) was killed. Two soldiers were wounded and ten Indians were killed. The army recovered one Mexican boy captive.

July 21, 1867: Capt. Benjamin T. Hutchins and detachments of Companies A and E, Sixth Cavalry, from Post at Buffalo Springs pursued Comanches who attacked a soldier wood detail on July 19. The Indians scattered and doubled back to attack the post.

July 21, 1867: Lt. Theodore Majtheny with detachments of Companies A and E, Sixth Cavalry, and civilian employees of the post quartermaster defended Post at Buffalo Springs during a two-day siege by three hundred Comanches. The Indians departed when the command under Capt. Benjamin T. Hutchins returned from a pursuit. One Indian was wounded.

August 22, 1867: Detachments of Companies D, G, and H, Fourth Cavalry, from Fort Chadbourne had a skirmish near the post.

August 23, 1867: A detachment of Company A, Fourth Cavalry, from Fort Chadbourne had a skirmish on the North Concho River.

August 30, 1867: Lt. Gustavus Schreyer and a detachment of Company F, Sixth Cavalry, from Fort Belknap had a skirmish near the post. Two soldiers were killed.

September 10, 1867: A detachment of Company K, Fourth Cavalry, from Fort Inge and a group of local citizens pursued and attacked a party of Indian raiders near Live Oak Creek. One Indian was killed.

September 16, 1867: A detachment of Company K, Fourth Cavalry, from Fort Inge pursued and attacked a party of Indian raiders near the post. One soldier was killed and the army recovered forty-six horses, one mule, and one Mexican boy captive.

September 20, 1867: A detachment of Company C, Fourth Cavalry, from Fort Clark had a skirmish on the Devils River.

October 1, 1867: A detachment of Company D, Ninth Cavalry, on mail escort had a skirmish at Howard's Spring. Two soldiers were killed.

October 17, 1867: Detachments of Companies F, I, K, and L, Sixth Cavalry, led by Sgt. W. A. T. Ahrberg from Fort Griffin had a skirmish on Deep Creek. Three Indians were killed and one was captured.

November 20, 1867: Sgt. W. A. T. Ahrberg and a detachment of Company L, Sixth Cavalry, from Fort Griffin had a skirmish with

Comanches. Three Indians were killed and one Indian was taken prisoner. The army captured nineteen horses.

December 5, 1867: A mail escort from Fort Davis to Eagle Spring was attacked by one hundred Apaches. The escort raced to the Eagle Spring mail station where Capt. Henry Carroll and a detachment of Company F, Ninth Cavalry, from Fort Davis ambushed the Indians, who broke off the pursuit. One soldier was killed.

December 26, 1867: A detachment of Company K, Ninth Cavalry, on a scout near Fort Lancaster was attacked by Indians and had to conduct a two-day defense. Three soldiers were killed.

January 1868: A detachment of Company D, Ninth Cavalry, from Fort Stockton had a skirmish near Fort Quitman.

March 7, 1868: Capt. Adna R. Chaffee and Companies I and F, Sixth Cavalry, and seven Tonkawa scouts from Fort Griffin were on a scout when they attacked a Comanche camp near Paint Creek. Three soldiers were wounded and seven Indians were killed. The army captured five horses and equipment.

March 10, 1868: A detachment of Company D, Fourth Cavalry, led by Sgt. C. Gale from Fort Concho had a skirmish near the headwaters of the Colorado River and captured ten horses.

September 14, 1868: Lt. Patrick Cusack and detachments of Companies C, F, and K, Ninth Cavalry, from Fort Davis attacked Lipan and Mescalero Apache Indians near Horsehead Hills. Three soldiers were wounded, twelve Indians were killed, one Indian girl was taken prisoner, and two Mexican boy captives were recovered. The army also captured supplies, and 198 horses and mules.

May 7, 1869: Capt. George W. Smith with detachments of Companies E and F, Thirty-fifth Infantry, and Indian scouts from Fort McKavett and Fort Griffin had a skirmish on Paint Creek near the Double Mountain Fork of the Brazos River.

June 9, 1869: Capt. John M. Bacon and Company G, Ninth Cavalry, from Fort Clark had a skirmish on the Pecos River with one hundred Lipan Apache. Two Indians were killed.

September 16, 1869: Capt. Henry Carroll and detachments of Companies B, E, F, and M, Ninth Cavalry, had a skirmish on the Brazos River.

September 20, 1869: Detachments of Companies B and E, Ninth Cavalry, had a skirmish on the Brazos River.

October 28, 1869: On the Fresh Water Fork of the Brazos River Comanches and Kiowas attacked the camp of a Fourth and Ninth Cavalry expedition. Capt. John M. Bacon and a detachment of Fourth and Ninth Cavalry pursued the Indians for thirty miles and attacked them. Eight Indians were killed, several Indians were wounded, and one Indian girl was taken prisoner.

November 24, 1869: Capt. Edward M. Heyl and a detachment of Companies L and M, Ninth Cavalry, had a skirmish with Apache Indians while on a scout of the headwaters of the Llano River. One officer (Captain Heyl) was wounded and one Indian was killed. The army captured six horses.

December 25, 1869: A sergeant with a detachment of Company E, Ninth Cavalry, defended Johnson's Mail Station on the Middle Concho River against an Indian attack. The Indians stole five army horses.

December 26, 1869: Lt. Howard B. Cushing and Company F, Third Cavalry, from Fort Stanton, New Mexico, along with twenty-eight civilian volunteers, attacked and destroyed a Mescalero Apache village at the old stage stop of Pine Spring in the Guadalupe Mountains. One officer was severely wounded.

December 30, 1869: Lt. Howard B. Cushing with a detachment of Company F, Third Cavalry, from Fort Stanton, New Mexico, and a small force of civilian volunteers attacked and destroyed a Mescalero Apache village at the mouth of McKitterick Canyon in the Guadalupe Mountains.

January 16, 1870: Capt. John M. Bacon with Company G and a detachment of Company L, Ninth Cavalry, from Fort Clark were on a scout on the Pecos River when they attacked an Indian village, putting the Indians to flight.

January 20, 1870: Detachments of Companies C, D, I, and K, Ninth Cavalry, from Fort Quitman had a skirmish on Delaware Creek while on scout of the Guadalupe Mountains.

February 6, 1870: Capt. John M. Bacon with Company G and a detachment of Company L, Ninth Cavalry, and detachments of Companies L and K, Twenty-fourth Infantry, from Fort Clark attacked an Indian camp while on a scout of the Pecos River and captured eighty-three horses.

February 10, 1870: Detachments of Companies H and I, Ninth Cavalry, had a skirmish while on scout of the Guadalupe Mountains.

April 3, 1870: Capt. Wirt Davis and a detachment of Company F, Fourth Cavalry, from Fort Griffin, and Tonkawa scouts were camped on North Hubbard Creek when Comanches attacked and tried to steal their horses. Two Indians were killed.

April 5, 1870: A sergeant and a detachment of Company H, Ninth Cavalry, had a skirmish at San Martin Springs. One Indian was killed.

April 6, 1870: A detachment of Company M, Tenth Cavalry, from New Mexico had a skirmish on Clear Creek.

April 25, 1870: Maj. Albert P. Morrow with detachments of Companies C and K, Ninth Cavalry, from Fort Quitman attacked an Indian camp at Crow Springs and captured thirty horses.

May 14, 1870: A detachment of Company M, Fourth Cavalry, had a skirmish at Mount Adams. Maj. William Russell Jr. died of wounds **May 15**.

May 20, 1870: Sgt. Emanuel Stance and a detachment of Company F, Ninth Cavalry, from Fort McKavett were on a scout to Kickapoo Springs when they attacked a party of Indians who were driving horses. Afterward, Stance discovered Indians raiding a small wagon train and attacked; the army drove off the Indians and captured more horses. Four soldiers were wounded and the army recovered two white boy captives and fifteen horses.

May 29, 1870: A detachment of Company K, Ninth Cavalry, from Fort Quitman had a skirmish at Bass Canyon.

May 30, 1870: Lt. Issac N. Walter with detachments of Companies C and D, Sixth Cavalry, from Fort Richardson, and a Professor Rossler of the Geological Survey, and five citizen volunteers were on a scout when they conducted a defense against a party of Kiowa that tried to capture the wagons and mules. One soldier and two citizens were killed.

July 12, 1870: Battle of the Little Wichita. Capt. Curwen B. McLellan and detachments of Companies A, C, D, H, K, and L, Sixth Cavalry, from Fort Richardson were on an expedition to pursue Comanches who on July 5 had attacked an overland mail stage at Rock Station, sixteen miles west of the post. On the North Fork of the Little Wichita River McLellan's sixty-man command attacked 250 Comanche under Kicking Bird. McLellan was forced into a six-hour fighting withdrawal to the South Fork of the Little Wichita River. Two soldiers were killed, eleven soldiers and one acting assistant surgeon were wounded, and fifteen Indians were killed. Eighteen Congressional Medals of Honor were earned in this battle.

July 14, 1870: Capt. Wirt Davis and detachments of Companies D and F, Fourth Cavalry, and Tonkawa scouts from Fort Griffin pursued and attacked Comanche cattle raiders at Mountain Pass. One Indian was killed and the army recovered 150 cattle.

August 1870: Maj. George A. Gordon, Fourth Cavalry, and Maj. Abraham K. Arnold, Fourth Cavalry, were leading combined units of the Fourth and Sixth Cavalry and nineteen Tonkawa scouts on an expedition to the Wichita River when the Tonkawa scouts attacked an Indian camp at the river and recovered twenty-eight stolen horses and mules.

September 30, 1870: A detachment of Company E, Fourth Cavalry, from Fort Concho had a skirmish near the post.

October 5, 1870: Capt. William A. Rafferty, a detachment of Company M, Sixth Cavalry, from Fort Richardson, and five Tonkawa scouts were on a scout when they found and attacked a party of Kichais Indians herding stolen horses on the Little Wichita River. The Indians were on a hunting pass from their Indian Territory reservation. Two Indians were killed and one wounded. The army recovered eighteen horses.

October 6, 1870: Capt. Tullius C. Tupper and Companies A and G, Sixth Cavalry, were on a scout from Camp Wichita when they were attacked in their camp on the Little Wichita River. The Indians captured twelve government horses.

October 8, 1870: Sgt. Lewis Strupp and twelve dismounted troopers of the Sixth Cavalry, who had their horses stolen from their camp October 6, were returning on foot to Camp Wichita when they conducted a dismounted attack on an Indian camp. Five horses belonging to citizens were recovered.

November 14, 1870: Capt. Adna R. Chaffee and a detachment of Company I, Sixth Cavalry, and two Tonkawa scouts were on a scout from Fort Richardson when they attacked a party of Comanche who were stealing cattle. The army captured seven horses.

May 12, 1871: A detachment of Company L, Ninth Cavalry, had a skirmish near the Red River.

May 20, 1871: Lt. Peter M. Boehm and a detachment of Company A,

Fourth Cavalry, from Fort Richardson were on a scout of the Brazos and Big Wichita divide when they attacked four Kiowas from Satanta's band who had remained behind to hunt buffalo after the Warren Raid on the Fort Richardson wagon train that killed seven teamsters on May 18. One soldier was wounded and one Indian was killed in the fight.

May 21, 1871: A detachment of Company K, Twenty-fifth Infantry, from Camp Melvin had a skirmish near the post.

May 28, 1871: A detachment of Company D, Eighth Cavalry, from New Mexico had a skirmish on the Canadian River in Texas.

June 30, 1871: Lt. Col. William R. Shafter, detachments of Company C, Tenth Cavalry, from Fort Davis, and a detachment of Ninth Cavalry from Fort Stockton pursued and attacked a band of Apache near the Pecos River northeast of Fort Davis. The Indians had stolen animals from the Barrilla Stage Station on June 16. The army recovered ten horses and five mules and captured one female prisoner, the Indian's provisions, and their lead and powder supply.

June 30, 1871: A detachment of Company I, Ninth Cavalry, had a skirmish on the Staked Plains.

July 4, 1871: A detachment of Company M, Fourth Cavalry, had a skirmish at Bandera Pass.

July 15, 1871: A detachment of Company G, Fourth Cavalry, had a skirmish near Double Mountain.

July 22, 1871: A detachment of Company F, Ninth Cavalry, had a skirmish near the headwaters of the Concho River.

July 31, 1871: Detachments of Company M, Ninth Cavalry, and Company A, Twenty-fourth Infantry, from Fort McKavett had a skirmish near the post.

August 2–September 13, 1871: Col. Ranald S. Mackenzie and the Fourth Cavalry's first expedition to the Staked Plains (no engagements).

September 1, 1871: Detachments of Company M, Ninth Cavalry, and Company E, Twenty-fourth Infantry, from Fort McKavett had a skirmish near the post.

September 24–November 8, 1871: Mackenzie's second expedition to the Staked Plains included the following engagements:

>   **October 9, 1871**: Col. Ranald S. Mackenzie and Companies A, F, G, H, and K, Fourth Cavalry, and Tonkawa scouts were on the

Freshwater Fork of the Brazos River during an expedition to the Staked Plains when they had to defend their camp against a night attack by Quahadis Comanches under Quanah Parker. The Indians captured sixty-six cavalry horses.

October 10, 1871: Capt. Edward M. Heyl and a detachment of Fourth Cavalry pursued and attacked a camp of Quahadis Comanches who had stolen horses from Mackenzie's camp on October 9. Captain Heyl's small command was soon forced into a dismounted defense by superior Indian numbers and was eventually relieved by the approach of Mackenzie's column. Lt. Robert G. Carter earned the Congressional Medal of Honor in this action. One soldier was killed.

October 15, 1871: Col. Ranald S. Mackenzie and Companies A, F, G, H, and K, Fourth Cavalry, and Tonkawa scouts were on a scout to Blanco Canyon when they attacked two Quahadis Comanches. One officer (Colonel Mackenzie) was wounded.

February 9, 1872: A three-man detachment of Company B, Fourth Cavalry, from Fort Richardson had a skirmish on the North Fork of the Concho River.

March 28, 1872: Sgt. William H. Wilson and a detachment of Company I, Fourth Cavalry, from Fort Concho were on a scout near the post when they attacked a group of Comancheros from New Mexico who were stealing cattle. Two Comancheros were killed, one was wounded, and one was taken prisoner. The prisoner, Polonis Ortiz, provided information on the location of Comanche camps that instigated Mackenzie's third expedition to the Staked Plains in July. Sergeant Wilson earned his first Congressional Medal of Honor, and soon became the only soldier so decorated twice in one year.

April 20, 1872: Capt. Michael Cooney and Companies A and H, Ninth Cavalry, from Fort Concho were on a scout near Howard's Springs when they pursued and attacked a Kiowa camp under Big Bow, who had raided a goverment wagon train and killed seventeen teamsters. Captain Cooney and his command were forced to withdraw when counterattacked. One soldier was killed in action, one officer (Lt. Frederick R. Vincent) died of wounds received in the battle, and two Indians were wounded.

May 18, 1872: Lt. John A. McKinney and a detachment of Company C,

Fourth Cavalry, from Fort Richardson pursued and attacked Indian raiders on the Wichita River. Three Indians were wounded.

May 20, 1872: Lt. Gustavus Valois with detachments of Company C, Ninth Cavalry; Company K, Twenty-fourth Infantry; and eight Indian scouts from Fort Duncan had a skirmish with Kickapoo Indians near La Pendencia.

May 23, 1872: Capt. Edward M. Heyl and detachments of Companies A and B, Fourth Cavalry, from Fort Richardson were on a scout to Lost Creek when they were attacked in camp. The army conducted a defense of the camp and then conducted a fighting withdrawal to the post. One soldier died of wounds received in the fight.

June 15, 1872: Corporal Hickey and a detachment of Company H, Eleventh Infantry, from Fort Concho had a skirmish at Johnson's Station. Two Indians were killed.

July 28, 1872: Corporal Walker and a detachment of Company K, Twenty-fifth Infantry, from Fort Stockton conducted a dismounted defense of Centralia Mail Station when Indians attempted to drive off the stock.

September 19, 1872: A sergeant and seven soldiers of the Fourth Cavalry with two Tonkawa scouts attacked fifty Comanche in Jones County. One Indian was killed and the soldiers recovered eleven horses.

September 29, 1872: The fight on the North Fork of the Red River during Mackenzie's third expedition to the Staked Plains (July 1–October 29, 1872). Col. Ranald S. Mackenzie and Companies A, D, F, I, and L, Fourth Cavalry; Company I, Twenty-fourth Infantry; and twenty Tonkawa scouts were on an expedition to the Staked Plains when they found and attacked a camp of 175 lodges of the Quahadis and Kotsoteka Comanche of Mow-way's band on the North Fork of the Red River near McClellan's Creek. Mackenzie captured the Indian herd of eight hundred ponies but that night the Comanches raided and recaptured all but fifty. Eight Congressional Medals of Honor were earned in this battle. Three soldiers were killed and seven soldiers were wounded. Fifty Indians were killed and seven were wounded. Three Mexican boy captives were recovered and 130 Indian women and children prisoners were taken to Fort Concho and then moved to Fort Sill, Indian Territory, in April 1873.

April 27, 1873: Sgt. Wilks and a detachment of Ninth Cavalry carrying mail from Fort Davis to Fort Bliss were attacked by Apaches at Eagle Spring and conducted a dismounted defense. Two soldiers and several Indians were killed.

May 18, 1873: Mackenzie's Kickapoo Expedition. Col. Ranald S. Mackenzie; Companies A, B, C, E, I, and M, Fourth Cavalry; and Lt. John L. Bullis and twenty-four Seminole-Negro Indian scouts left the vicinity of Fort Clark on May 17 on a punitive raid against a Kickapoo and Lipan Apache village near Remolina, Mexico. On the morning of May 18, the command attacked and destroyed three villages. One soldier was killed, two soldiers were wounded, and nineteen Indians were killed. The army captured sixty-five horses. Forty women and children were taken prisoner and transported to Fort Clark and then to Fort Gibson, Indian Territory.

July 14, 1873: A detachment of Company L, Fourth Cavalry, from Fort Clark had a skirmish on Lipan Creek.

August 31, 1873: Capt. Theodore A. Baldwin and detachments of Companies E and I, Tenth Cavalry, from Fort Richardson were attacked by Indians near the Pease River. One Indian was wounded.

September 30, 1873: Capt. Theodore A. Baldwin and detachments of Companies E and I, Tenth Cavalry, attacked a band of Indians at Mesquite Flats and recovered nine stolen horses.

October 1, 1873: Sgt. Benjamin Stow and three soldiers of Company K, Twenty-fifth Infantry, were on stage escort from Fort Stockton when fifteen Indians attacked them at Centralia Mail Station.

October 25, 1873: Lt. John B. Kerr and a detachment of Sixth Cavalry from the Indian Territory were on a scout near Little Cabin Creek, Texas, when they attacked a party of Indian raiders. The army recovered seventy horses and two hundred cattle.

December 5, 1873: Lt. Edward P. Turner and a detachment of Company D, Tenth Cavalry, from Fort Griffin had a skirmish with Indian cattle thieves on Elm Creek.

December 10, 1873: Lt. Charles L. Hudson and detachments of Companies A, B, C, and I, Fourth Cavalry, from Fort Clark were on a scout near Kickapoo Springs when they intercepted and attacked a party of Comanche and Kiowa who had been horse raiding in Mexico and were returning to the Fort Sill Reservation. One soldier was wounded and nine Indians were killed, including Tau-ankia, the son of the Kiowa chief Lone Wolf, and Guitain, Lone Wolf's nephew. The army recovered eighty-one horses and mules.

December 31, 1873: A sergeant and three soldiers of Company B, Twenty-fifth Infantry, were attacked at Eagle Spring by fifteen Indians. One Indian was wounded.

February 2, 1874: A detachment of Company A, Tenth Cavalry, from Fort Concho had a skirmish on Home Creek.

February 5, 1874: Lt. Col. George P. Buell; detachments of Companies G and D, Tenth Cavalry; Companies A and G, Eleventh Infantry; and Indian scouts were on a scout from Fort Griffin when they attacked a party of Comanche and Kiowa near Double Mountain. Eleven Indians were killed and the army captured sixty-five horses.

May 2, 1874: Lt. Quincy O. Gillmore and a detachment of Company K, Tenth Cavalry, from Fort Sill, Indian Territory, attacked a band of Indians on the Wichita River in Texas.

May 18, 1874: Capt. Charles Bentzoni and a detachment of Company B, Twenty-fifth Infantry, from Fort Quitman attacked a group of Indians near Carrizo Mountain.

July 3, 1874: Companies F and L, Fourth Cavalry, from Fort Clark received intelligence that Kiowa Chief Lone Wolf was going to Kickapoo Springs to recover the body of his son, who was killed in the fight with Lieutenant Hudson on December 10, 1873. The Fourth Cavalry went to intercept Lone Wolf and when they were on the South Fork of the Concho they discovered a detachment of Ninth Cavalry that had been attacked and lost their horses. The Fourth Cavalry companies pursued the Kiowa raiders and recovered twenty-two cavalry horses. One soldier was killed.

June–December 1874: The Red River or Buffalo War. Angered by the commercial destruction of the buffalo and other grievances, a coalition of seven hundred Comanche, Kiowa, and Southern Cheyenne attacked a Texas buffalo hunter's station called Adobe Walls on the North Canadian River June 27–July 1, 1874. The event precipitated a five-column army campaign into the Red River region of the Texas Panhandle.

> **August 19, 1874**: A detachment of Sixth Cavalry and Indian scouts from the Indian Territory had a skirmish near Adobe Walls.

August 20, 1874: A detachment of Sixth Cavalry and Indian scouts from the Indian Territory had a skirmish near Chicken Creek.

August 30, 1874: Battle of the Red River. As part of Col. Nelson A. Miles' column from Kansas Maj. James Biddle and detachments of Companies A, D, F, G, H, I, L, and M, Sixth Cavalry, and detachments of Companies C, D, and E, Fifth Cavalry, along with twenty Delaware scouts were ambushed by Cheyenne on Mulberry Creek and pursued the Indians twenty miles to Tule Canyon. One soldier and two Delaware scouts were wounded and one Indian was killed.

September 8, 1874: A detachment of Indian scouts had a skirmish on the Wichita River.

September 9, 1874: A detachment of Company H, Sixth Cavalry, from the Indian Territory had a skirmish on Sweetwater Creek.

September 10–12, 1874: Lyman's Wagon Train Fight. Capt. Wyllys Lyman, Fifth Infantry, with detachments of Company H, Sixth Cavalry and Company I, Fifth Infantry, were escorting a supply train for Miles's column when they were attacked by Comanche and Kiowa on the Dry Fork of the Washita River. After advancing under fire September 10, the command formed a defense at Gageby Creek and fought for two days. Two soldiers were killed; one officer (Lt. Granville Lewis) and four soldiers were wounded.

September 12, 1874: Maj. William R. Price and Companies C, K, and L, Eighth Cavalry, formed a column from New Mexico while searching for Lyman's Wagon Train and attacked a party of Comanche and Kiowa near the Dry Fork of the Washita River.

September 12, 1874: A detachment of Company I, Sixth Cavalry, from the Indian Territory had a skirmish on the Canadian River.

September 12, 1874: A detachment of Company M, Sixth Cavalry, sent as couriers from Miles's column to Camp Supply, had a skirmish on McClellan Creek. One soldier was killed.

September 25, 1874: Lt. William A. Thompson, a detachment of six Fourth Cavalry soldiers, and twenty-seven Seminole, Tonkawa, and Lipan scouts were scouting ahead of Col. Ranald S. Mackenzie's column of Fourth Cavalry near Tule Canyon when Comanche and Kiowa attacked. The soliders and scouts conducted a dismounted fighting withdrawal back to the column.

September 26, 1874: Indians attacked Col. Ranald S. Mackenzie's Fourth Cavalry column camp in Tule Canyon at night by attempting to stampede the horses. A dawn attack by Company E and Lt. William A. Thompson's scouts drove them off. Three cavalry horses were wounded and one Indian was killed. The army captured one horse.

September 28, 1874: Battle of Palo Duro Canyon. Col. Ranald S. Mackenzie and a column of Companies A, D, E, H, I, K, and L, Fourth Cavalry, and a detachment of Seminole, Tonkawa, and Lipan scouts with a camp and train guard of Companies A, C, I, and K, Tenth Infantry, and Company H, Eleventh Infantry, attacked a camp of Comanche, Kiowa, and Southern Cheyenne in Palo Duro Canyon. One soldier was wounded and four Indians were killed. All Indian provisions and lodges were destroyed and the army captured 1,274 horses and 150 mules. After his experience on September 29, 1872, of Comanches re-capturing their horses, Mackenzie had most of the animals taken to Tule Canyon and shot on September 29.

October 9, 1874: Lt. Col. George P. Buell and a column of Companies A, E, F, H, and I, Eleventh Infantry, and twenty-seven Indian scouts attacked an Indian camp on the Salt Fork of the Red River. One Indian was killed.

October 9, 1874: Capt. Ambrose E. Hooker and detachments of Companies E and K, Ninth Cavalry, had a skirmish near the Canadian River in Texas. One Indian was killed.

November 3, 1874: Col. Ranald S. Mackenzie and a column of Companies A, D, F, H, I, K, and L, Fourth Cavalry, with thirty-two Indian scouts on a scout near Las Lagunas Quatras attacked a Comanche camp. Two Indians were killed and nineteen women and children were taken prisoner. The army captured 144 horses.

November 5, 1874: While scouting for Mackenzie's column, Lt. William A. Thompson and nine Indian scouts attacked a Comanche camp near Laguna Tahoka. Two Indians were killed and the army captured twenty-six horses and mules.

November 6, 1874: From the Indian Territory column of Lt. Col. John W. Davidson a detachment of Company H, Eighth Cavalry, led by Lt. Henry J. Farnsworth on a scout to McClellan Creek, was ambushed by Cheyenne under Gray Beard and had to conduct a defense. Two soldiers were killed and four were wounded.

November 8, 1874: From Col. Nelson A. Miles's column, Lt. Frank D. Baldwin and detachments of Company D, Sixth Cavalry, and Company D, Fifth Infantry, while escorting wagons to pick up supplies, found Gray Beard's Cheyenne camp on McClellan Creek. Baldwin put his infantry in the empty wagons, attacked the camp, and pursued the Indians for ten miles. Lieutenant Baldwin earned his second Congressional Medal of Honor in this action.

November 29, 1874: From Col. Nelson A. Miles's column, Capt. Charles A. Hartwell and detachments of Companies C, H, K, and L, Eighth Cavalry, were on a scout of the Canadian River when they attacked a Cheyenne camp on Muster Creek. Two Indians were killed and two were wounded.

December 8, 1874: While on a scout from Col. Ranald S. Mackenzie's column, Lt. Lewis Warrington attacked a Comanche camp in the Muchaqua Valley. Two Indians were killed, one was wounded, and one was taken prisoner.

January 26, 1875: A detachment of Company G, Ninth Cavalry, from Ringgold Barracks had a skirmish with Indians at Solis Ranch near the post.

January 27, 1875: Detachments of Company B and G, Ninth Cavalry, from Ringgold Barracks had a skirmish with Indians near the post.

April 26, 1875: Lt. John L. Bullis, three Seminole-Negro scouts, and a detachment of Twenty-fourth Infantry were on a scout when they attacked a party of Indians at the Eagle's Nest crossing of the Pecos River. Three Indians were killed and two were wounded.

May 5, 1875: An expedtion of detachments of Companies A, F, G, I, and L, Tenth Cavalry, from Fort Concho had a skirmish near Battle Point.

June 29, 1875: A detachment of Company A, Fourth Cavalry, from Fort Sill, Indian Territory, had a skirmish near Reynolds Ranch, Texas.

September 13, 1875: Shafter Expedition of 1875. Lt. Col. William R. Shafter, 220 soldiers of the Tenth Cavalry, and twenty Seminole-Negro scouts were on an exploration of the Staked Plains when Apaches attacked their camp at night. The Indians stole four horses.

October 17, 1875: Part of Shafter's 1875 expedition to the Staked Plains.

Lt. John L. Bullis and a detachment of Seminole-Negro scouts attacked an Apache camp near Cedar Lake or Lagunas Sabinas. The army captured twenty-five horses and mules, fifty packs of provisions, and three thousand pounds of dried meat.

November 2, 1875: Shafter Expedition of 1875. Lt. Andrew Geddes, Twenty-fifth Infantry, and detachments of Companies G and L, Tenth Cavalry, from Lt. Col. William R. Shafter's column, followed a trail of Apaches that the Seminole-Negro scouts under Lt. John L. Bullis had found. Geddes attacked the Apache camp near the Pecos River. One Indian was killed and four Indian women and one boy were taken prisoner.

February 18, 1876: A detachment of Company B, Twenty-fifth Infantry, on a mounted scout to the Carrizo Mountains from Fort Quitman attacked an Indian camp and destroyed provisions.

July 30, 1876: As part of Lt. Col. William R. Shafter's expedition to Mexico in the summer of 1876, Lt. George H. Evans; a detachment of Company B, Tenth Cavalry; and Lt. John L. Bullis with twenty Seminole-Negro scouts were detached from the main column on the San Diego River, Mexico, and sent to attack a Lipan Apache camp the Mexican guides had reported. Near Zaragoza, Mexico, the detachment attacked and destroyed a camp of twenty-three lodges before the Mexican army pursued the detachment back to the main column. Three soldiers were wounded and twelve Indians were killed. The army captured four women prisoner and one hundred horses and mules.

August 12, 1876: As part of Lt. Col. William R. Shafter's expedition to Mexico in the summer of 1876, Capt. Thomas C. Lebo and two Companies of Tenth Cavalry, acting on information supplied by an Lipan woman prisoner captured by Lieutenant Bullis on July 30, attacked a Kickapoo camp of ten lodges in the Santa Rosa Mountains, Mexico. The army captured sixty horses and mules.

April 1, 1877: A detachment of Seminole-Negro scouts had a skirmish on the Rio Grande near the mouth of the Devils River.

May 4, 1877: Capt. Phillip L. Lee and Company G, Tenth Cavalry, from Fort Griffin attacked a Comanche camp near Lake Quemado. 1st Sgt. Charles Baker and four Indians were killed. The army captured six women prisoners and sixty-nine horses.

September 29, 1877: As part of Lt. Col. William R. Shafter's second expedition to Mexico in September 1877, detachments of Companies A and F, Eighth Cavalry, with Lt. John L. Bullis and a detachment of Seminole-Negro scouts, attacked a Lipan Apache camp near Zaragoza, Mexico. Four Indian women and one boy were captured.

November 1, 1877: Lt. John L. Bullis and a detachment of Seminole-Negro scouts had a skirmish with Apaches in the area of the Big Bend of the Rio Grande.

November 29, 1877: Capt. Samuel B. M. Young and Companies A and K, Eighth Cavalry; Company C, Tenth Cavalry; and Lt. John L. Bullis and a detachment of Seminole-Negro scouts were on a scout into Mexico when they attacked a camp of Mescalero Apaches. One officer (Lt. Frederick E. Phelps) was wounded, two Indians were killed, and three Indians were wounded. The army captured thirty horses.

July 25, 1879: Capt. Michael L. Courtney and detachments of Company H, Twenty-fifth Infantry, and Company H, Tenth Cavalry, from Fort Davis were camped at Eagle Spring when they pursued and attacked dismounted a party of Comanche horse raiders near Sulphur Springs. Two soldiers were wounded, two Indians were killed, and one Indian was wounded. The army recovered ten horses.

September 16, 1879: Capt. Michael L. Courtney and detachments of Company H, Twenty-fifth Infantry, and Company H, Tenth Cavalry, from Fort Davis were on a scout when they pursued and attacked a party of Indians at Eagle Mountain. They captured all the Indians' horses and equipment.

April 2, 1880: Lt. Calvin Esterly and a detachment of Companies F and L, Tenth Cavalry, from Fort Stockton pursued and attacked a party of Comanches who had stolen horses. One Indian was wounded and the army recovered eight horses.

April 9, 1880: Capt. Thomas C. Lebo and Company K, Tenth Cavalry, were at a temporary camp at Salada Water Holes while on a scout of the Guadalupe Mountains when they attacked a camp of Apaches at Shake Hand Springs, New Mexico. One Indian was killed and four women and one child were taken prisoner. The army captured twenty-one horses and mules and recovered an eleven year-old Mexican boy (Coyetano Garcia), who the Apaches had kidnapped in March at Presidio.

June 11, 1880: Indians attacked Lt. Frank H. Mills and a Pueblo Indian scout detachment from Fort Davis at Viejo Pass near present Valentine, Texas. Simon Olgin, the Pueblo scout and Ysleta headman, was killed.

July–August 1880: Grierson's Victorio Campaign

> **July 30, 1880:** During his campaign against the Texas raids of the Mimbres Apache leader Victorio Col. Benjamin H. Grierson, Tenth Cavalry, and his son Robert and a detachment of the regimental headquarters and band from Fort Davis received word that Victorio was near Quitman Canyon moving north. Grierson took his small party and established a defense at Tenaja de Las Palmas and denied Victorio a crucial waterhole. Reinforced by Lt. Leighton Finley and a detachment of Company G, Tenth Cavalry, Grierson had Finley and ten men attack the approaching Indian party. With the arrival of further reinforcements, Victorio broke off the engagement and returned to Mexico.

> **July 30, 1880:** While riding from Eagle Spring to reinforce Col. Benjamin H. Grierson's defense at Tenaja de Las Palmas (see above), Capt. Charles D. Viele and detachments of Companies G and C, Tenth Cavalry, attacked Victorio's Apache party and forced it to withdraw to Mexico. One soldier was killed, one officer (Lt. Samuel R. Colladay) was wounded, and seven Indians were killed.

> **August 3, 1880:** Cpl. A. Weaver and a detachment of Company H, Tenth Cavalry, were on picket at Alamo Springs when they had a skirmish with Apaches from Victorio's band. One soldier was listed as missing in action.

> **August 4, 1880:** Sergeant Richardson and a detachment of Company F, Tenth Cavalry, were on a scout of the Guadalupe Mountains near Bowen Springs when they attacked an Apache camp but were repulsed and driven from their horses. One soldier was killed and the Apache captured five cavalry horses.

> **August 5, 1880:** Capt. John C. Gilmore and Company H, Twenty-fifth Infantry, were attacked by Apaches while escorting a supply train eight miles northeast of Rattlesnake Springs. One Indian was killed and one wounded.

> **August 6, 1880:** Capt. William B. Kennedy and Company F, Tenth Cavalry, pursued the Indians who had attacked Sergeant

Richardson's detachment on August 4 (see above). One Apache woman was killed and the army captured one horse.

August 6, 1880: Capt. Charles D. Viele and Company G, Tenth Cavalry, set an ambush for Victorio's Apache party in Rattlesnake Canyon. Victorio reacted to the ambush by launching an immediate attack. One soldier was wounded.

August 6, 1880: Capt. Louis H. Carpenter and detachments of Companies B, C, and H, Tenth Cavalry, attacked Victorio's Apache party that was attacking Company G at Rattlesnake Springs. Victorio broke off the action and attacked a nearby supply train but Captain Carpenter's command pursued him into the mountains. One Indian was killed.

October 28, 1880: Detachments of Company B and K, Tenth Cavalry, were on a scout of the Rio Grande when they were attacked in camp by Indians near Ojo Caliente. Two soldiers were killed.

May 3, 1881: Lt. John L. Bullis and thirty Seminole-Negro scouts from Fort Clark pursued a party of Lipan Apache raiders who killed a settler, Mrs. McLauren, on the Rio Frio on April 24. Bullis followed the raiders' trail for six days into the Sierra del Burros of Mexico, then surrounded and attacked their camp at dawn. Four Indians were killed and one woman and child were taken prisoner, The army captured twenty-one horses.

---

* Francis B. Heitman, "Chronological list of battles, actions, etc., in which troops of the Regular Army have participated, and troops engaged," in *Historical Register and Dictionary of the United States Army* . . . (2 vols.; Washington, D.C.: Government Printing Office, 1903), II, 400–446; Letters and combat reports in the Report of the Secretary of War for the years 1849–1881 as found in *House of Representatives Executive Documents* no. 1 or 2 for each session of Congress; National Archives Microfilm Publication M617, Returns From United States Military Posts 1800–1916, Records of the United States Army Adjutant General's Office, 1780–1917, Record Group (RG) 94; National Archives (NA) Record Group 98, Records of United States Army Commands, 1784–1821, Letters Received, Department of Texas, and RG 393 Records of United States Army Continental Commands, 1821–1920, Department of Texas and the Eighth Military Department, Letters Received, 1866–1868, 1868–1870, Tabular Statements of Expeditions and Scouts 1869–1890; General Orders No. 14, Headquarters, United States Army, 13 November 1857; and General Orders No. 22, Headquarters, United States Army, 10 November 1858, RG 94 (NA).

See also Capt. Robert G. Carter, *On the Border with Mackenzie; or, Winning West Texas from the Comanches* (Washington, D.C.: Eynon, 1935), 349–372; Robert G. Carter,

The Old Sergeant's Story: Fighting Indians and Bad Men in Texas, 1870 to 1876 (New York: Hitchcock, 1926; reprint, Mattituck, N.Y.: John M. Carroll, 1982), 72, 82–87, 97, 104–110; John Bell Hood, *Advance and Retreat: Personal Experiences in the United States and Confederate States Armies* (New Orleans: G.T. Beauregard, 1880), 11; Brig. Gen. Richard W. Johnson, *A Soldier's Reminiscences in Peace and War* (Philadelphia: J.B. Lippincott Company, 1886), 109–111, 125–126; H. H. McConnell, *Five Years a Cavalryman, Or, Sketches of Regular Army Life on the Texas Frontier, 1866–1871* (Jacksboro, Texas: J. N. Rogers, 1889; reprint with foreword by William H. Leckie, Norman: University of Oklahoma Press, 1996), 93, 94–95; Gen. Philip Henry Sheridan, *Personal Memoirs of P. H. Sheridan, General, United States Army* (2 vols.; New York: D. Appleton & Company, 1904), I, 22–23; and Jesse Sumpter, *Paso del Águila: A Chronicle of Frontier Days on the Texas Border as Recorded in the Memoirs of Jesse Sumpter*, comp. Harry Warren, ed. Ben Pingenot (Austin: Encino Press, 1969), 18–20.

Other sources are Lt. Col. William H. Carter, *From Yorktown to Santiago with the Sixth U.S. Cavalry* (Baltimore: Lord Baltimore Press, 1900; reprint, Austin: State House Press, 1989), 137–169, 277–278; Maj. Edward L. N. Glass, *The History of the Tenth Cavalry, 1866–1921* (1921; reprint, Fort Collins, Colo.: Old Army Press, 1972), 21–22, 96, 100; Joseph I. Lambert, *One Hundred Years with the Second Cavalry* (Fort Riley, Kans.: Capper Printing, 1939), 264–267; John H. Nankivell (ed.), *History of the Twenty-Fifth Regiment United States Infantry, 1869–1926* (Denver, Colo.: Smith-Brooks Printing Company, 1927; reprint, Fort Collins, Colo.: Old Army Press, 1972), 23–30; George Frederick Price, *Across the Continent with the Fifth Cavalry* (New York: Van Nostrand, 1883), 44–96, 650–651; Theo. F. Rodenbough, *From Everglade to Cañon with the Second Dragoons . . .* (New York: D. Van Nostrand, 1875), 165; Robert Wooster (ed.), *Recollections of Western Texas: Descriptive and Narrative Including An Indian Campaign, 1852–1855, Interspersed With Illustrative Anecdotes By Two of the Mounted Rifles*. Preface by Robert Utley. (Austin: Book Club of Texas, 1995), 79–84; Harold B. Simpson, *Cry Comanche: the Second U.S. Cavalry in Texas, 1848–1861* (Hillsboro, Tex.: Hill Junior College Press, 1979), 53–64, 83–93; Thomas T. Smith, *Fort Inge: Sharps, Spurs, and Sabers on the Texas Frontier, 1849–1869* (Austin: Eakin Press, 1991), 26–28, 40–44, 117–118, 186–188; Thomas Wilhelm, *History of the Eighth U.S. Infantry* (2 vols.; Headquarters, Eighth Infantry, 1873), II, 43, 48, 80–90; Ty Cashion, *A Texas Frontier: The Clear Fork Country and Fort Griffin, 1849–1887* (Norman: University of Oklahoma Press, 1996), 299; William Y. Chalfant, *Without Quarter: The Wichita Expedition and the Fight on Crooked Creek* (Norman: University of Oklahoma Press, 1991), 80–90; John M. Carroll (ed.), *The Black Military Experience in the American West* (New York: Liveright Publishing Corp., 1971), 71–72, 335–336, 390, 403–404; and Arlen Fowler, *Black Infantry In the West, 1869–1891* (Westport, Conn.: Greenwood Publishing Corp., 1971; reprint with foreword by William H. Leckie, Norman: University of Oklahoma Press, 1996), 25–26, 37–38.

See also James L. Haley, *The Buffalo War: The History of the Red River Uprising of 1874* (Garden City, N.Y.: Doubleday, 1976; reprint, Norman: University of Oklahoma Press, 1985), 50–51, 127–137, 154–164, 192–197; Allen Lee Hamilton, *Sentinel of the Southern Plains: Fort Richardson and the Northwest Texas Frontier, 1866–1878* (Fort Worth: Texas Christian University Press, 1988), 23–24, 54–63, 83, 125–126; Herbert M. Hart, *Old Forts of the Southwest* (New York: Bonanza Books), 47; San Antonio *Herald*,

May 9, 1857; William H. Leckie, *The Buffalo Soldiers: A Narrative History of the Negro Cavalry in the West* (Norman: University of Oklahoma Press, 1967), 150–151; Col. W. S. Nye, *Carbine and Lance: The Story of Old Fort Sill* (Norman: University of Oklahoma Press, 1937), 152–153; Rupert Norval Richardson, *The Frontier of Northwest Texas, 1846 to 1876* . . . (Glendale, Calif.: The Arthur H. Clark Company, 1963), 190–193; Carl Coke Rister, *The Southwestern Frontier: 1865–1881* . . . (Cleveland: The Arthur H. Clark Company, 1928), 114–121; Carl Coke Rister, *Fort Griffin on the Texas Frontier* (Norman: University of Oklahoma Press, 1956), 74–76; A. J. Sowell, *Early Settlers and Indian Fighters of Southwest Texas* (2 vols; 1900; reprint, New York: Argosy-Antiquarian, 1964), II, 696–698; Robert M. Utley, *Frontier Regulars: The United States Army and the Indian, 1866–1891* (New York: Macmillan Publishing Company, 1973), 227; Paul H. Carlson, *"Pecos Bill:" A Military Biography of William R. Shafter* (College Station: Texas A&M University Press, 1989), 57–60, 81–84, 94, 101–102; James T. King, *War Eagle: A Life of General Eugene A. Carr* (Lincoln: University of Nebraska Press, 1963), 15–16; Ernest Wallace, *Ranald S. Mackenzie on the Texas Frontier* (Lubbock: West Texas Museum Association, 1964; reprint, College Station: Texas A&M University Press, 1993), 34, 50–54, 64, 77–91, 98–104, 118–120, 136–146, 155–156, 197; and Clayton W. Williams, *Texas' Last Frontier: Fort Stockton and the Trans-Pecos, 1861–1895* (College Station: Texas A&M University Press, 1982), 102, 115–116, 119, 120–121.

Other sources include Martin L. Crimmins (ed.), "Colonel Robert E. Lee's Report on Indian Combats in Texas," *Southwestern Historical Quarterly*, 39 (July, 1935), 21–32; Marvin E. Kroeker, "William B. Hazen," in *Soldiers West: Biographies from the Military Frontier*, ed. Paul Andrew Hutton (Lincoln: University of Nebraska Press, 1987), 193–212; Kenneth F. Neighbours, "Tonkaway Scouts and Guides," *West Texas Historical Association Yearbook*, 49 (1973), 90–112; Martin L. Crimmins, "Notes on the Establishment of Fort Elliott and the Buffalo Wallow Fight," *Panhandle-Plains Historical Review*, 25 (1952), 45; "Record of Engagements With Hostile Indians In Texas 1868 To 1882," *West Texas Historical Association Year Book*, 9 (October, 1933), 101–118; Thomas T. Smith, "U.S. Army Combat Operations in the Indian Wars of Texas, 1849–1881," *Southwestern Historical Quarterly*, 99 (April, 1996), 501–531; Robert Wooster, *History of Fort Davis, Texas* (Southwest Cultural Resources Center, Professional Paper No. 34. Santa Fe: Southwest Region, National Park Service, Department of the Interior, 1990), 79–80, 87, 94–95, 97, 101–102, 186, 205, 212, 233, 239.

---

[1] Army reports require the officer to establish some proof that horses were stolen, such as brands, descriptions, etc. because either the horses are returned to the owners or sold at auction. If the horses are not stolen the quartermaster department stands to profit; therefore it is not in the army's fiscal interest to report stolen horses. However, the integrity of the officer corps demands a true accounting—if the report says the horses were stolen there is no reason to doubt it.

Sgt. M. Lauderdale, Company B, Twenty-fourth Infantry Regiment. Formed under the command of Col. Ranald S. Mackenzie at Fort McKavett in 1869, companies of the Twenty-fourth served continuously on the Texas frontier until 1888, longer than any other infantry regiment of the army. *Photograph courtesy Lawrence T. Jones III, Austin.*

PART VI

SELECTED BIBLIOGRAPHY OF THE U.S. ARMY IN NINETEENTH-CENTURY TEXAS

Outline

RESEARCH SOURCES FOR REGULAR ARMY SOLDIERS AND UNITS

Government Documents and Records

National Archives and Records Service, Washington, D.C.
  Records of the United States Army Adjutant General's Office,
    1780–1917, Record Group 94
    (Guide) *Military Service Records: A Select Catalog of National
    Archives Microfilm Publications*. (Washington, D.C.: National
    Archives and Service Administration, 1985).

(Officers)
    Appointment, Commission, and Personal Branch, Documents Files
      (APC Service Files). (Search request).
    Letters Received by the Commissioned Branch of the Adjutant Gen-
      eral's Office, 1863–1870. Microfilm no. M1064, 527 rolls.
    Name and Subject Index to the Appointment, Commission, and Per-
      sonal Branch of the Adjutant General's Office, 1871–1894.
      Microfilm no. M1125, 4 rolls.
    United States Military Academy Cadet Application Papers, 1805–
      1866. Microfilm no. M688, 242 rolls (arranged by year).
    Selected documents Relating to Blacks Nominated for Appointment
      to the United States Military Academy During the 19th Century,
      1870–1887. Microfilm no. M1002, 21 rolls.

(Enlisted Men)
    Registers of Enlistments in the United States Army, 1798–1914.
      Microfilm no. M233, 81 rolls.
    Muster Rolls. (Can be microfilmed by request if provided the compa-
      ny, regiment, place, and date. Payday musters were normally

held every third month, February, April, June, August, October, and December).

General Index to Pension Files, 1861–1934. Microfilm no. T288, 544 rolls, 16mm (arranged alphabetically).

Organizational Index to Pension Files of Veterans Who Served Between 1861 and 1900. Microfilm no. T289, 765 rolls, 16mm (arranged by unit and branch).

Old War Index to Pension Files, 1815–1926. (Death or disability in regular forces). Microfilm no. T316, 7 rolls, 16mm.

Index to Mexican War Pension Files, 1887–1926. Microfilm no. T288, 544 rolls, 16mm (arranged alphabetically).

Index to Indian Wars Pension Files, 1892–1926. Microfilm no. T318, 12 rolls, 16mm (arranged alphabetically).

(Army Units)

Returns From Regular Army Infantry Regiments, June 1821–December 1916, microfilm no. M665, 300 rolls (for periods the unit was stationed in Texas).

First Infantry Regiment:
January 1844–December 1848, roll 3
January 1849–December 1855, roll 4
January 1856–December 1864, roll 5
January 1874–December 1881, roll 7
Third Infantry Regiment:
January 1843–December 1849, roll 31
January 1850–December 1859, roll 32
Fourth Infantry Regiment:
January 1843–December 1850, roll 43
Fifth Infantry :
January 1843–December 1851, roll 55
January 1852–December 1861, roll 56
January 1880–December 1889, roll 59
January 1890–December 1898, roll 60
Sixth Infantry Regiment:
January 1844–December 1848, roll 66

Seventh Infantry Regiment:

    January 1832–December 1842, roll 78

    January 1843–December 1850, roll 79

    January 1851–December 1859, roll 80

Eighth Infantry Regiment:

    January 1838–December 1847, roll 90

    January 1848–December 1857, roll 91

    January 1858–December 1865, roll 92

Tenth Infantry Regiment:

    January 1863–December 1870, roll 114

    January 1871–December 1879, roll 115

    January 1880–December 1890, roll 116

Eleventh Infantry Regiment:

    January 1866–December 1872, roll 125

    January 1873–December 1882, roll 126

Thirteenth Infantry Regiment:

    January 1887–December 1895, roll 147

Fifteenth Infantry Regiment:

    January 1866–December 1872, roll 165

    January 1873–December 1880, roll 166

    January 1881–December 1889, roll 167

Sixteenth Infantry Regiment:

    January 1880–December 1889, roll 176

Seventeenth Infantry Regiment:

    January 1866–December 1871, roll 183

Eighteenth Infantry Regiment:

    January 1890–December 1897, roll 186

    January 1898–December 1900, roll 187

Nineteenth Infantry Regiment:

    January 1866–December 1870, roll 203

    January 1871–December 1879, roll 204

    January 1880–December 1888, roll 205

    January 1889–December 1897, roll 206

Twentieth Infantry Regiment:

    January 1874–December 1881, roll 212

    January 1882–December 1889, roll 213

Twenty-first Infantry Regiment:
    January 1873–December 1880, roll 220
Twenty-second Infantry Regiment:
    January 1874–December 1881, roll 228
    January 1882–December 1889, roll 229
Twenty-third Infantry Regiment:
    January 1874–December 1882, roll 237
    January 1883–December 1890, roll 238
    January 1891–December 1897, roll 239
    January 1898–December 1900, roll 240
Twenty-fourth Infantry Regiment:
    January 1866–December 1872, roll 245
    January 1873–December 1880, roll 246
    January 1881–December 1889, roll 247
Twenty-fifth Infantry Regiment:
    January 1867–December 1873, roll 254
    January 1874–December 1882, roll 255
    January 1898–December 1900, roll 258
Twenty-sixth Infantry Regiment:
    December 1866– June 1869, roll 262
Thirty-fifth Infantry Regiment:
    December 1866–August 1869, roll 290
Thirty-eighth Infantry Regiment:
    February 1867–December 1869, roll 293
Forty-first Infantry Regiment:
    December 1866–December 1869, roll 296

Returns From Regular Army Cavalry Regiments, 1833–1916, microfilm
    no. M744, 117 rolls (for periods the unit was stationed in Texas):
First Cavalry Regiment (First Dragoons):
    June 1836–March 1843, roll 1
    1845–1847, roll 2
Second Cavalry Regiment (Second Dragoons):
    April 1844–December 1845, roll 14
    1846–1848, roll 15
    1849–1855, roll 16

Third Cavalry Regiment (Mounted Rifles):
  October 1846–December 1850, roll 27
  1885–1893, roll 32
Fourth Cavalry Regiment:
  1864–1871, roll 41
  1872–1876, roll 42
  1877–1883, roll 43
  1884–1889, roll 44
Fifth Cavalry Regiment (Second Cavalry):
  March 1855–December 1863, roll 51
  1887–1893, roll 55
Sixth Cavalry Regiment:
  August 1861–December 1867, roll 61
  1868–1874, roll 62
Seventh Cavalry Regiment:
  1889–1896, roll 74
Eighth Cavalry Regiment:
  1875–1882, roll 80
  1883–1889, roll 81
Ninth Cavalry Regiment:
  October 1866–December 1872, roll 87
  1873–1880, roll 88
  1881–1887, roll 89
  1896–1900, roll 91
Tenth Cavalry Regiment:
  September 1866–December 1872, roll 95
  1873–1880, roll 96
  1881–1888, roll 97

Returns From Regular Army Artillery Regiments, June 1821–January 1901, microfilm no. M727, 38 rolls.
  First Regiment of Artillery:
    January 1841–December 1850, roll 3
    January 1851–December 1860, roll 4
    January 1861–December 1870, roll 5
    January 1896–December 1901, roll 8

Second Regiment of Artillery:
    January 1841–December 1850, roll 11
    January 1861–December 1870, roll 13
    January 1871–December 1880, roll 14
    January 1881–December 1893, roll 15
Third Regiment of Artillery:
    January 1841–December 1850, roll 19
    January 1871–December 1888, roll 22
    January 1889–December 1897, roll 23
Fourth Regiment of Artillery:
    January 1841–December 1850, roll 27
    January 1851–December 1860, roll 28

Returns of the Corps of Engineers, April 1832–December 1916, micro film no. M851, 22 rolls.
Returns From Regular Army Engineer Battalions, September 1846–June 1916, microfilm no. M690, 10 rolls.
Returns of the Corps of Topographical Engineers, November 1831–February 1863, microfilm no. M852, 2 rolls.

Papers and Archives

Bancroft Library, Berkeley, California:
    Edward R. S. Canby Papers
    Edward O. C. Ord Papers.
Beinecke Rare Book and Manuscript Library, Yale University, New Haven, Connecticut:
    William H. Emory Papers.
Center for American History, University of Texas at Austin, Texas:
    Zenas R. Bliss, "Recollections," 2 vols, manuscripts.
    Samuel H. Starr Papers.
Chestatee Regional Library, Gainesville, Georgia:
    James Longstreet Papers (Texas letters).
Fort Concho Research Library, San Angelo, Texas:
    George Gibson Huntt, microfilm papers (MF 13–15).
    Benjamin H. Grierson, Texas letters, microfilm (MF 16, 17).
The Library of Congress, Washington, D.C.:

Edward R. S. Canby Papers
George Croghan Papers.
Winfield S. Hancock Papers
Edward L. Hartz Papers.
William B. Hazen Papers
Samuel P. Heintzelman Papers.
Ethan Allan Hitchcock Papers.
George B. McClellan Papers.
Albert J. Myer Papers.
Edward O. C. Ord Papers
John M. Schofield Papers
Zachary Taylor Papers.
Emory University Library, Atlanta, Georgia:
James Longstreet Papers (Texas letters).
Gilcrease Institute Museum, Tulsa, Oklahoma:
Ranald S. Mackenzie Papers
Illinois State Historical Library, Springfield, Illinois:
Christopher C. Augur Papers.
Benjamin H. Grierson Papers
Winfield S. Hancock Papers
University of Michigan, Ann Arbor, Michigan:
William R. Shafter Collection
Missouri Historical Society, St. Louis, Missouri:
William S. Harney Papers.
Ethan Allan Hitchcock Papers.
Edward O. C. Ord Papers
Samuel H. Starr Papers, Bixby Collection.
New York State Library, Albany, New York:
John E. Wool Papers.
University of North Carolina Library, Chapel Hill, North Carolina:
Edward R. S. Canby Papers
Edmund Kirby Smith Papers.
University of Oklahoma Library, Norman, Oklahoma:
William B. Hazen Papers
The Historical Society of Pennsylvania, Philadelphia, Pennsylvania:
George G. Meade Papers.
Persifor F. Smith Papers.

Stanford University Libraries, Stanford, California:
  Edward O. C. Ord Papers
  William R. Shafter Papers.
Texas Tech University, Southwest Collection, Lubbock, Texas:
  Benjamin H. Grierson Papers.
U.S. Army Military History Institute, Carlisle Barracks, Pennsylvania:
  Eugene A. Carr Papers
  Winfield S. Hancock Papers
  Ranald S. Mackenzie Papers.
  Simon Snyder Papers.
United States Military Academy Library, Special Collections, West
    Point, New York:
  John Bigelow Jr. Papers.
  John Gregory Bourke Diaries (available on microfilm).
  William Chapman Family Papers.
  Napoleon Jackson Tecumseh Dana Papers.
  James Duncan Papers.
  Ulysses S. Grant Papers (Mexican War typescripts).
  Joseph Jones Reynolds Papers.
  William R. Shafter Papers (microfilm).
  Samuel Davis Sturgis Jr. Family Papers.
  John C. Tidball, "First Experiences," manuscript.
Western Michigan University, Kalamazoo, Michigan:
  William R. Shafter Collection
Wyoming Archives, Cheyenne, Wyoming:
  William H. Carter Papers

Books, Articles, and Biographical Collections

Alberts, Don E. *Brandy Station to Manila Bay: A Biography of General Wesley Merritt*. Austin: Presidial Press, 1981.
Armes, George A. *Ups and Downs of An Army Officer*. Washington, D.C.: Privately printed, 1900.
Babcock, Elkanah. *A War History of the Sixth U.S. Infantry from 1789 To 1903. . . .* Edited by S. T. Fish. Kansas City, Mo.: Hudson-Kimberly Publishing Co., 1903.
Bauer, K. Jack. *Zachary Taylor: Soldier, Planter, Statesman of the Old Southwest*. Baton Rouge: Louisiana State University Press, 1985.

Boatner, Mark Mayo III. *The Civil War Dictionary*. New York: David McKay Company, Inc., 1959.

Brackett, Albert G. *History of the United States Cavalry, from the Formation of the Federal Government To the 1st of June 1863. . .*. New York: Harper & Brothers, Publishers, 1865.

Brown, Capt. Fred R. *History of the Ninth U.S. Infantry, 1799–1909*. Chicago: R. R. Donnelley & Sons Co., 1909.

Carlson, Paul H. *"Pecos Bill": A Military Biography of William R. Shafter*. College Station: Texas A&M University Press, 1989.

_____. "Baseball's Abner Doubleday on the Texas Frontier." *Military History of Texas and the Southewest*, 12 (Spring, 1976), 235–244.

Carter, Lieut. Col. William H. *From Yorktown to Santiago With the Sixth U.S. Cavalry*. Baltimore: Lord Baltimore Press, 1900. Reprint, with introduction by John M. Carroll, Austin: State House Press, 1989.

Cashin, Herschel V., et. al. *Under Fire With the Tenth U.S. Cavalry*. New York: F. Tennyson Neely, 1899. Reprint, New York: Arno Press, 1969.

Chance, Joseph E., ed. *My Life In the Old Army: The Reminiscences of Abner Doubleday from the Collection of the New-York Historical Society*. Illustrated by Wil Martin. Fort Worth: Texas Christian University Press, 1998.

Cleaves, Freeman. *Rock of Chickamauga: The Life of General George H. Thomas*. Norman: University of Oklahoma Press, 1948.

Crimmins, Martin L. "Robert E. Lee in Texas: Letters and Diary."*West Texas Historical Association Year Book*, 15 (June, 1932), 3–24.

Cullum, Bvt. Maj. Gen. George W. *Biographical Register of the Officers and Graduates of the U.S. Military Academy at West Point, N.Y. from Its Establishment, in 1802, to 1890*. 3 vols. New York. Houghton, Mifflin and Company, 1891.

_____. *Biographical Register of the Officers and Graduates of the U.S. Military Academy at West Point, N.Y. Since its Establishment, in 1802. Supplement IV*. Edited by Edward S. Holden. Cambridge: The Riverside Press, 1901.

Dawson, Joseph G. III. *The Late 19th Century U.S. Army, 1865–1898: A Research Guide*. Westport, Conn.: Greenwood Press, 1990.

Deibert, Chaplain Ralph C. *A History of the Third United States Cavalry: The Regiment of Mounted Riflemen, the First Regiment of Mounted*

Riflemen, the Third United States Cavalry. Harrisburg, Pa.: Telegraph Press, 1933.

Dupuy, Trevor N., Curt Johnson, and David L. Bongard. *The Harper Encyclopedia of Military Biography*. New York: HarperCollins, Publishers, 1992.

Freeman, Douglas Southall. *R. E. Lee: A Biography*. 4 vols. New York: Charles Scribner's Sons, 1936.

Gibson, John M. *Physician to the World: The Life of General William C. Gorgas*. Durham, N.C.: Duke University Press, 1950.

Glass, Maj. Edward L. N. *The History of the Tenth Cavalry, 1866–1921*. 1921. Reprint, Fort Collins, Colo.: Old Army Press, 1972.

Hamersly, Thomas H. *Army Register, 1799 to 1879*. Washington, D.C.: T. H. S. Hamersly, 1880.

Haskin, Bvt. Maj. William L. *The History of the First Regiment of Artillery. . . .* Fort Preble, Portland, Maine: B. Thurston and Company, 1879.

Headquarters, Fourth Cavalry. *Fourth Cavalry, United States Army, 1855–1930*. Fort Meade, S.D.: [n.p.], 1930.

Heitman, Francis B. *Historical Register and Dictionary of the United States Army*. 2 vols. Washington, D.C.: Government Printing Office, 1903.

Henry, Guy V. *Military Record of Civilian Appointments in the United States Army*. 2 vols. New York: Carleton, Publishers, 1869.

Heyman, Max L. *Prudent Soldier: A Biography of Major General E. R. S. Canby, 1817–1873. . . .* Glendale, Calif.: The Arthur H. Clark Co., 1959.

Hughes, Nathaniel C. *General William J. Hardee: Old Reliable*. Baton Rouge: Louisiana State University Press, 1965.

Hughes, Robert M. *General [Joseph E.] Johnston*. New York: D. Appleton and Co., 1897.

Hutton, Paul Andrew. *Phil Sheridan and His Army*. Lincoln: University of Nebraska Press, 1985.

———, ed. *Soldiers West: Biographies from the Military Frontier*. With an introduction by Robert M. Utley. Lincoln: University of Nebraska Press, 1987.

Jordan, David M. *Winfield Scott Hancock: A Soldier's Life*. Bloomington: Indiana University Press, 1988.

Kajencki, Francis C. "Charles Radzemenski: Soldier of the American Southwest." *New Mexico Historical Review,* 66 (Oct., 1991), 371–391.

Kieffer, Chester L. *Maligned General: The Biography of Thomas Sidney Jesup.* San Rafael, Calif.: Presido Press, 1979.

King, James T. *War Eagle: A Life of General Eugene Carr.* Lincoln: University of Nebraska Press, 1963.

Kroeker, Marvin E. *Great Plains Command: William B. Hazen in the Frontier West.* Norman: University of Oklahoma Press, 1976.

Lambert, Joseph I. *One Hundred Years with the Second Cavalry.* Fort Riley, Kans.: Capper Printing, 1939.

Leckie, William H. and Shirley A. *Unlikely Warriors: General Benjamin H. Grierson and His Family.* Norman: University of Oklahoma Press, 1975.

Lewis, Lloyd. *Captain Sam Grant.* Boston: Little, Brown and Company, 1950.

Mahon, John K. and Romana Danysh. *Infantry, Part I: Regular Army.* Army Lineage Series. Washington, D.C.: U.S. Army Center of Military History, 1972.

Marcy, Randolph B. *Border Reminiscences.* New York: Harper and Brothers, 1872.

McKenney, Janice E., complier. *Field Artillery.* Army Lineage Series. Washington, D.C.: U.S. Army Center of Military History, 1985.

McLung, Donald R. "Second Lieutenant Henry O. Flipper: Negro Officer on the West Texas Frontier." *West Texas Historical Year Book,* 48 (1971), 20–31.

E. V. D. Miller, ed. *A Soldier's Honor: With Reminiscences of Major-General Earl Van Dorn by His Comrades.* New York: Abbey Press, 1902.

Morris, Roy. *Sheridan: The Life & Wars of General Phil Sheridan.* New York: Random House, 1992.

Muller, William G. *The Twenty Fourth Infantry, Past and Present.* 1922. Reprint, with introduction by John M. Carroll, Fort Collins, Colo.: Old Army Press, 1972

Nankivell, John H., ed. *History of the Twenty-Fifth Regiment United States Infantry, 1869–1926.* Denver, Colo.: Smith-Brooks Printing Co., 1927. Reprint, Fort Collins, Colo.: Old Army Press, 1972.

Parks, Joseph H. *General Edmund Kirby Smith, CSA*. Baton Rouge: Louisiana State University Press, 1965.

Pierce, Michael D. *The Most Promising Young Officer: A Life of Ranald Slidell Mackenzie*. Norman: University of Oklahoma Press, 1993.

Porter, Joseph C. *Paper Medicine Man: John Gregory Bourke and His American West*. Norman: University of Oklahoma Press, 1986.

Powell, William H. *List of Officers of the Army of the United States from 1779 to 1900*. New York: L. S. Hamersley and Company, 1900. Reprint, Detroit: Gale Research Company, 1967.

————. *A History of the Organization and Movements of the Fourth Regiment of Infantry, United States Army, from May 30, 1796, to December 31, 1870*. Washington, D.C.: M'Gill & Witherow, Printers and Stereotypers, 1871.

Price, George Frederick. *Across the Continent with the Fifth Cavalry*. New York: Van Nostrand, 1883.

Reavis, L. U. *The Life and Military Services of Gen. William Selby Harney*. St. Louis: Bryan, Brand & Co., Publishers, 1878.

The Register of Graduates and Former Cadets of the United States Military Academy. West Point, N.Y.: West Point Alumni Foundation, Inc., 1964.

Robinson, Charles III. *Bad Hand: A Biography of General Ranald S. Mackenzie*. Austin: State House Press, 1993.

Rodenbough, Theo. F. *From Everglade to Cañon With the Second Dragoons . . . .* New York: D. Van Nostrand, 1875.

Rodenbough, Theo. F. and William L. Haskin, eds. *The Army of the United States: Historical Sketches of Staff and Line with Portraits of General-in-Chief*. New York: Maynard, Merrill, & Co., 1896.

Roland, Charles P. *Albert Sidney Johnston: Soldier of Three Republics*. Austin: University of Texas Press, 1964.

Rister, Carl Coke. *Robert E. Lee in Texas*. Norman: University of Oklahoma Press, 1946.

————. *Border Command: General Phil Sheridan In the West*. Norman: University of Oklahoma Press, 1944.

Scheips, Paul J. "Albert James Myer, an Army Doctor in Texas, 1854–1857." *Southwestern Historical Quarterly*, 82 (July, 1978), 1–24.

Schmidt, Daniel and Carol Schmidt. "From the Memoirs of Alfred Lacey Hough." *Fort Concho Report*, 15 (Spring, 1983), 3–19.

Schubert, Frank N. *The Trail of the Buffalo Soldier: Biographies of African Americans in the U.S. Army, 1866–1917.* Wilmington, Del.: Scholarly Resources, Inc., 1995.

Scott, Florence Johnson. "George Washington Clutter in the Mexican War." *Texas Military History,* 4 (Summer, 1964), 119–131.

Sears, Stephen W. *George B. McClellan: The Young Napoleon.* New York: Ticknor & Fields, 1988.

Sigerfoos, Edward. *Historical Sketch of the 5th United States Infantry.* [N.p.]: Regimental Press, 1902.

Silver, James W. *Edmund Pendleton Gaines, Frontier General.* Baton Rouge: Louisiana State University Press, 1949.

Simpson, Harold B. *Cry Comanche: The 2nd U.S. Cavalry in Texas, 1848–1861.* Hillsboro, Tex.: Hill Junior College Press, 1979.

Spiller, Roger J. and Joseph G. Dawson III, eds. *Dictionary of American Military Biography.* 3 vols. Westport Conn.: Greenwood Press, 1984.

_____. *American Military Leaders.* New York: Praeger, 1989.

Steinbach, Robert H. *The Long March: The Lives of Frank and Alice Baldwin.* Austin: University of Texas Press, 1989.

Stubbs, Mary Lee and Stanley Russell Conner. *Armor-Cavalry, Part I: Regular Army and Army Reserve.* Army Lineage Series. Washington, D.C.: U.S. Army Center of Military History, 1969.

Thompson, Jerry D. *Henry Hopkins Sibley: Confederate General of the West.* Natchitoches, La.: Northwestern State University Press, 1987. Reprint, with a foreword by Frank E. Vandiver, College Station: Texas A&M University Press, 1996.

_____. "Henry Hopkins Sibley: Military Inventor on the Texas Frontier." *Military History of the Southwest,* 11, No. 4 (1972), 227–248.

Tyler, Ron, Douglas E. Barnett, Roy R. Barkley, Penelope C. Anderson, and Mark F. Odintz, eds. *The New Handbook of Texas.* 6 vols. Austin: Texas State Historical Association, 1996.

Wallace, Edward S. "General William Jenkins Worth and Texas." *Southwestern Historical Quarterly,* 54 (Oct., 1950), 159–168.

_____. *General William Jenkins Worth: Monterey's Forgotten Hero.* Dallas: Southern Methodist University Press, 1953.

_____. "General John Lapham Bullis: The Thunderbolt of the Texas Frontier." *Southwestern Historical Quarterly,* 54 (Apr., 1951), 452–461; 55 (July, 1951), 77–85.

Wallace, Ernest. *Ranald S. Mackenzie on the Texas Frontier*. Lubbock: West Texas Museum Association, 1964. Reprint, with a foreword by David J. Murrah, College Station: Texas A&M University Press, 1993.

————. "General Ranald Slidell Mackenzie: Indian Fighting Cavalryman." *Southwestern Historical Quarterly*, 56 (Jan., 1953), 378–396.

Warner, Ezera J. *Generals in Gray: The Lives of the Confederate Commanders*. Baton Rouge: Louisiana State University Press, 1959.

————. *Generals in Blue: The Lives of the Union Commanders*. Baton Rouge: Louisiana State University Press, 1964.

Webb, Walter Prescott and H. Bailey Carroll, eds. *The Handbook of Texas*. 2 vols. Austin: Texas State Historical Association, 1952. Supplement, edited by Eldon Stephen Branda, 1964.

Webster's American Military Biographies. Springfield, Mass.: G. & C. Merriam Company, 1978.

Wert, Jeffry D. *General James Longstreet: The Confederacy's Most Controversial Soldier, a Biography*. New York: Simon & Schuster, 1993.

Whilhelm, Thomas. *History of the Eighth U.S. Infantry*. 2 vols. Headquarters, Eighth Infantry, 1873.

Wooster, Robert. *Nelson A. Miles and the Twilight of the Frontier Army*. Lincoln: University of Nebraska Press, 1993.

Histories of Forts, Garrison Life, and Civil-Military Relations in Texas

Fort and Camp Histories: Government Documents and Records

National Archives and Records Service, Washington, D.C.

Records of the United States Army Adjutant General's Office, 1780–1917, Record Group 94

Historical Information Relating to Military Posts and Other Installations ca. 1700–1900, microfilm no. 661, 8 rolls.

Returns from United States Military Posts 1800–1916, microfilm no. M617, 1,550 rolls.

Camp Jacob A. Auger, Tex.: Aug. 1909, roll 1516

Austin, Tex.: Nov. 1848–Aug. 1875, roll 59

Austin Arsenal, Tex.: Oct. 1845–Feb. 1846, roll 1493

Beaumont, Tex.: July 1865, roll 1495

Fort Belknap, Tex.: June 1851–Aug. 1867, roll 95

Belton, Tex.: July 1866–Feb. 1869, roll 1495

Camp Blake, Tex.: Apr.–Sept. 1854, roll 1496

Fort Bliss, Tex.: Jan. 1854–Dec. 1871, roll 116; Jan. 1872–Dec. 1885, roll 117; Jan. 1886–Dec. 1897, roll 118; Jan. 1898–Dec. 1908, roll 119; Jan. 1909–Dec. 1916, roll 120

Boston, Tex.: Feb.–June 1869, roll 1496

Camp at Brazos Agency, Tex.: Mar.–June 1859, roll 1497

Brazos Island, Tex.: June 1846–Aug.1848, roll 140

Brazos Santiago, Tex.: Mar. 1864–July 1867, roll 142

Brenham, Tex.: July 1865–May 1870, roll 144

Fort Brown, Tex.: May 1846–Feb. 1861, roll 151; June 1866–Dec. 1886, roll 152; Jan. 1887–Dec. 1902, roll 153; Jan. 1903–Sept. 1915, roll 154

Brownsville, Tex.: May 1865–Sept. 1915, May 1914–Sept. 1915, roll 155

Bryan, Tex.: Oct. 1868–Sept. 1869, roll 1497

Camp Buchanan, Tex.: Nov. 1855, roll 1497

Buffalo, Tex.: Aug. 1849, roll 1497

Buffalo Bayou, Tex.: Oct. 1914, roll 1497

Buffalo Springs, Tex.: Apr.–Dec. 1867, roll 1497

Camp Burbank, Tex.: Dec. 1854, roll 1498

Camp Burwell, Tex.: Nov. 1855, roll 1498

Calvert, Tex.: Oct. 1869–May 1870, roll 1499

Cameron, Tex.: Jan.–May 1870, roll 1500

Canton, Tex.: Nov. 1868–July 1869, roll 1500

Carrizo, Tex.: Jan.–June 1893, roll 1501

Centerville, Tex.: Mar. 1867–Apr. 1868, roll 1502

Fort Chadbourne, Tex.: Apr. 1849–Nov. 1867, roll 195

Camp Charlotte, Tex.: June 1880, roll 1502

Fort Clark, Tex.: June 1852–Feb. 1861, roll 213; Dec. 1866–Dec. 1881, roll 214; Jan. 1882–Dec. 1892, roll 215; Jan. 1893–Dec. 1905, roll 216; Jan. 1906–Dec. 1916, roll 217

Clarksville, Tex.: Oct. 1868–Feb. 1870, roll 1503

Post on the Clear Fork of Brazos (see Fort Phantom Hill)

Camp Colorado, Tex.: Aug. 1856–Jan. 1861, roll 226

Columbus, Tex.: Apr. 1869–May 1870, roll 1504

Camp Near Comanche Agency, Tex.: Mar.–May 1859, roll 1504

Comstock, Tex.: June 1916, roll 1504

Fort Concho, Tex.: Dec. 1867–Dec. 1878, roll 241; Jan. 1879–June 1889, roll 242

Camp Concordia, Tex.: Feb.–Dec 1868, roll 1504

Camp Cooper, Tex.: July 1851–Jan. 1861, roll 253

Corpus Christi, Tex.: Sept. 1845–Nov. 1898, roll 255

Corsicana, Tex.: Jan.–May 1870, roll 1505

Fort Crockett, Tex.: Mar. 1911–Sept. 1915, roll 269

Fort Croghan, Tex.: Mar. 1849–Nov. 1853, roll 270

Dallas, Tex.: July–Oct. 1868; Oct. 1915, roll 1507

Fort Davis, Tex.: Sept. 1854–Dec. 1878, roll 297; Jan. 1879–June 1891, roll 298

Camp Del Rio, Tex.: Feb. 1884–Apr. 1916, roll 304

Dryden, Tex.: June 1916, roll 1508

Fort Duncan, Tex.: Mar. 1849–Mar. 1861, roll 335; Mar. 1868–Aug. 1883, roll 336

Camp Eagle Pass, Tex.: Jan. 1892–Sept. 1916, roll 340

Eatmans Ferry, Tex.: Oct. 1914, roll 1509

Edinburg, Tex.: May 1853–Dec. 1865, roll 1509

Fort Elliott, Tex.: Sept. 1874–Oct. 1890, roll 346

El Paso, Tex.: Feb. 1848–Sept. 1916, roll 351

Fort Ewell, Tex.: May 1852–Nov. 1855, roll 356

Fabens, Tex.: May and June 1916, roll 1510

Franklin, Tex.: Mar. 1863–Oct. 1865, roll 378

Galveston, Tex.: July 1865–May 1870, roll 391

Camp Gardenier, Tex.: May–July 1854, roll 1511

Fort Gates, Tex.: Oct. 1849–Feb. 1852, roll 398

Camp Genoa, Tex.: Apr. 1914, roll 1511

Goliad, Tex.: Aug. 1866–Mar. 1868, roll 1512

Fort Graham, Tex.: Apr. 1849–Oct. 1853, roll 412

Fort Griffin, Tex.: July 1867–May 1881, roll 429

Camp Hainey [Harney], Tex.: Feb.–July 1853, roll 1514

Camp Hamilton, Tex.: Aug. 1853, roll 1514

Fort Hancock, Tex.: July 1884–Sept. 1895, roll 1895

Harlingen, Tex.: Aug. 1915–Apr. 1916, roll 1514

Hart's Mill, Tex.: Aug. 1862–Mar. 1863, roll 1514

Helena, Tex.: Mar. 1868–Apr. 1870, roll 1514

Hempstead, Tex.: July 1865–Mar. 1868, roll 474

Highbridge, Tex.: Mar. 1911, roll 1515

Hot Wells, Tex.: July 1916, roll 1515

Houston, Tex.: Dec. 1848–Apr. 1868, roll 484

Camp Hunt, Tex.: May 1902, roll 1515

Huntsville, Tex.: Oct.–Dec. 1868, roll 1515

Camp Hudson, Tex.: Sept. 1856–Mar. 1868, roll 495

Indianola, Tex.: Sept. 1866–July 1969, roll 515

Fort Inge, Tex.: Mar. 1849–Jan. 1869, roll 517

Camp Ives, Tex.: Oct. 1859–Dec. 1860, roll 1516

Jefferson, Tex.: Dec. 1867–May 1871, roll 544

Camp Johnson, Tex.: Sept. 1862, roll 1516

Camp Johnston, Tex.: Mar.–Oct. 1852, roll 1516

Kaufman, Tex.: Oct. 1867–Feb. 1868, roll 1517

La Feria, Tex.: Sept. 1915, roll 1518

Lampasas, Tex.: May 1867–June 1870, roll 587

Fort Lancaster, Tex.: Aug. 1855–Mar. 1861, roll 589

La Pena, Tex.: May–Sept. 1854, roll 1518

Camp Near Laredo, Tex.: Jan. 1860, roll 1519

Laredo, Tex.: Mar. 1914–June 1916, roll 1519

Las Animas, Tex.: May–Oct. 1854, roll 1519

Camp Las Vegas [Laxas], Tex.: May–July 1854, roll 1519

Lavaca, Tex.: Aug. 1866, roll 1519

Camp Lawson, Tex.: Oct. 1859–Apr. 1860, roll 1519

Leon Springs, Tex.: June 1908–Aug. 1910, roll 622

Leona, Tex.: Aug.–Nov. 1866, roll 1519

Fort Lincoln, Tex.: Jan. 1849–July 1852, roll 632

Livingston, Tex.: Oct. 1868–June 1870, roll 640

Llano Grande, Tex.: Aug. 1916, roll 1519

Lockhart, Tex.: July–Oct. 1867, roll 1520

Camp Lopeno, Tex.: Apr. 1856, roll 1520

Lyford, Tex.: Oct. 1915–Apr. 1916, roll 1521

Camp McAllen, Tex.: July and Aug. 1916, roll 1522

Fort McIntosh, Tex.: Mar. 1849–Dec. 1870, roll 681; Jan. 1871–Dec. 1880, roll 682; Jan. 1881–Dec. 1891, roll 683; Jan. 1892–Dec. 1902, roll 684; Jan. 1903–Dec. 1908, roll 685; Jan. 1909–Dec. 1916, roll 686

Fort McKavett, Tex.: Mar. 1852–Dec. 1872, roll 687; Jan. 1873–June 1883 , roll 688

Camp Mabry, Tex.: July–Sept. 1906, roll 713

Marathon, Tex.: Jan.–Mar. 1911, roll 1523

Marfa, Tex.: Mar. 1911; May 1915, roll 1523

Marshall, Tex.: Jan. 1866–Dec. 1868, roll 1524

Fort Martin Scott, Tex.: May 1849–Nov. 1853, roll 1139; Oct.–Nov. 1866, roll 1524

Fort Mason, Tex.: July 1851–Dec. 1869, roll 759

Matagorda Island, Tex.: Jan. 1864, roll 1524

Cantonment at Mayer's Springs, Tex.: Sept. 1880–Jan. 1881, roll 1524

Fort Merrill, Tex.: Mar. 1850–Nov. 1855, roll 771

Mexican Border Patrol Districts, Feb. 1915–Nov. 1916, roll 774

Minera, Tex.: Mar. 1911, roll 1525

Mission, Tex.: Sept. 1915, roll 1525

Mount Pleasant, Tex.: June 1867–Mar. 1868, roll 1526

Nacogdoches, Tex.: July 1836–Feb. 1870, roll 828

Camp Olmus [Olmos], Tex.: Dec. 1845–Feb. 1846, roll 1528

Palestine, Tex.: Sept. 1868–Jan. 1869, roll 1529

Camp Palo Blanco, Tex.: Aug. 1855, roll 1529

Camp Pecan, Tex.: July 1856, roll 1531

Camp on the Pecos River, Tex.: Sept. 1857–Apr. 1858, roll 1531

Camp at the Mouth of the Rio Pecos, Tex.: Sept. 1880–Feb. 1881, roll 1536

Camp Peña Colorado, Tex.: Mar. 1880–Feb. 1893, roll 901

Pendencia, Tex.: Oct. 1859, roll 1531

Fort Phantom Hill, Tex.: Feb. 1857, Jan. 1872, roll 1531

[Fort Phantom Hill] Post on the Clear Fork of Brazos, Tex.: Sept. 1851–Mar. 1854, roll 141

Pharr, Tex.: Sept. and Oct. 1915, roll 1531

Camp Phelps, Tex.: Jan.–Feb. 1852, roll 1531

Pilot Grove, Tex.: July 1868–Feb. 1869, roll 1531

Fort Point, Tex.: Mar. 1898–June 1900, roll 1533

Point Isabel, Tex.: Oct. 1867–Feb. 1869, roll 1533

Fort Polk, Tex.: Mar. 1846–Jan. 1850, roll 947

Camp Near Presidio, Tex.: Sept. 1880–Feb. 1881, roll 1534

Progreso, Tex.: Oct. 1915, roll 1534

Fort Quitman, Tex.: Sept. 1858–Jan. 1877, roll 985

Refugio, Tex.: Sept. 1867–Feb. 1868, roll 1536

Fort Richardson, Tex.: June 1866–May 1878, roll 1008

Richmond, Tex.: June–Oct. 1866, roll 1536

Camp Ricketts, Tex.: Dec. 1851–Mar. 1852, roll 1536

Camp at the Mouth of the Rio Grande, Dec. 1846, roll 1536

Fort Ringgold, Tex. (Ringgold Barracks): Oct. 1848–Apr. 1861, roll 1019; July 1865–Dec. 1874, roll 1020; Jan. 1875–Dec. 1884, roll 1021; Jan. 1885–Dec. 1894, roll 1022; Jan. 1895–Dec. 1904, roll 1023; Jan. 1905–Sept. 1915, roll 1024

Roma, Tex.: Jan. 1852–Dec. 1865, roll 1537

Camp Rosario, Tex.: June 1860, roll 1537

Round Top, Tex.: Apr.–Dec. 1867, roll 1537

Camp Sabinal, Tex.: July–Aug. 1856, roll 1538

Camp Salinena, Tex.: May 1854–Apr. 1856, roll 1538

Camp at Salt Lake, Tex.: May–Nov. 1854, roll 1538

Sam Fordyce, Tex.: Mar. 1911, Sept. 1915, roll 1539

Fort Sam Houston, Tex.: Sept. 1890–Dec. 1900, roll 1079; Jan. 1901–Dec. 1907, roll 1080; Jan. 1908–Dec. 1911, roll 1081; Jan. 1912–Dec. 1916, roll 1082

San Antonio, Tex.: Oct. 1845–Dec. 1872, roll 1083; Jan. 1873–Dec. 1882, roll 1084; Jan. 1883–Aug. 1890, roll 1085

San Antonio Arsenal, Tex.: Aug. 1870–Dec. 1880, roll 1086; Jan. 1881–Dec. 1895, roll 1087; Jan. 1896–Dec. 1907, roll 1088; Jan. 1908–Dec. 1816, roll 1089

San Antonio Barracks, Tex.: July 1857–Mar. 1861, roll 1090

San Antonio Wells, Tex.: May–Aug. 1854, roll 1539

San Augustine, Tex.: Oct. 1868–Mar. 1869, roll 1539

San Benito, Tex.: Sept. 1915–Mar. 1916, roll 1539

San Diego, Tex.: Apr. 1878–Apr. 1882, roll 1095

San Elizario, Tex.: Nov. 1849–Aug. 1851, roll 1105

San Felipe, Tex.: Sept. 1876–Jan. 1881, roll 1106

San Ignacio, Tex.: May–Oct. 1868, roll 1539

Fort San Jacinto, Tex.: Feb. 1899–June 1914, roll 1108

Camp on the San Pedro [Devils River], Tex.: July 1854, roll 1540

Camp J. M. Scott, Tex.: May–Dec. 1854, roll 1541

Seguin, Tex.: Sept. 1867–Feb. 1868, roll 1542

Sherman, Tex.: Mar.–Aug. 1867, roll 1542

Fort Stockton, Tex.: Apr. 1859–Dec. 1874, roll 1229

Camp E. B. Strong, Tex.: Nov.–Dec. 1854, roll 1544

Fort Terrett, Tex.: Feb. 1852–Jan. 1854, roll 1259

Texas City, Tex.: Jan. 1913–Sept. 1915, roll 1263

Texas Indian Agency Camp, Indian Territory, Sept. 1859, roll 1545

Camp Thornton, Tex.: March 1849, roll 1545

Fort Travis, Tex.: Aug. 1911–June 1914, roll 1288

Camp Trinidad, Tex.: Mar. 1868–Feb. 1869, roll 1546

Tyler, Tex.: Mar. 1867–Apr. 1870, roll 1302

Camp Verde, Tex.: July 1856–Mar. 1869, roll 1327

Victoria, Tex.: Jan. 1866–Jan. 1867, roll 1540

Waco, Tex.: Aug. 1866–Sept. 1870, roll 1333

Weatherford, Tex.: June 1867–Mar. 1868, roll 1549

Wharton, Tex.: Sept. 1868–Mar. 1869, roll 1549

Whitesboro, Tex.: Dec. 1898, roll 1549

Camp Wood, Tex.: Jan. 1860–Feb. 1861, roll 1550

Camp G. W. F. Wood, Tex.: May–Sept 1857, roll 1550

Woodland, Tex.: Oct. 1866, roll 1550

Woodville, Tex.: Apr. 1867–May 1868, roll 1550

Camp Worth, Tex.: Feb. 1854, roll 1550

Fort Worth, Tex.: June 1849–Aug. 1853, roll 1465

Descriptive Commentaries from the Medical Histories of Posts, microfilm no. M903, 5 rolls.

Records of the United States Army Commands, Record Group 98, Brief Histories of U.S. Army Commands (Army Posts) and Description of Their Records, microfilm no. T-912, 1 roll.

Records of the Headquarters of the Army, Record Group 108, Headquarters, U.S. Army, "Descriptive Book of the District of Texas, July 1st 1868." Entry 51, Vol. 220, microfilm no. M253, 1 roll.

Records of the United States Army Continental Commands, 1821–1920, Record Group 393, Headquarters Records of Fort Stockton, Texas 1867–1870, microfilm no. M1381, 5 rolls.

Headquarters of the Military Division of the Missouri. *Outline Descriptions of the Posts in the Military Division of the Missouri, Commanded by Lieutenant General P. H. Sherdian.* Chicago: Headquarters, Military Division of the Missouri, 1876. Reprint, Bellevue, Neb.: The Old Army Press, 1969.

Inspector General's Office. *Outline Descriptions of the Posts and Stations of Troops in the Geographic Divisions and Departments of the United States (1872).* Washington, D.C.: Government Printing Office, 1872.

Office of the Judge Advocate General, *United States Military Reservations, National Cemeteries and Military Parks: Title, Jurisdiction, Etc.* Washington, D.C.: Government Printing Office, 1910.

Quartermaster General's Office. *Outline Description of U.S. Military Posts and Stations in the Year 1871.* Washington, D.C.: Government Printing Office, 1872.

FORT AND CAMP HISTORIES: BOOKS, ARTICLES, AND DISSERTATIONS

General Studies:

Barrett, Arrie. "Western Frontier Forts of Texas, 1845–1861." *West Texas Historical Association Year Book*, 7 (June, 1931), 115–139.

_____. "Federal Military Outposts in Texas, 1845–1861." M.A. thesis, University of Texas, 1927.

Conway, Walter C., ed. "Colonel Edmund Schriver's Inspector-General's Report on Military Posts in Texas November, 1872–January, 1873." *Southwestern Historical Quarterly*, 67 (April, 1964), 559–583.

Crimmins, Martin L., ed. "Colonel J. F. K. Mansfield's Report of the Inspection of the Department of Texas in 1856." *Southwestern Historical Quarterly*, 42 (Oct., 1938), 122–148; (Jan., 1939), 215–217; (Apr., 1939), 351–387.

_____, ed. "W. G. Freeman's Report on the Eighth Military Department." *Southwestern Historical Quarterly*, 51 (July, 1947), 54–58; (Oct., 1947), 167–174; (Jan., 1948), 252–258; (Apr., 1948), 350–357; 52 (July, 1948), 100–108; (Oct., 1948), 227–233; (Jan., 1949): 349–353; (Apr., 1949), 444–447; 53 (July, 1949), 71–77; (Oct., 1949), 202–208; (Jan., 1950), 308–319; (Apr., 1950), 443–473; 54 (Oct., 1950), 204–218.

Fox, Daniel E. *Traces of Texas History: Archeological Evidence of the Past 450 Years*. San Antonio: Corona Publishing Company, 1983.

Frantz, Joe B. "The Significance of Frontier Forts to Texas." *Southwestern Historical Quarterly*, 74 (Oct., 1970), 204–205.

Frazer, Robert W. *Forts of the West*. Norman: University of Oklahoma Press, 1965.

Graham, Roy E. *Texas Historic Forts*. 5 vols. University of Texas School of Architecture, Austin: Texas Parks and Wildlife Department, 1968.

_____. "Federal Fort Architecture in Texas during the Nineteenth Century." *Southwestern Historical Quarterly*, 74 (Oct., 1970), 165–188.

Hart, Herbert M. *Tour Guide to Old Western Forts*. Fort Collins, Colo.: Old Army Press, 1980.

National Park Service. *Soldier and Brave: Historic Places Associated with Indian Affairs and the Indian Wars in the Trans–Mississippi West.* The National Survey of Historic Sites and Buildings, vol. 12. Edited by Robert G. Ferris. Washington, D.C.: United States Department of the Interior, National Park Service, 1971.

Roberts, Robert B. *Encyclopedia of Historic Forts: The Military, Pioneer, and Trading Posts of the United States.* New York: Macmillan Publishing Company, 1988.

Simons, Helen, Rachel Feit, and Michael Davis, compilers. *Texas Military Sites: A Guide to Materials in the Holdings of the Office of the State Archeologist, Texas Historical Commission.* Office of the State Archeologist Special Report 34. Austin: Texas Historical Commission, 1996.

Simpson, Harold B., coordinator. *Frontier Forts of Texas.* Waco: Texian Press, 1966.

Thompson, Jerry Don, ed. *Texas and New Mexico on the Eve of the Civil War: J. F. K. Mansfield and Joseph E. Johnston's Inspections of the Department of Texas and New Mexico, 1859–1860.* Albuquerque: University of New Mexico Press, forthcoming.

Toulouse, James R. and Joseph H. *Pioneer Posts of Texas.* San Antonio: The Naylor Company, 1936.

Utley, Robert M. and J. U. Salvant. *If These Walls Could Speak: Historic Forts of Texas.* Austin: University of Texas Press, 1985.

Fort and Camp Histories

Fort Belknap:

Braly, Earl Burk. "Fort Belknap on the Texas Frontier." *West Texas Historical Association Year Book,* 30 (Oct., 1954), 83–114.

Ledbetter, Barbara A. Neal. *Fort Belknap Frontier Saga: Indians, Negroes and Anglo-Americans on the Texas Frontier.* Burnet, Tex.: Eakin Press, 1982.

"Letters about the End of Fort Belknap and the Beginning of Fort Griffin." *West Texas Historical Association Year Book,* 34 (Oct., 1958), 141–148.

Fort Bliss:

Christian, Garna Loy. "Sword and Plowshare: The Symbiotic Development of Fort Bliss and El Paso, Texas, 1848–1918." Ph.D diss., Texas Tech University, 1977.

Crimmins, Martin L. "The Border Command at Fort Bliss." *West Texas Historical and Scientific Society* Bulletin 21 (Dec., 1926), 16–20.

Harris, Charles H. and Louis R. Sadler. *Bastion On the Border: Fort Bliss, 1854–1943*. Historical and Natural Resources Report 6. Fort Bliss, Tex: Management Branch, Directorate of Environment, U.S. Army Air Defense Artillery Center, 1993.

Jamieson, Perry. *A Survey History of Fort Bliss, 1890–1940*. Historical and Natural Resources Report 5. Fort Bliss, Tex.: Management Branch, Directorate of Environment, U.S. Army Air Defense Artillery Center, 1993.

McMaster, Richard K. *Musket, Saber and Missle: A History of Fort Bliss*. El Paso, Tex.: Complete Printing & Letter Service, 1962.

Metz, Leon C. *Fort Bliss: An Illustrated History*. El Paso, Tex.: Mangan Books, 1981.

————. *Desert Army: Fort Bliss on the Texas Border*. El Paso: Mangan Books, 1988.

Thomlinson, Mathew H. *The Garrison of Fort Bliss, 1849–1916*. El Paso, Tex.: Hertzog and Resler, 1945.

Timmons, W. H. "The Merchants and the Military, 1849–1854." *Password*, 28 (Summer, 1982), 51–61.

Brazos Santiago:

Banks, Cynthia Richelle. "Brazos Santiago Depot and Fort Polk, Cameron County, Texas: Contexts of Sites and Analysis of Ceramics from 1967 and 1980 Investigations." M.A. Thesis, University of Texas at Austin, 1983.

Hoyt, Steven D. "Underwater Investigations, Brazos Island Harbor Navigation Project, Cameron County, Texas." Austin: Espey, Huston and Associates, Inc., Document 910040, 1992.

Nichols, Peter W., Dan Prikryl, and Peggy Jodry. "Cultural Resources Technical Report: Survey and Limited Testing-

Proposed Deep Water Channel and Multipurpose Terminal, Brownsville, Cameron County, Texas." Austin: Espey, Huston and Associates, Inc., Document 85568, 1981.

Tunnell, Curtis and J. Richard Ambler. *Proposal for the Acquisition and Archeological Study of Brazos Island.* Office of the State Archeologist Special Report 4. Austin: Texas Historical Commission, 1971.

Fort Brown:

Ashcraft, Allan C. "Fort Brown, Texas, in 1861." *Texas Military History*, 3 (Winter, 1963), 243–247.

Carlson, Shawn Bonath, Joe Sanders, Frank Winchell, and Bruce Aiken. *Archeological Investigations at Fort Brown (41CF96), Cameron County, Texas.* Archeological Resources Lab, Reports of Investigations 11. College Station: Texas A&M University, 1990.

Marcum, Richard T. "Fort Brown, Texas: The History of a Border Post." Ph.D diss., Texas Tech University, 1977.

Sides, Joseph C. *Fort Brown Historical: History of Fort Brown, Texas Border Post on the Rio Grande.* San Antonio, Tex.: The Naylor Company, 1942.

Buffalo Springs:

Thompson, Theronne. "Fort Buffalo Spring, Texas, Border Post." *West Texas Historical Association Year Book*, 36 (Oct., 1960), 156–175.

Fort Chadbourne:

Crimmins, Martin L. "Experiences of an Army Surgeon at Fort Chadbourne." *West Texas Historical Association Year Book*, 15 (Oct., 1939), 31–39.

Fort Clark:

Fort Clark Records, Center for American History, University of Texas at Austin.

Pingenot, Ben E. "Fort Clark, Texas: A Brief History." *The Journal of Big Bend Studies*, 7 (Jan., 1995), 103–122.

Pirtle, Caleb III and Michael F. Cusack. *Fort Clark: The Lonely Sentinel*. Austin, Tex.: Eakin Press, 1985.

Warren, James E. "A Cultural Resources Survey of the Fort Clark/Bracketville Wastewater Improvement Project, Kinney County, Texas." George West, Tex.: Archaeology Consultants, Inc. Report 352, 1994.

Camp Colorado:

Crimmins, Martin L. "The Military History of Camp Colorado." *West Texas Historical Association Year Book*, 28 (Oct., 1952), 71–81.

Havins, Thomas R. *Camp Colorado: A Decade of Frontier Defense*. Brownwood, Tex.: Brown Press, 1964.

Fort Concho:

Boggs, Herschel. "A History of Fort Concho." M.A. thesis, University of Texas at Austin, 1940.

Haley, J. Evetts. *Fort Concho and the Texas Frontier*. San Angelo, Tex.: San Angelo Standard Times, 1952.

Melton, Greg. "Trials by Nature: The Harsh Environment of Fort Concho, Texas." M.A. thesis, Abilene Christian University, 1981.

Miles, Susan. *Fort Concho in 1877*. San Angelo, Tex.: Bradley Co., 1952.

————. "Fort Concho in 1877." *West Texas Historical Association Year Book*, 35 (1959), 29–49.

Mobley, Charles M. *Archaeological Investigations at Fort Concho, Texas*. Southern Methodist University Archaeology Research Program Research Report 98. Dallas: Southern Methodist University, 1976.

Pettingill, Shirley J. *Report for 1975 and 1976 of Archeological Investigations at Fort Concho*. San Angelo, Tex.: Fort Concho Museum, 1977.

Stevens, Joanne Darsey. "Fort Concho, Guardian of the Conchos, 1867–1874." M.A. thesis, Angelo State University, 1975.

Sutton, Mary. "Glimpses of Fort Concho Through the Military Telegraph." *West Texas Historical Association Year Book*, 32 (Oct., 1956), 122–134.

Camp Cooper:

Crimmins, Martin L. "Camp Cooper and Fort Griffin, Texas." *West Texas Historical Association Year Book*, 17 (1941), 32–43.

Crum, Tom. "Camp Cooper, A Different Look." *West Texas Historical Association Year Book*, 68 (1992), 62–65.

Mayhall, Mildred P. "Camp Cooper—First Federal Fort in Texas to Fall, 1861, and Events Preceding its Fall." *Texana*, 5 (Winter, 1967), 318–342.

Richardson, Rupert N. "The Saga of Camp Cooper." *West Texas Historical Association Year Book*, 56 (1980), 14–33.

Fort Croghan:

Cox, Mike. "Old Fort Croghan." *Texas Military History*, 5 (Spring, 1965), 15–19.

Fort Davis:

Crimmins, Martin L. "The Border Command at Fort Davis." *West Texas Historical and Scientific Society* Bulletin 21 (Dec., 1926), 7–15.

Scobee, Barry. *Old Fort Davis*. San Antonio: The Naylor Co., 1947.

_____. *Old Fort Davis, Texas, 1583–1960*. El Paso, Tex.: Hill Printing Co., 1963.

Thomas, W. Stephen. *Fort Davis and the Texas Frontier: Paintings by Arthur T. Lee, Eighth U.S. Infantry*. College Station: Texas A&M University Press for the Amon Carter Museum, 1976.

Utley, Robert M. *Fort Davis National Historic Site, Texas*. National Park Service Historical Handbook Series No. 38. Washington, D.C.: United States Department of the Interior, 1965.

Wooster, Robert. *Fort Davis: Outpost on the Texas Frontier*. Austin: Texas State Historical Association, 1994.

_____. *History of Fort Davis, Texas*. Southwest Cultural Resources Center, Professional Paper No. 34. Santa Fe: Southwest Region, National Park Service, Department of the Interior, 1990.

Fort Duncan:

Fort Duncan Records, Center for American History, University of Texas at Austin.

Field, William T. "Fort Duncan and Old Eagle Pass." *Texas Military History*, 6 (Summer, 1967), 160–71.

Sellers, Rosella R. "The History of Fort Duncan, Eagle Pass, Texas." M.A. thesis, Sul Ross State College, 1960.

Fort Elliott:

Fort Elliott Papers, Center for American History, University of Texas at Austin.

Anderson, John Q. "Fort Elliot, Texas: Last Guard of the Plains." *Texas Military History*, 2 (Nov., 1962), 243–254.

Crimmins, Martin L. "Notes on the Establishment of Fort Elliott and the Buffalo Wallow Fight." *Panhandle-Plains Historical Review*, 25 (1952), 45.

Crimmins, Martin L. "Fort Elliott, Texas." *West Texas Historical Association Year Book*, 23 (Oct., 1947), 3–12.

Kyvig, David E. "Policing the Panhandle: Fort Elliott, Texas, 1875–1890." *Red River Valley Historical Review*, 1 (Autumn, 1974), 222–232.

Oswald, James M. "History of Fort Elliott." *Panhandle-Plains Historical Review*, 32 (1959), 1–59.

Fort Ewell:

McGuire, T. C. "A Model of Fort Ewell Constructed under the Gillmore Method of Historical Site Identification." Manuscript. Center for Archaeological Research, University of Texas at San Antonio, [n.d.].

Galveston:

Freeman, Martha Doty and Sandra L. Hunnum. "A History of Fortifications at Fort San Jacinto, Galveston Island, Texas." Austin: Prewitt & Associates, Inc., Reports of Investigations 80, 1991.

Young, Earle B. *Galveston and the Great West*. College Station: Texas A&M University Press, 1997.

Fort Gates:

 Lemmons, Thomas C. "Fort Gates and the Central Texas Frontier, 1849–1852." M.A. thesis, Abilene Christian College, 1967.

 Mears, Mildred Watkins. "The Three Forts in Coryell County." *Southwestern Historical Quarterly*, 67 (July, 1963), 1–14.

Fort Graham

 Myres, Sandra L. "Fort Graham: Listening Post on the Texas Frontier." *West Texas Historical Association Year Book*, 59 (1983), 33–51.

Fort Griffin:

 Cashion, Ty. *A Texas Frontier: The Clear Fork Country and Fort Griffin, 1849–1887*. Norman: University of Oklahoma Press, 1996.

 Clark, O. D. *Fort Griffin*. Albany, Tex.: Albany Chamber of Commerce, 1935.

 Fox, Anne A. *Archaeological Investigations at Fort Griffin State Historic Park, Texas*. Archaeological Survey Report No. 21. San Antonio: Center for Archaeological Research, University of Texas at San Antonio, 1976.

 _____. *Archaeological Investigations at Fort Griffin State Historic Park, Shackelford County, Texas*. Archaeological Survey Report No. 23. San Antonio: Center for Archaeological Research, University of Texas at San Antonio, 1976.

 _____. *Archeological Investigations at Fort Griffin, Part 2*. Archeological Completion Report, Series 10. Washington, D.C.: Office of Archeological and Historic Preservation, National Park Service, Department of the Interior, 1975.

 Haskew, Eula. "Stribling and Kirkland of Fort Griffin." *West Texas Historical Association Year Book*, 32 (Oct., 1956), 55–69.

 Lynch, Vernon. "1879 in the Echo: A Year at Fort Griffin on the Texas Frontier." *West Texas Historical Association Year Book*, 41 (Oct., 1965), 51–79.

 Olds, Dorris L. *Archaeological Investigation at Fort Griffin Military Post, Shackelford County, Texas*. Austin: Texas Archeological Research Laboratory, 1969.

Rister, Carl Coke. *Fort Griffin on the Texas Frontier*. Norman: University of Oklahoma Press, 1956.

Robinson, Charles M. III. *The Frontier World of Fort Griffin: The Life and Death of a Western Town*. Spokane, Wash.: The Arthur H. Clark Company, 1992.

Yates, C. *Archeological Investigations at Fort Griffin*. Archeological Completion Report, Series 3. Washington, D.C.: Office of Archeological and Historic Preservation, National Park Service, Department of the Interior, 1975.

_____. *Archeological Investigations at Fort Griffin State Historic Park, 1971, Shackelford County, Texas*. Texas Archeological Survey Research Report 24. Austin: University of Texas, 1973.

Fort Hancock:

Ruhlen, George. "Fort Hancock—Last of the Frontier Forts." *Password*, 4 (Jan., 1959), 19–30.

Indianola:

Malsch, Brownson. *Indianola: The Mother of Western Texas*. Austin: Shoal Creek Publishers, 1977.

Fort Inge:

Nelson, George. *Preliminary Archaeological Survey and Testing at Fort Inge, Texas*. Uvalde, Tex.: Uvalde County Historical Commission, 1981.

_____. *Additional Archaeological Survey and Testing at Fort Inge, Texas*. Uvalde, Tex.: Uvalde County Historical Commission, 1981.

Smith, Thomas Tyree. *Fort Inge: Sharps, Spurs, and Sabers on the Texas Frontier, 1849–1869*. Austin: Eakin Press, 1991.

_____. "Fort Inge and Texas Frontier Military Operations, 1849–1869." *Southwestern Historical Quarterly*, 96 (July, 1992), 1–25.

_____. "Fort Inge and the Texas Frontier Economy." *Military History of the Southwest*, 21 (Fall, 1991), 135–156.

_____. "Fort Inge and the Texas Frontier, 1849–1869." M.A. thesis, Texas A&M University, 1991.

Fort Lancaster:

Black, Art. *Fort Lancaster State Historic Site, Crockett County, Texas: Archeological Excavations.* Texas Parks and Wildlife Department Archeological Report No. 18. Austin: Historic Sites and Restoration Branch, Texas Parks and Wildlife Department, 1975.

Clark, John W. Jr. *Archeological Investigations at Fort Lancaster State Historic Site, Crockett County, Texas.* Texas Archeological Salvage Project Research Report No. 12. Austin: University of Texas at Austin, 1972.

_____. "The 'Digs' At Fort Lancaster, Texas, 1966 and 1971." *Military History of Texas and the Southwest,* 12 (1974), 284–299.

Fletcher, Henry T. "Old Fort Lancaster." *West Texas Historical and Scientific Society* Bulletin 44 (Dec., 1932), 33–34.

Francell, Lawrence John. *Fort Lancaster: Texas Frontier Sentinel.* Austin: Texas State Historical Association, 1999.

_____. *Ft. Lancaster State Historic Park, Crockett County, Texas.* Austin: Historic Sites and Restoration Branch, Texas Parks and Wildlife Department, 1969.

Hays, T. R. and Edward B. Jelks. *Archeological Explorations at Fort Lancaster, 1966: A Preliminary Report.* Office of the State Archeologist Report 4. Austin: Texas Historical Commission, 1966.

Fort Lincoln:

Crook, Garland and Cornelia Crook. "Fort Lincoln, Texas." *Texas Military History,* 4 (Fall, 1964), 145–161.

Fort McIntosh:

Briggs, Alton. "Archeological Investigation of an Area Proposed for Vegetation Management at Fort McIntosh, U.S.A. 1849–1946." Georgetown, Tex.: Lone Star Archeological Services, Report 19, 1982.

Fox, Daniel E. *Archaeological Testing at Fort McIntosh, Laredo Junior College Campus, Laredo, Texas.* Archaeological Survey Report No. 68. San Antonio: Center for Archaeological Research, University of Texas at San Antonio, 1979.

Ivey, James E., Thomas Medlin, and Jack D. Eaton. *An Initial Archaeological Assessment of Areas Proposed for Modification at Fort McIntosh, Webb County, Texas.* Archaeological Survey Report No. 23. San Antonio: Center for Archaeological Research, University of Texas at San Antonio, 1977.

Ivey, James E. and Thomas W. Medlin. "The Fort McIntosh Problem." *La Tierra*, 4, no. 3 (1977), 1–6.

Warren, James E. "Historical Archeology at Fort McIntosh, Webb County, Texas." George West, Tex.: Archaeology Consultants, Inc., Report 199, 1989.

———. "Historic Archeology at Fort McIntosh in Laredo, Webb County, Texas." George West, Tex.: Archaeology Consultants, Inc., Report 175, 1989.

———. "Historic Archeology at Fort McIntosh in Webb County, Texas." George West, Tex.: Archaeology Consultants, Inc., Report 180, 1989.

———. "Historical Archeology at Fort McIntosh (41WB11) in Laredo, Webb County, Texas." George West, Tex.: Archaeology Consultants, Inc., Report 239, 1991.

Fort McKavett:

Bierschwale, Margaret. *Fort McKavett, Texas: Post on the San Saba.* Salado, Tex.: Anson Jones, 1966.

Black, Art and J. David Ing. *Fort McKavett State Historic Site: Archeological Investigations, 1974–1977.* Austin: Historic Sites and Restoration Branch, Texas Parks and Wildlife Department, 1980.

Carter, E. Suzanne. *Fort McKavett–Menard County, Texas: Archeological and Architecural Details of the Bakery, Barracks, and Headquarters Buildings, Spring 1973.* Texas Archeological Survey 20. Austin: University of Texas at Austin, 1974.

Crimmins, Martin L. "Fort McKavett, Texas." *Southwestern Historical Quarterly*, 38 (July, 1934), 28–39.

Earls, Amy C. and John Leffler. *Fort McKavett: Archeological Investigations for Fort Stabilization and Restoration, Fort McKavett State Historical Park, Menard County, Texas: 1978–1990 Seasons.* Austin: Historic Sites and Restoration Branch, Texas Parks and Wildlife Department, 1996.

Green, F. E. *Report on Preliminary Archeological Investigations at Fort McKavett, Texas*. Lubbock: Texas Tech University, 1969.

Sullivan, Jerry M. *Fort McKavett: A Texas Frontier Post*. Lubbock: West Texas Museum Association, Texas Tech University, 1981.

―――――. "Fort McKavett, 1852–1883." *West Texas Historical Association Year Book*, 45 (1969), 138–149.

Fort Martin Scott:

Labadie, Joseph H. *Archaeological Investigations at Fort Martin Scott (41GL52) in Gillespie County, Texas*. Archaeological Survey Report No. 169. San Antonio: Center for Archaeological Research, University of Texas at San Antonio, 1987.

Fort Mason:

Bierschwale, Margaret. "Mason County, Texas, 1845–1870." *Southwestern Historical Quarterly*, 52 (Apr., 1949), 379–397.

Jaquier, J. A. "Archeological Investigations at Fort Mason (1987–1988), Mason County, Texas." TAC Permit 617. [N.p.], 1991.

Ponder, Jerry. *Fort Mason, Texas: Training Ground for Generals*. Mason, Tex.: Ponder Books, 1997.

Camp Melvin:

Ramsey, Grover C. "Camp Melvin, Crockett County, Texas." *West Texas Historical Association Year Book*, 37 (Oct., 1961), 137–146.

Fort Merrill:

Warren, James E. "Fort Merrill, Texas, 1850–55." George West, Tex.: Archaeology Consultants, Inc., Report 174, 1990.

Camp Peña Colorado:

Crimmins, Martin L. "Camp Pena Colorado, Texas." *West Texas Historical and Scientific Society* Bulletin 6 (Dec., 1935), 8–22.

Guffee, E. J. "Camp Pena Colorado, Texas, 1879–1893." M.A. thesis, West Texas State University, 1976.

Fort Phantom Hill:

Anderson, Hugh Allen. "Fort Phantom Hill: Outpost on the Clear Fork of the Brazos." M.A. thesis, Texas Tech University, 1975.

Hatcher, John H. "Fort Phantom Hill." *Texas Military History*, 3 (Fall, 1963), 154–164.

Rister, Carl Coke. "The Border Post of Phantom Hill." *West Texas Historical Association Year Book*, 14 (1938), 3–38.

Fort Quitman:

Ruhlen, George. "Quitman: Worst Post at Which I Ever Served." *Password*, 11 (Fall, 1966). Reprinted in John M. Carroll, ed. *The Black Military Experience in the American West*. New York: Liveright Publishing Corp., 1971, 103–114.

_____. "Quitman's Owners: A Sidelight on Frontier Realty." *Password*, 5 (Apr., 1960), 54–63.

Fort Richardson:

Dickson, D. B. *Archeological Research at Fort Richardson State Park, Summer 1975*. Anthropology Lab Report No. 28. College Station: Texas A&M University, 1976.

Hamilton, Allen Lee. *Sentinel of the Southern Plains: Fort Richardson and the Northwest Texas Frontier, 1866–1878*. Fort Worth: Texas Christian University Press, 1988.

Ippolito, John E. and William A. Westbury. *Archeological Investigations at Fort Richardson State Park, Fall 1976*. Anthropology Lab Report No. 39. College Station: Texas A&M University, 1976.

Lorrain, Dessamae. *Archeological Investigations at Fort Richardson State Historic Site, Jack County, Texas*. Archeological Salvage Project Research Report No. 10. Austin: University of Texas, 1972.

_____. *Fort Richardson Commissary and Quartermaster's Storehouse: Archeological Tests, August 1972*. Austin: Historic Sites and Restoration Branch, Texas Parks and Wildlife Department, 1973.

Olsen, S. C. *Fort Richardson*. Archeological Completion Report, Series 6. Washington, D.C.: Office of Archeological and Historic

Preservation, National Park Service, Department of the Interior, 1975

Westbury, William A. *Archeological Investigations at Fort Richardson State Park, 1976.* Anthropology Labratory Report No. 31. College Station: Texas A&M University, 1976.

Whisenhunt, Donald W. "Fort Richardson." *West Texas Historical Association Year Book,* 39 (1963), 19–27.

_____. "Frontier Military Life at Fort Richardson, Texas." *West Texas Historical Association Year Book,* 42 (Oct., 1966), 15–27.

_____. *Fort Richardson: Outpost on the Texas Frontier.* Southwestern Studies Monograph No. 20. El Paso, Tex.: Texas Western Press, 1968.

Fort Ringgold:

Simmons, Thomas E. *Fort Ringgold: A Brief Tour.* Edinburg: University of Texas Pan-American Press, 1991.

San Antonio Area:

Cagle, Eldon Jr. *Quadrangle: The History of Fort Sam Houston.* Austin: Eakin Press, 1985.

Eaton, Jack D. *Excavations at the Alamo Shrine (Mission San Antonio de Valero).* Special Report No. 10. San Antonio: Center for Archaeological Research, University of Texas at San Antonio, 1980.

Fox, Anne A. *Archeological Investigations at the United States Arsenal Site (41BX622), San Antonio, Texas.* Archaeological Survey Report No. 137. San Antonio: Center for Archaeological Research, University of Texas at San Antonio, 1986.

Gerstle, Andrea, Thomas C. Kelly, and Cristi Assad. *The Fort Sam Houston Project: An Archaeological and Historical Assessment.* Archaeological Survey Report No. 40. San Antonio: Center for Archaeological Research, University of Texas at San Antonio, 1978.

Giglio, Donald F. "A Historical Retrospection of Fort Sam Houston." *Texana,* 7 (Spring. 1969), 38–55.

Greer, John W. *A Description of the Stratigraphy, Features, and Artifacts from an Archeological Excavation at the Alamo*. Office of the State Archeologist Special Report 3. Austin: Texas Historical Commission, 1967.

Handy, Mary Olivia. *History of Fort Sam Houston*. San Antonio: The Naylor Company, 1951.

Fort Stockton:

Hopper, W. L. "The Birth and Death of an Army Fort [Fort Stockton]." *Military History of Texas and the Southwest*, 10 (1972), 273–277.

Williams, Clayton W. *Texas' Last Frontier: Fort Stockton and the Trans–Pecos, 1861–1895*. College Station: Texas A&M University Press, 1982.

Fort Terrett:

King, Grace, Sherwood Noël McGuigan, and Gem Meacham. *From Muskets To Mohair: The History of Fort Terrett*. Waco: Texian Press, 1992.

Camp Verde:

Hunter, Marvin J. *Old Camp Verde, The Home of the Camels*. Bandera, Tex.: *Frontier Times*, 1939.

Fort Worth:

Knight, Oliver. *Fort Worth on the Trinity*. Norman: University of Oklahoma Press, 1954.

Garrett, Julia Kathryn. *Fort Worth: A Frontier Triumph*. Austin: Encino Press, 1972.

Selcer, Richard F. "Setting the Record Straight: Fort Worth and the Historians." *Southwestern Historical Quarterly*, 100 (Jan., 1997), 361–379.

Selcer, Richard F. and William B. Potter. *The Fort That Became a City: An Illustrated Reconstruction of Fort Worth, Texas, 1849–1853*. Abilene: Texas Christian University Press, 1995.

GARRISON LIFE: PRIMARY SOURCES; GOVERNMENT DOCUMENTS, BOOKS AND ARTICLES

Government Documents

United States Congressional Records:

34th Congress, 1st Session. *Senate Executive Documents*, no. 96, serial 827 (Statistical Report on the Sickness and Mortality in the Army of the United States . . . from January, 1838 to January, 1855).

36th Congress, 1st Session. *Senate Executive Documents*, no. 52, serial 1035 (Statistical Report on the Sickness and Mortality in the Army of the United States . . . from January, 1855, to January, 1860).

52nd Congress, 1st Session. *House Executive Documents*, no.1, pt.2, serial 2921 (Report of the Surgeon-General of the Army, 22 Sept. 1891).

Books and Articles

Abbot, Frederick V. *History of the Class of 'Seventy-Nine at the U.S. Military Academy*. New York: G. P. Putnam's Sons, 1884.

Alexander, Eveline Martin. *Cavalry Wife: The Diary of Eveline M. Alexander, 1866–1867*. Edited by Sandra L. Myres. College Station: Texas A&M University Press, 1977.

Boyd, Mrs. Orsemus B. *Cavalry Life in Tent and Field*. New York: J. S. Tait, 1894. Reprint, with an introduction by Darlis A. Miller, Lincoln: University of Nebraska Press, 1982.

Bluthard, Robert F. "The Men of Company F." *Fort Concho Report*, 15 (Summer, 1983), 3–9.

Buck, Maj. Gen. Beaumont B. *Memories of Peace and War*. San Antonio: Naylor Co., 1935.

Byrne, James Bernard. *A Frontier Army Surgeon*. New York: Exposition Press, 1935.

Clary, David A., ed. "'I Am Already Quite a Texan': Albert J. Myer's Letters from Texas, 1854–1856." *Southwestern Historical Quarterly*, 82 (July, 1978), 25–76.

Coker, Caleb and Janet G. Humphrey. "The Texas Frontier in 1850: Dr. Ebenezer Swift and the View from Fort Martin Scott." *Southwestern Historical Quarterly*, 96 (Jan., 1993), 392–413.

Coker, Caleb, ed. *The News From Brownsville: Helen Chapman's Letters from the Texas Military Frontier, 1848–1852*. Austin: Texas State Historical Association, 1992.

Crane, R. C., "Letters From Texas." *West Texas Historical Association Year Book*, 25 (Oct., 1949), 110–126.

Crook, George. *General George Crook: His Autobiography*. Edited by Martin F. Schmitt. Norman: University of Oklahoma Press, 1960.

Duke, Escal F. "O. M. Smith—Frontier Pay Clerk." *West Texas Historical Association Year Book*, 45 (1969), 45–57.

First Class Annual of the Class of '86, United States Military Academy, West Point, N.Y. [Letters From Texas]. Poughkeepsie, N.Y.: Haight & Dudley, Printers, 1887.

Green, Bill. *The Dancing Was Lively: Fort Concho, Texas: A Social History, 1867–1882*. San Angelo, Tex.: Fort Concho Sketches Publishing Co., 1974.

Howe, Edgar W. *The History of the Class of 'Seventy-Eight, at the U.S. Military Academy*. New York: Homer Lee Bank Note Company, 1881.

Lane, Lydia Spencer. *I Married A Soldier: Or, Old Days in the Army*. Philadelphia: J. B. Lippincott Co., 1893. Reprint, with an introduction by Darlis A. Miller, Albuquerque: University of New Mexico Press, 1987.

Laurence, Mary Leefe. *Daughter of the Regiment: Memoirs of a Childhood in the Frontier Army, 1878–1898*. Edited by Thomas T. Smith. Lincoln: University of Nebraska Press, 1996.

Leckie, Shirley Anne, ed. *The Colonel's Lady on the Western Frontier: The Correspondence of Alice Kirk Grierson*. Lincoln: University of Nebraska Press, 1989.

McChristian, Douglas C., ed. *Garrison Tangles in the Friendless Tenth: The Journal of First Lieutenant John Bigelow Jr., Fort Davis, Texas*. Bryan, Tex.: J. M. Carroll & Company, 1985.

Moore, Ike. *The Life and Diary of Reading W. Black*. Uvalde, Tex.: The El Progreso Club, 1934.

Neilson, John. "'I Long To Return to Fort Concho': Acting Assistant Surgeon Samuel Smith's Letters from the Texas Military Frontier, 1878–1879." *Military History of the West*, 24 (Fall, 1994), 122–186.

Notson, William M. "Fort Concho, 1868–1872: The Medical Officers Observations." Edited by Stephen Schmidt. *Military History of Texas and the Southwest*, 12, no. 1 (1975), 125–149.

Olmsted, Frederick Law. *A Journey through Texas; Or, a Saddle-Trip on the Southwestern Frontier*. New York: Dix, Edwards & Co., 1857. Reprint, Austin: University of Texas Press, 1978.

Parkhurst, Lt. C. D. "Electricity and the Art of War." *Journal of the United States Artillery*, 1 (Oct., 1892), 315–363.

Richardson, Rupert N., ed. "Report of the Post Surgeon at Fort Phantom Hill for 1852." *West Texas Historical Association Year Book*, 1 (1924), 73–77.

Roland, Charles P. and Richard C. Robbins (eds.). "The Diary of Eliza (Mrs. Albert Sidney) Johnston: The Second Cavalry Comes to Texas." *Southwestern Historical Quarterly*, 60 (Apr., 1957), 463–500.

Scannell, Jack C. "A Survey of the Stagecoach Mail in the Trans–Pecos, 1850–1861." *West Texas Historical Association Year Book*, 47 (1971), 115–126.

Schmidt, Carol. "The Chaplains of Fort Concho." *Fort Concho Report*, 16 (Spring, 1984), 27–32.

Smith, Thomas T., ed. *A Dose of Frontier Soldiering: The Memoirs of Corporal E. A. Bode, Frontier Regular Infantry, 1877–1882*. Lincoln: University of Nebraska Press, 1994.

Steuart, Lt. George H. "Correspondence, 1853–1855." Eberstadt Collection, Box 3N182, Center for American History, University of Texas at Austin.

Summerhayes, Martha. *Vanished Arizona: Recollections of My Army Life*. Philadelphia: Lippincott, 1908. Reprint, Lincoln: University of Nebraska Press, 1979.

Todd, Albert. *The Class of 1877*. Cambridge, Mass.: Riverside Press, 1878.

Turnley, Parmenas Taylor. *Reminiscences of Parmenas Taylor Turnley from the Cradle to Three-Score and Ten*. Chicago: Donohue & Henneberry, 1892.

United States Military Academy. *First Class Annual of the Class of '86, United States Military Academy, West Point, N.Y. for the Year 1887*. Poughkeepsie, N.Y.: Haight & Dudley Printers, 1887.

Vielé, Teresa Griffin. *Following the Drum: A Glimpse of Frontier Life*. New York: Rudd & Carleton, 1858. Reprint, with a foreword by Sandra L. Myres, Lincoln: University of Nebraska Press, 1984.

Wynes, Charles E., ed. "Lewis Harvie Blair: Texas Travels, 1851–1855." *Southwestern Historical Quarterly*, 66 (Oct., 1962), 262–270.

GARRISON LIFE: SECONDARY SOURCES; BOOKS AND ARTICLES

Austerman, Wayne R. *Sharps Rifles and Spanish Mules: The San Antonio-El Paso Mail, 1851–1881*. College Station: Texas A&M University Press, 1985.

Bluthhardt, Robert F. "Baseball on the Military Frontier." *Fort Concho Report*, 19 (Spring, 1987), 17–26.

Breeden, James O. "Health of Early Texas: The Military Frontier." *Southwestern Historical Quarterly*, 80 (Apr., 1977), 357–398.

Carlson, Paul H. "Baseball's Abner Doubleday on the Texas Frontier." *Military History of Texas and the Southwest*, 12 (Spring, 1976), 235–244.

Cashion, Ty. "(Gun)Smoke Gets in Your Eyes: A Revisionist Look at 'Violent' Fort Griffin." *Southwestern Historical Quarterly*, 99 (July, 1995), 80–94.

Christian, Garna. *Black Soldiers in Jim Crow Texas, 1899–1917*. College Station: Texas A&M University Press, 1995.

_____. "Adding on Fort Bliss to Black Military Historiography." *West Texas Historical Association Year Book*, 54 (1978), 41–54.

_____. "The Twenty-Fifth Regiment at Fort McIntosh: Precursor to Retaliatory Racial Violence." *West Texas Historical Association Year Book*, 55 (1979), 149–161.

_____. "Rio Grande City: Prelude to the Brownsville Raid." *West Texas Historical Association Year Book*, 57 (1981), 118–132.

Clary, David A. "The Role of the Army Surgeon in the West: Daniel Weisel at Fort Davis, 1868–1872." *Western Historical Quarterly*, 3 (Jan., 1972), 53–66.

Coffman, Edward M. *The Old Army: A Portrait of the American Army in Peacetime, 1784–1898*. New York: Oxford University Press, 1986.

Conkling, Roscoe and Margaret B. Conkling. *The Butterfield Overland Mail, 1857–1869.* 3 vols. Glendale, Calif.: The Arthur H. Clark Co., 1947.

Dawson, Joseph G. III, ed. *The Texas Military Experience.* College Station: Texas A&M University Press, 1995.

Delo, David Michael. *Peddlers and Post Traders: The Army Sutler on the Frontier.* Salt Lake City: University of Utah Press, 1992.

Dinges, Bruce J. "The Court-Martial of Lieutenant Henry O. Flipper: An Example of Black-White Relationships in the Army, 1881." *The American West,* 9 (Jan., 1972), 12–17, 19, 21.

_____. "Colonel Grierson Invests on the West Texas Frontier." *Fort Concho Report,* 16 (Fall, 1984), 6–11.

_____. "Scandal in the Tenth Cavalry." *Arizona and the West,* 28 (Summer, 1986), 125–140.

Eales, Anne Bruner. *Army Wives on the American Frontier.* Boulder, Colo.: Johnson Books, 1996.

Garesche, Louis. *Biography of Lieut. Col. Julius P. Garesche: Assistant Adjutant General, U.S. Army.* Philadelphia: J. B. Lippincott Co., 1887.

Gates, John M. "The Alleged Isolation of U.S. Army Officers in the Late 19th Century." *Parameters: Journal of the U.S. Army War College,* 10 (Sept., 1980), 32–45.

Greaves, Rex E. "Commentary: A Glimpse of Life in the Old Army on the Frontier." *Military History of Texas and the Southwest,* 10, no. 1 (1972), 51–54.

Greene, A. C. *900 Miles on the Butterfield Trail.* Denton, Tex.: University of North Texas Press, 1994.

Ingalls, Joan. "Family Life on the Southwestern Frontier." *Military History of Texas and the Southwest,* 14 (1978), 203–213.

Johnson, Barry C. *Flipper's Dismissal.* London: Privately published, 1980.

Knight, Oliver. *Life and Manners in the Frontier Army.* Norman: University of Oklahoma Press, 1978.

Leckie, Shirley. "Fort Concho: A Paradise for Children." *Fort Concho Report,* 19 (Spring, 1989), 1–15.

_____. "Reading Between the Lines: Another Look at Officers'

Wives in the Post-Civil War Army." *Military History of the Southwest*, 19 (Fall, 1989), 137–160.

Lenny, John J. *Rankers: The Odyssey of the Enlisted Regular Soldier of America and Britain*. New York: Greenburg, 1950.

Mahon, Emmie Giddings W. and Chester V. Kielman. "George H. Giddings and the San Antonio-San Diego Mail Line." *Southwestern Historical Quarterly*, 61 (Oct., 1957), 220–239.

McChristian, Doug. "The Commissary Sergeant: His Life at Fort Davis." *Military History of Texas and the Southwest*, 14, no. 1 (1978), 21–32.

Miller, Darlis A. "Foragers, Army Women, and Prostitutes." In Joan M. Jensen and Darlis A. Miller (eds.). *New Mexico Women: Intercultural Perspectives*. Alburquerque: University of New Mexico Press, 1986.

Mulroy, Kevin. *Freedom on the Border: The Seminole Maroons in Florida, the Indian Territory, Coahuila, and Texas*. Lubbock: Texas Tech University Press, 1993.

Myres, Sandra L. "Romance and Reality on the American Frontier: Views of Army Wives." *Western Historical Quarterly*, 13 (Oct., 1982), 409–427.

————. "Frontier Historians, Women, and the 'New' Military History." *Military History of the Southwest*, 19 (Spring, 1989), 27–37.

Nalty, Bernard C. *Strength for the Fight: A History of Black Americans in the Military*. New York: The Free Press, 1986.

Reese, James V. "The Murder of Major Ripley A. Arnold." *West Texas Historical Association Year Book*, 41 (1965), 144–155.

Scheips, Paul J. "Albert James Myer, an Army Doctor in Texas, 1854–1857." *Southwestern Historical Quarterly*, 82 (July, 1978), 1–24.

Smith, Sherry L. *The View From Officers' Row: Army Perceptions of Western Indians*. Tucson: University of Arizona Press, 1990.

Sohn, Anton Paul. *A Saw, Pocket Instruments, and Two Ounces of Whiskey: Frontier Medicine in the Great Basin*. Frontier Military Series 20. Spokane, Wash.: Arthur H. Clark, 1998.

Stallard, Patricia Yeary. *Glittering Misery: Dependents of the Indian*

Fighting Army. Fort Collins, Colo.: The Old Army Press, 1978. Reprint, with a foreword by Darlis A. Miller, Norman: University of Oklahoma Press, 1992.

Steward, T. G. *The Colored Regulars in the U.S. Army*. Philadelphia: [n.p.], 1904.

Stewart, Miller J. "Army Laundresses: Ladies of 'Soap Suds Row.'" *Nebraska History*, 61 (Winter, 1980), 421–36.

_____. "A Touch of Civilization: Culture and Education in the Frontier Army." *Nebraska History*, 65 (Summer, 1984), 257–82.

Temple, Frank M. "Discipline and Turmoil in the Tenth U.S. Cavalry." *West Texas Historical Association Year Book*, 58 (1982), 103–118.

Thompson, Edwin N. "The Negro Soldier on the Frontier: A Fort Davis Case Study." *Journal of the West*, 7 (Apr., 1968), 217–235.

Wheeler, David L. and William H. Landis. "'It is beef every day . . .': The Army Ration and the Enlisted Man, 1865–1890."*Military History of the West*, 26 (Fall, 1996), 129–157.

Williams, Clayton. "A Threatened Mutiny of Soldiers at Fort Stockton in 1873 Resulted in Penitentiary Sentences of Five to Fifteen Years." *West Texas Historical Association Year Book*, 52 (1976), 78–83.

Wilson, Aubrey A. "A Soldier of the Texas Frontier: Brevet Major Robert Patterson Wilson, United States Army." *West Texas Historical Association Year Book*, 34 (1958), 86.

Wooster, Robert. *Soldiers, Sutlers, and Settlers: Garrison Life on the Texas Frontier*. Illustrated by Jack Jackson. College Station: Texas A&M University Press, 1987.

CIVIL-MILITARY RELATIONS: BOOKS, ARTICLES, AND DISSERTATIONS

Ball, Larry Durwood. "Filibusters and Regular Troops in San Francisco, 1851–1855." *Military History of the West*, 28 (Fall, 1998), 161–183.

Cantrell, Gregg. "Racial Violence and Reconstruction Politics in

Texas, 1867–1868." *Southwestern Historical Quarterly*, 93 (Jan., 1990), 333–355.

Coakley, Robert W. *The Role of Federal Military Forces in Domestic Disorders*. Army Historical Series. Washington, D.C.: Center of Military History, 1988.

Cooper, Jerry M. *The Army and Civil Disorder: Federal Military Intervention in Labor Disputes, 1877–1900*. Contributions in Military History No. 19. Westport, Conn.: Greenwood Press, 1980.

Crouch, Barry A. *The Freedman's Bureau and Black Texans*. Austin: University of Texas Press, 1992.

_____. "'Unmanacling' Texas Reconstruction: A Twenty-Year Perspective." *Southwestern Historical Quarterly*, 93 (Jan., 1990), 274–302.

Crouch, Dr. Thomas W. "The Funston-Gambrell Dispute: An Episode in Military-Civil Relations [1915–1916]." *Military History of Texas and the Southwest*, 9, no. 2 (1972), 79–105.

Dawson, Joseph G. III. *Army Generals and Reconstruction: Louisiana, 1862–1877*. Baton Rouge: Louisiana State University Press, 1992.

_____. "Army Generals and Reconstruction: Mower and Hancock as Case Studies." *Southern Studies*, 17 (Fall, 1978), 255–272.

Gates, John M. "The Alleged Isolation of U.S. Army Officers in the Late 19th Century." *Parameters: Journal of the US Army War College*, 13 (Mar., 1983), 59–68.

Huntington, Samuel P. *The Soldier and the State: The Theory and Politics of Civil-Military Relations*. Cambridge, Mass.: Harvard University Press, 1957.

Ifera, Raymond Philip. "Crime and Punishment at Fort Davis, 1867–1891." M.A. thesis, Sul Ross State College, 1974.

Lale, Max S. "Military Occupation of Marshall, Texas, by the Eighth Illinois Volunteer Infantry, U.S.A, 1865." *Military History of Texas and the Southwest*, 13, no. 3 (1976), 39–47.

Langley, Lester. "The Democratic Tradition and Military Reform, 1878–1885." *Southwestern Social Science Quarterly*, 48 (Sept., 1967), 192–200.

Ramsdell, Charles W. *Reconstruction in Texas*. New York: Columbia

University Press, 1910. Reprint, Austin: University of Texas Press, 1970.

Richter, William L. *The Army in Texas During Reconstruction*. College Station: Texas A&M University Press, 1987.

_____. *Overreached on All Sides: The Freedman's Bureau Administrators in Texas, 1865–1868*. College Station: Texas A&M University Press, 1992.

_____. "Devil Take Them All: Military Rule in Texas, 1862–1870." *Southern Studies*, 25 (Spring, 1986), 5–30.

_____. "General Phil Sheridan, the Historians, and Reconstruction." *Civil War History*, 33 (June, 1987), 131–154.

_____. "Outside . . . My Profession: The Army and Civil Affairs in Texas Reconstruction." *Military History of Texas and the Southwest*, 9, no. 1 (1971), 5–14.

_____. "'The Revolver Rules the Day': Colonel Dewitt C. Brown and the Freedmen's Bureau in Paris, Texas, 1867–1868." *Southwestern Historical Quarterly*, 93 (Jan., 1990), 303–332.

Sefton, James E. *The United States Army and Reconstruction, 1865–1877*. Baton Rouge: Louisiana State University Press, 1967.

Shook, Robert W. "The Federal Military in Texas, 1865–1870." *Texas Military History*, 6 (Spring, 1967), 3–54.

_____. "Federal Occupation and Administration of Texas, 1865–1870. Ph.D diss., North Texas State University, 1970.

Skelton, William B. *An American Profession of Arms: The Army Officer Corps, 1784–1861*. Lawrence: The University Press of Kansas, 1992.

Thompson, Jerry Don. *Warm Weather and Bad Whiskey: The 1886 Laredo Election Riot*. El Paso: Texas Western Press, 1991.

Weaver, John D. *The Brownsville Raid*. New York: W. W. Norton, 1970. Reprint, College Station: Texas A&M University Press, 1992.

Weigley, Russell F. *History of the United States Army*. New York: Macmillan, 1967. Enlarged edition, Bloomington: Indiana University Press, 1984.

Wooster, Robert. "The Army and the Politics of Expansion: Texas and the Southwest Borderlands, 1870–1886." *Southwestern Historical Quarterly*, 93 (Oct.,1989), 151–167.

The Mexican War, 1846–1848

Primary Sources: Government Documents and Records, Books and Articles

Government Documents and Records

National Archives and Records Service, Washington, D.C.:

Records of the United States Army Adjutant General's Office, 1780–1917, Record Group 94

Orders of Gen. Zachary Taylor to the Army of Occupation in the Mexican War, 1845–1847, microfilm no. M29, 3 rolls.

Orders and Special Orders by Maj. Gen. William O. Butler and Maj. Gen. W. J. Worth to the Army in Mexico, 1848, microfilm no. T1114, 1 roll.

United States Congressional Records:

30th Congress, 1st Session:

Senate Executive Documents, no. 32, serial 562, Capt. George W. Hughes. "Memoir Descriptive of the March of a Division of the United States Army, under the Command of Brigadier General John E. Wool from San Antonio de Bexar, in Texas, to Saltillo, in Mexico."

House Executive Documents, no. 60, Mexican War Correspondence.

Primary Sources: Books and Articles

Chamberlain, Samuel E. *My Confession*. Introduction by Roger Butterfield. New York: Harper & Brothers, 1956.

———. *My Confession: Recollections of a Rogue*. Annotated and with an introduction by William H. Goetzmann. Austin: Texas State Historical Association, 1996.

Clayton, Lawrence R. and Joseph E. Chance, eds. *The March to Monterrey: The Diary of Lt. Rankin Dilworth, U.S. Army*. El Paso: Texas Western Press, 1996.

Deas, George. "Reminiscences of the Campaign on the Rio Grande." *Historical Magazine*, 7 (Jan.-May, 1870), 19–22, 99–103, 236-238, 311–316.

Ferrell, Robert H., ed. *Monterrey is Ours! The Mexican War Letters of Lieutenant Dana, 1845–1847*. Lexington: The University Press of Kentucky, 1990.

Foote, H. S. [Lt. Daniel H. Hill]. "The Army in Texas." *Southern Quarterly Review*, 9 (Apr., 1846), 434–457.

French, Samuel G. *Two Wars: An Autobiography of Gen. Samuel G. French*. Nashville, Tenn.: Confederate Veteran, 1901.

Goetzmann, William H., ed. *Sam Chamberlain's Mexican War: The San Jacinto Museum of History Paintings*. Austin: Texas State Historical Association, 1996.

Grant, Ulysses S. *Personal Memoirs of U. S. Grant: Selected Letters 1839–1865*. New York: Charles L. Webster and Company, 1885. 2 vols. Reprint, New York: The Library of America, 1990.

Hamlin, Captain Percy, ed. *The Making of a Soldier: Letters of General R. S. Ewell*. Richmond, Va.: Whitlet & Sheppardson, 1935.

Hitchcock, Ethan Allen. *Fifty Years in Camp and Field: Diary of Major-General Ethan Allen Hitchcock, U.S.A.*. Edited by W. A. Croffut. New York: G. P. Putnam's Sons, 1909.

Kendall, George Wilkins. *The War between the United States and Mexico, Illustrated*. Introduction by Ron Tyler. Austin: Texas State Historical Association, 1996.

Manning, Dan R. "The Mexican War Journal of John James Dix: A Texian." *Military History of the West*, 23 (Spring, 1993), 46–74.

Meade, George, ed. *The Life and Letters of George Gordon Meade, Major General United States Army*. 2 vols. New York: Charles Scribner's Sons, 1913.

Smith, Franklin. *The Mexican War Journal of Captain Franklin Smith*. Edited by Joseph E. Chance. Jackson: University Press of Mississippi, 1991.

Turnley, Parmenas Taylor. *Reminiscences of Parmenas Taylor Turnley from the Cradle to Three-Score and Ten*. Chicago: Donohue & Henneberry, 1892.

Secondary Sources: Books, Articles, and Dissertations

Bauer, K. Jack. *The Mexican War, 1846–1848*. New York: Macmillan Publishing Co., 1974.

Dawson, Joseph G. III. *Doniphan's Epic March: The 1st Missouri Volunteers in the Mexican War*. Lawrence: University Press of Kansas, 1999.

DePalo, William A. Jr. *The Mexican National Army, 1822–1852*. College Station: Texas A&M University Press, 1997.

Dillon, Lester R. Jr. *American Artillery in the Mexican War, 1846–1847*. Austin: Presidial Press, 1975.

_____. "American Artillery in the Mexican War." *Military History of Texas and the Southwest*, 11, no. 1 (1973), 7–29; no. 2 (1973), 109–127; no. 3 (1973), 149–172; no. 4 (1973), 233–250.

Eisenhower, John S. D. *So Far From God: The U.S. War with Mexico, 1846–1848*. New York: Random House, 1989.

Flores, Dan L. *Jefferson and Southwestern Exploration: The Freeman and Custis Accounts of the Red River Expedition of 1806*. Norman: University of Oklahoma Press, 1984.

Gruber, Robert H. "The Cross, Porter, and Thornton Episodes: America's Inauspicious Entry into the Mexican War." *Military History of Texas and the Southwest*, 12, no. 3 (1975), 185–201.

Haecker, Charles M. A. *Thunder of Cannon: Archeology of the Mexican-American War Battlefield of Palo Alto*. Southwest Cultural Resources Center Professional Papers No. 52. Santa Fe: Divisions of Anthropology and History, Southwest Regional Office, National Park Service, 1994.

Johannsen, Robert W. *To the Halls of the Montezumas: The Mexican War in the American Imagination*. New York: Oxford University Press, 1985.

McCaffery, James M. *Army of Manifest Destiny: The American Soldier in the Mexican War, 1846–1848*. New York: New York University Press, 1992.

_____. "Wearing Army Blue (and Green, and Red, and Gray. . .) During the Mexican War." *Military History of the West*, 23 (Spring, 1993), 39–45.

Miller, Robert Ryal. *Shamrock and Sword: The Saint Patrick's Battalion in the U.S.-Mexican War*. Norman: University of Oklahoma Press, 1989.

Miller, Roger G. "Winfield Scott and the Sinews of War: The Logistics of the Mexico City Campaign, October 1846–September 1847." M.A. thesis, North Texas State University, 1976.

Payne, Darwin. "Camp Life in the Army of Occupation: Corpus Christi, July 1845 to March 1846." *Southwestern Historical Quarterly*, 73 (Jan., 1970), 326–342.

Pulver, Dale R. "Handling the U.S. Military Mails During the War With Mexico: 1846–48." *Stamp Chronicle*, 98 (May, 1978), 86–93; 99 (Aug., 1978), 172–175; 100 (Nov., 1978), 240–247.

Silver, James W. *Edmund Pendleton Gaines, Frontier General*. Baton Rouge: Louisiana State University Press, 1949.

Singletary, Otis A. *The Mexican War*. Chicago: University of Chicago Press, 1960.

Smith, George Winston and Charles Judah. *Chronicles of the Gringos: The U.S. Army in the Mexican War, 1846–1848*. Albuquerque: University of New Mexico Press, 1968.

Smith, Justin H. *The War With Mexico*. 2 vols. New York: Macmillan, 1919.

Thonhoff, Robert H. "Taylor's Trail in Texas." *Southwestern Historical Quarterly*, 70 (July, 1966), 7–22.

Trass, Adrian George. *From the Golden Gate to Mexico City: The U.S. Army Topographical Engineers in the Mexican War, 1846–1848*. Washington, D.C.: Office of History, Corps of Engineers and Center of Military History, 1993.

Watson, Samuel J. "Manifest Destiny and Military Professionalism: Junior U.S. Army Officers' Attitudes toward War with Mexico, 1844–1846." *Southwestern Historical Quarterly*, 99 (Apr., 1996), 466–498.

Weems, John Edward. *To Conquer a Peace: The War between the United States and Mexico*. Garden City, N.Y.: Doubleday, 1974.

Winders, Richard Bruce. *Mr. Polk's Army: The American Military Experience in the Mexican War*. College Station: Texas A&M University Press, 1997.

ARMY OPERATIONS ON THE TEXAS FRONTIER, 1849–1900

Primary Sources: Government Documents and Records

National Archives and Records Service, Washington, D.C.:

Records of the Office of the Quartermaster General, Record Group 92

Letters Sent by the Office of the Quartermaster General, Main Series, 1818–1870, microfilm no. M745, 61 rolls.

Records of the United States Army Continental Commands, 1821–1920, Record Group 393

Letters Sent by Headquarters, Department of Texas, 1870–1898, microfilm no. M1114, 10 rolls.

Letters Sent by the Department of Texas and the Fifth Military District, 1856–1858, 1865–1870, microfilm no. M1165, 3 rolls.

Registers of Letters Received and Letters Received of the Department of Texas, the District of Texas, and the Fifth Military District, 1865–1870, microfilm no. M1193, 33 rolls.

Headquarters Records of the District of the Pecos, 1878–1881, microfilm no. M1381, 5 rolls.

United States Congressional Records:

The Annual Report of the Secretary of War is usually contained in *Senate Executive Documents* or *House Executive Documents*, no. 1 or 2 of each serial set. Contracts with the War Department are a separate document in the serial set. The serial sets are usually available on microform at most university libraries. Of special interest are the following:

30th Congress, 1st Session:

Senate Executive Documents, no. 26, serial 554 (The contracts made . . . 1849).

Senate Executive Documents, no. 64, serial 562 (Reports of the Secretary of War with Reconnaissances of Routes from San Antonio to El Paso, 24 July 1850).

Senate Executive Documents, no. 69, serial 562 (The Commerce of Brazos de St. Iago [1849]).

31st Congress, 2d Session:

House Executive Documents, no. 23, serial 599 (Statements of contracts and purchases, &c. [1850]).

32d Congress, 1st Session:

House Executive Documents, no. 2, serial 634 (Report of the Quartermaster General, 22 Nov. 1851).

House Executive Documents, no. 23, serial 640 (Contracts—War Department [1851]).

32d Congress, 2d Session:

House Executive Documents, no. 21, serial 676 (Contracts [1852]).

33d Congress, 1st Session:

Senate Executive Documents, no. 37, serial 698 (Contracts made under the authority of the War Department during the year 1853).

33d Congress, 2d Session:

House Executive Documents, no. 68, serial 788 (Contracts—War Department, 1854).

House Executive Documents, no. 91, serial 801 (Reports of Explorations and Surveys to Ascertain the Most Practicable and Economic Route for a Railroad from the Mississippi River to the Pacific Ocean [1855]).

34th Congress, 1st Session:

Senate Executive Documents, no. 7, serial 815 (List of contracts. . . during the year 1855).

34th Congress, 3d Session:

Senate Executive Documents, no. 32, serial 880 (Statements showing the contracts made. . . during the year 1856).

35th Congress, 1st Session:

Senate Executive Documents, no. 31, serial 924 (A statement of contracts. . . during the year 1857).

House Executive Documents, no. 13, serial 947 (General Account of the receipts and expenditures of the United States for the fiscal year ending June 30, 1857).

35th Congress, 2d Session:

House Executive Documents, no. 2, pt. 2, vol. 2, serial 998 (Artesian Well Experiment, Reports of Captain John Pope; Report on On Camels).

House Executive Documents, no. 50, serial 1006 (Contracts—War Department [1858]).

36th Congress, 1st Session:

House Executive Documents, no. 22, serial 1047 (War Department—Contracts [1859]).

House Executive Documents, no. 52, serial 1050 (Difficulties on the Southwestern Frontier).

House Executive Documents, no. 81, serial 1056 (Troubles on the Texas Frontier).

36th Congress, 2d Session:

Senate Executive Documents, no. 1, pt. 2, serial 1057 (Report of the Engineer Bureau, Nov. 14, 1860; Report of the Topographical Bureau, Nov. 14, 1860).

Senate Executive Documents, no. 1, pt. 2, serial 1079 (Affairs in the Department of Texas, Aug. 30, 1860).

House Executive Documents, no. 47, serial 1099 (Contracts of the War Department for 1860).

37th Congress, 2d Session:

House Executive Documents, no. 54, serial 1100 (Army Register, 1861).

39th Congress, 2d Session:

House Executive Documents, no. 1, serial 1285 (Report of Maj. Gen. P. H. Sheridan, Department of the Gulf, Nov. 14, 1866).

40th Congress, 3d Session:

House Executive Documents, no. 1, serial 1367 (Report of the Secretary of War, Nov. 20, 1868; Report of the Quartermaster General, Oct. 20, 1868).

House Executive Documents, no. 124, serial 1513 (Letter from the Secretary of War Showing Expenditures for Construction and Repairs of Buildings at Each Fort and Military Post in Texas, Feb. 9, 1872).

44th Congress, 1st Session:

House Executive Documents, no. 1, pt. 2, serial 1674 (Report of Brig. Gen. E. O. C. Ord, Headquarters, Department of Texas, Sept. 10, 1875).

52nd Congress, 2d Session:

House Executive Documents, no.1, pt.2, vol. 4, serial 3084 (Report of the Inspector-General, Sept. 15, 1892).

Pacific Railroad Reports. 13 vols. Washington, D.C.: A. O. P. Nicholson, Printer, 1855–1860.

War Department. *The War of the Rebellion: A Compilation of the Official Records of the Union and Confederate Armies.* 128 parts in 70 vols. Washington, D.C.: Government Printing Office, 1880–1901.

Primary Sources: Books, Articles, and Manuscripts:

Archambeau, Ernest P., ed. "The Battle of Lyman's Wagon Train." *The Panhandle Plains Historical Review*, 36 (1963), 89–101.

Baker, T. Lindsay, ed. *The Texas Red River Country: The Official Surveys of the Headwaters, 1876.* Foreword by Dan. L. Flores. College Station: Texas A&M University Press, 1998.

Brackett, Albert G. "Our Cavalry on the Frontier." *Army and Navy Journal* (Nov. 10, 1883), 283–284.

Burg, Maclyn P. "Service on the Vanishing Frontier, 1887–1889."*Military History of Texas and the Southwest*, 13, no. 3 (1976), 5–21; no. 4 (1976), 19–28.

Carter, Robert G. *The Old Sergeant's Story: Winning the West from the Indians and Bad Men in 1870 to 1876.* New York: Frederick H. Hitchcock, 1926.

_____. *On the Border with Mackenzie; Or, Winning West Texas from the Comanches.* Washington, D.C.: Eynon, 1935.

Crane, Charles J. *Experiences of a Colonel of Infantry.* New York: The Knickerbocker Press, 1923.

Crimmins, Martin L., ed. "Two Thousand Miles by Boat in the Rio Grande in 1850." *West Texas Historical and Scientific Society* Bulletin 48 (Dec., 1933), 44–52.

_____, ed. "Colonel Robert E. Lee's Report on Indian Combats in Texas." *Southwestern Historical Quarterly*, 39 (July, 1935), 21–32.

_____. "The Second Dragoon Indian Campaign in Texas." *West Texas Historical Association Year Book*, 21 (Oct., 1945), 50–56.

Custer, Gen. G. A., U.S.A. *My Life on the Plains, or Personal Experiences with Indians.* New York: Sheldon and Company, 1874.

Dodge, Richard Irving. *Our Wild Indians: Thirty-three Years' Personal Experience among the Red Men of the Great West.* Hartford, Conn.: 1882. Reprint, New York: Archer House, 1959.

Dorst, Lt. Joseph ("One Who Was There"). "Scouting on the Staked Plains." *United Services Magazine* (Oct.–Nov. 1885), 400–412.

Duke, Escal F., ed. "A Description of the Route from San Antonio to El Paso by Captain Edward S. Meyer." *West Texas Historical Association Year Book*, 49 (1973), 128–141.

Eastman, Seth. *Seth Eastman Sketchbook, 1849–1849*. San Antonio: Marion Kooger McNay Art Museum and University of Texas Press, 1961.

Ellis, Tuffly L., ed. "Lieutenant A. W. Greely's Report on the Installation of Military Telegraph Lines in Texas, 1875–1876."*Southwestern Historical Quarterly*, 69 (July, 1965), 66–87.

Ford, John Salmon. *Rip Ford's Texas*. Edited by Stephen B. Oates. Austin: University of Texas Press, 1963.

French, Samuel G. *Two Wars: An Autobiography of Gen. Samuel G. French*. Nashville, Tenn.: Confederate Veteran, 1901.

Greely, Maj. Gen. A. W. *Reminiscences of Adventure and Service: A Record of Sixty-Five Years*. New York: Charles Scribner's Sons, 1927.

Hancock, Almira R. *Reminiscences of Winfield Scott Hancock by His Wife*. New York: Charles L. Webster & Company, 1887.

Harris, Theodore D., ed. *Negro Frontiersman: The Western Memoirs of Henry O. Flipper, First Negro Graduate of West Point*. El Paso: Texas Western College Press, 1963.

——————, ed. *Black Frontiersman: The Memoirs of Henry O. Flipper, First Black Graduate of West Point*. Fort Worth: Texas Christian University Press, 1997.

Hatfield, Charles A. P. "Diary; Campaign of Col. R. S. McKenzie . . . in 1874." Ranald S. Mackenzie File, Southwest Library, Texas Tech University, Lubbock.

Hazen, General William B. *A Narrative of Military Service*. Boston: Ticknor and Company, 1885.

Hood, John Bell. *Advance and Retreat: Personal Experiences in the United States and Confederate States Armies*. New Orleans: G. T. Beauregard, 1880.

Jenkins, John H., ed. *Robert E. Lee on the Rio Grande: The Correspondence of Robert E. Lee on the Texas Border, 1860*. Austin: The Jenkins Publishing Co., 1988.

Johnson, Richard W. *A Soldier's Reminiscences in Peace and War.* Philadelphia: J. B. Lippincott Company, 1886.

Larson, James. "Memoirs." Manuscript, Arthur W. Arndt Collection, 2L158, Center for American History, University of Texas at Austin.

Lesley, Lewis Burt, ed. *Uncle Sam's Camels: The Journal of May Humphreys Stacy Supplemented by the Report of Edward Fitzgerald Beale (1857–1858).* Cambridge, Mass.: Harvard University Press, 1929. Reprint, Glorieta, N.M.: The Rio Grande Press, 1970.

McConnell, H. H. *Five Years a Cavalryman, or, Sketches of Regular Army Life on the Texas Frontier, 1866–1871.* Jacksboro, Tex.: J. N. Rogers, 1889. Reprint, with a foreword by William H. Leckie, Norman: University of Oklahoma Press, 1996.

McIntyre, Benjamin F. *Federals on the Frontier: The Diary of Benjamin F. McIntyre, 1862–1864.* Edited by Nannie M. Tilley. Austin: University of Texas Press, 1963.

McKinley, J. W. "Narrative [Battle of Adobe Walls]." *Panhandle-Plains Historical Review*, 36 (1963), 61–70.

Marcy, Capt. Randolph B. *The Prairie Traveler.* New York: Harper & Brothers, 1859.

————. *Thirty Years of Army Life on the Border.* New York: Harper, 1966.

————. *Border Reminiscences.* New York: Harper & Brothers, 1872.

Marshall, J. T. *The Miles Expedition of 1874–1875: An Eyewitness Account of the Red River War.* Edited by Lonnie J. White. Austin: Encino Press, 1971.

Maury, Dabney Herndon. *Recollections of a Virginian in the Mexican, Indian, and Civil Wars.* New York: Charles Scribner's Sons, 1894.

Mills, Anson. *My Story.* Edited by C. H. Claudy. Washington, D.C.: Anson Mills, 1918.

Parker, James. *The Old Army: Memoirs, 1872–1918.* Philadelphia: Dorrance & Company, 1929.

Parker, W. B. *Through Unexplored Texas.* 1856. Reprint, with an introduction by George B. Ward, Austin: Texas State Historical Association, 1992.

Pingenot, Ben E., ed. *Paso Del Águila: A Chronicle of Frontier Days on the Texas Border as Recorded in the Memoirs of Jesse Sumpter.* Complied by Harry Warren. Austin: The Encino Press, 1969.

_____. "Journal of a Wagon Train Expedition from Fort Inge to El Paso del Norte in 1850." *Military History of the West*, 25 (Spring, 1995), 69–105.

Pratt, Richard Henry. *Battlefield and Classroom: Four Decades with the American Indian, 1867–1904.* Edited by Robert M. Utley. New Haven, Conn.: Yale University Press, 1964.

Reeve, Frank D. "Frederick E. Phelps: A Soldier's Memoirs." *New Mexico Historical Review*, 25 (Jan., 1950), 37–56; (Apr., 1950), 109–135; (July, 1950), 187–221; (Oct., 1950), 305–327.

Rodríquez, José Policarpo. *The Old Guide.* Dallas: Publishing House of the Methodist-Episcopal Church, Smith and Lamar, Agents, [n.d].

Rodríquez, José Policarpo and D. W. Carter "The Old Guide: His Life in His Own Words." *Old West*, 5 (1968), 77–96.

Roosevelt, Theodore. *The Rough Riders.* New York: Charles Scribner's Sons, 1899.

Russel, Lt. Edgar. "Notes on Field Practice, Light Battery 'F' Third Artillery." *Journal of the United States Artillery*, 1, no. 1 (1892), 110–113.

Santleben, August. *A Texas Pioneer: Early Staging and Overland Freighting Days on the Frontiers of Texas and Mexico.* Edited by I. D. Affleck. New York: The Neal Publishing Company, 1910. Reprint, Castroville, Tex.: Castro Colonies Heritage Association, 1994.

Schneider, George A., ed. "A Border Incident of 1878 from the Journal of Captain John S. McNaught [20th In.]." *Southwestern Historical Quarterly*, 70 (Oct., 1966), 314–320.

Schofield, Lt. Gen. John M. *Forty-Six Years in the Army.* New York: The Century Co., 1897.

Sheffy, L.F., ed. "Letters and Reminiscences of General Theodore A. Baldwin: Scouting after Indians on the Plains of West Texas." *Panhandle-Plains Historical Review*, 11 (1938), 7–30.

Sheridan, Philip H. *Personal Memoirs of P. H. Sheridan, General United States Army.* 2 vols. New York: Charles L. Webster & Co., 1888.

Shook, Robert, ed. "Lee's Farewell to Texas, February 9, 1861." *Military History of Texas and the Southwest,* 14, no. 6 (1978), 244–245.

Stanley, David S. *Personal Memoirs of Major-General D. S. Stanley, U.S.A..* Cambridge, Mass.: Harvard University Press, 1917.

Stewart, Edgar I. *Custer's Luck*. Norman: University of Oklahoma Press, 1955.

Storey, Brit Allan, ed. "An Army Officer in Texas, 1866–1867 [Lt. Adam Kramer, 6th Cav.]." *Southwestern Historical Quarterly*, 72 (Oct., 1968), 241–251.

Strong, Henry W. *My Frontier Days and Indian Fights on the Plains of Texas*. Waco, Tex.: [N.p.], 1926.

Sullivan, Jerry M., ed. "Lieutenant Colonel William R. Shafter's Pecos River Expedition of 1870." *West Texas Historical Association Year Book*, 47 (1971), 146–152.

"Target Practice." *Army and Navy Journal* (Nov. 10, 1883), 290.

Taylor, Joe F. *The Indian Campaign on the Staked Plains, 1874–1875: Military Correspondence from War Department Adjutant General's Office, File 1815–1874*. Canyon, Tex.: Panhandle-Plains Historical Society, 1962.

Thompson, Jerry D., ed. *Fifty Miles and a Fight: Major Samuel Peter Heintzelman's Journal of Texas and the Cortina War*. Austin: Texas State Historical Association, 1998.

Wallace, Ernest, ed. *Ranald S. Mackenzie's Official Correspondence Relating to Texas [1871–1979]*. 2 vols. Lubbock: West Texas Museum Association, 1967.

————. "Colonel Ranald S. Mackenzie's Expedition of 1872 across the Plains." *West Texas Historical Association Year Book*, 38 (Oct., 1962), 3–18.

White, Lonnie, ed. "Letters of a Sixth Cavalryman Stationed at 'Cantonment' in the Texas Panhandle, 1875." *Texas Military History*, 7 (Summer, 1968), 77–101.

Wooster, Robert, ed. *Recollections of Western Texas: Descriptive and Narrative Including an Indian Campaign, 1852–1855, Interspersed with Illustrative Anecdotes by Two of the Mounted Rifles*. Preface by Robert Utley. Austin: Book Club of Texas, 1995.

Secondary Sources: Books, Articles, and Dissertations

Alprin, Lynn M. *Custodians of the Coast: History of the United States Army Engineers at Galveston*. Galveston, Tex.: Galveston District, United States Army Corps of Engineers, 1977.

Archambeau, Ernest P., ed. "Monthly Reports of the Fourth Cavalry,

1872–1874." *The Panhandle Plains Historical Review*, 38 (1965), 95–154.

Aston, B. W. "Federal Military Reoccupation of the Texas Southwestern Frontier, 1865–1871." *Texas Military History*, 8, no. 3 (1970), 123–134.

Athern, Robert G. *William Tecumseh Sherman and the Settlement of the West.* Norman: University of Oklahoma Press, 1956.

Austerman, Wayne R. "José Policarpo Rodríquez: Chicano Plainsman." *West Texas Historical Association Year Book*, 59 (1983), 52–74.

Ball, Larry Durwood. "The United States Army on the Interwar Frontier, 1848–1861." Ph.D. diss., University of New Mexico, 1994.

Ballew, Elvis Joe. "Supply Problems of Fort Davis, Texas, 1867–1880. M.A. thesis, Sul Ross State College, 1971.

Barr, Alwyn. "Texas Coastal Defense, 1861–1865." *Southwestern Historical Quarterly*, 65 (July, 1961), 14–18.

Barrett, Lenora. "Transportation, Supplies, and Quarters for the West Texas Frontier under the Federal Military System, 1848–1861." *West Texas Historical Association Year Book*, 5 (1929), 87–89.

Beck, Paul N. "Military Officer's Views of Indian Scouts." *Military History of the West*, 23 (Spring, 1993), 1–19.

Bowden, J. J. *The Exodus of Federal Forces From Texas, 1861.* Austin: Eakin Press, 1985.

Britten, Thomas A. "The History of the Seminole Negro-Indian Scouts." M.A. thesis, Hardin-Simmons University, 1990.

———. "The Dismissal of the Seminole-Negro Indian Scouts, 1880–1914." *Fort Concho and the South Plains Journal*, 24, no. 2 (1992), 55–77.

Carlson, Paul. H. "William R. Shafter Commanding Black Troops in West Texas." *West Texas Historical Association Year Book*, 50 (1974), 104–116.

Carroll, John M., ed. *The Black Military Experience in the American West.* New York: Liveright Publishing Corp., 1971.

———, ed. *Custer in Texas: An Interrupted Narrative.* New York: Sol Lewis, 1975.

Chalfant, William Y. *Without Quarter: The Wichita Expedition and the Fight on Crooked Creek.* Norman: University of Oklahoma Press, 1991.

Clendenen, Clarence C. *Blood on the Border: The United States Army and the Mexican Irregulars*. New York: Macmillan, 1969.

Connelly, Thomas L. "The American Camel Experiment: A Reappraisal." *Southwestern Historical Quarterly*, 69 (Apr., 1966), 442–462.

Cosmas, Graham A. *An Army For Empire: The United States Army in the Spanish-American War*. Columbia: University of Missouri Press, 1971. 2nd edition, Shippensburg, Pa.: White Mane Publishing Company, Inc., 1994.

Crane, R. C. "Robert E. Lee's Expedition in the Upper Brazos and Colorado Country." *West Texas Historical Association Year Book*, 13 (1937), 53–63.

Crimmins, Martin L. "General B. H. Grierson in West Texas." *West Texas Historical and Scientific Society* Bulletin 18 (Dec., 1937), 30–44.

_____. "Shafter's Explorations in Western Texas, 1875." *West Texas Historical Association Year Book*, 9 (1933), 82–96.

_____. "Captain Nolan's Lost Troop on the Staked Plains." *West Texas Historical Association Year Book*, 10 (1934). Reprinted in John M. Carroll, ed. *The Black Military Experience in the American West*. New York: Liveright, 1971.

_____. "General Randolph B. Marcy's Last Tour of Texas." *West Texas Historical Association Year Book*, 25 (1949), 74–76.

_____. "First Sergeant John W. Spangler, Company H, Second United States Cavalry." *West Texas Historical Association Year Book*, 26 (Oct., 1950), 68–75.

Davenport, B. T. "The Watch along the Rio Grande." *The Journal of Big Bend Studies*, 7 (Jan., 1995), 149–156.

Douglas, James Ridley. "Juan Cortina: El Caudillo de la Frontera." M.A. thesis, University of Texas at Austin, 1987.

Dunlay, Thomas W. *Wolves for the Blue Soldiers: Indian Scouts and Auxiliaries with the United States Army, 1860–90*. Lincoln: University of Nebraska Press, 1982.

Emmett, Chris. *Texas Camel Tales*. Austin: Steck Vaughn, 1969.

Essin, Emmett M. *Shavetails and Bell Sharps: The History of the U.S. Army Mule*. Lincoln: University of Nebraska Press, 1997.

_____. "Mules, Packs, and Pack Trains." *Southwestern Historical Quarterly*, 74 (July, 1970), 52–80.

Foner, Jack D. *The United States Soldier between Two Wars: Army Life and Reforms, 1865–1898.* (New York: Humanities Press, 1969.

Fowler, Arlen. *Black Infantry in the West, 1869–1891.* Westport, Conn.: Greenwood Publishing Corp., 1971. Reprint, with a foreword by William H. Leckie, Norman: University of Oklahoma Press, 1996.

Frazer, Robert W. *Forts and Supplies: The Role of the Army in the Economy of the Southwest, 1846–1861.* Albuquerque: University of New Mexico Press, 1983.

Freedom, Gary S. "'Forticide' Policies on the Northern Great Plains." *Periodical: Journal of America's Military Past,* 19 (Fall, 1992), 118–127.

Frysinger, Victor Francis. "The Smith Plan, Texas Frontier Defense in the 1850s." M.A. thesis, Texas A&M University, 1975.

Ganoe, William Addleman. *The History of the United States Army.* New York: D. Appleton and Company, 1924.

Goetzmann, William H. *Army Exploration in the American West, 1803–1863.* New Haven, Conn.: Yale University Press, 1959. Reprint, Lincoln: University of Nebraska Press, 1979.

Haley, James L. *The Buffalo War: The History of the Red River Indian Uprising of 1874.* Garden City, N.Y.: Doubleday & Company, 1976. Reprint, Norman: University of Oklahoma Press, 1985.

Harrison, Lowell H. "Supplying Texas Military Posts in 1876." *Texas Military History,* 4 (Spring, 1964), 23–24.

Havins, Thomas R. "The Texas Mounted Regiment at Camp Colorado." *Texas Military History,* 4 (Summer, 1964), 67–79.

Heidler, Jeanne T. "'Embarrassing Situation': David E. Twiggs and the Surrender of United States Forces in Texas, 1861." *Military History of the Southwest,* 21 (Fall, 1991), 156–172.

Hoig, Stan. *The Battle of the Washita: The Sheridan-Custer Indian Campaign of 1867–69.* New York: Doubleday & Company, Inc., 1976.

Holden, W. C. "Frontier Defense, 1865–1889." *Panhandle-Plains Historical Review,* 2 (1929), 43–64.

Huston, James A. *The Sinews of War: Army Logistics, 1775–1953.* Washington, D.C.: United States Army Center of Military History, 1988.

Jackson, W. Turrentine. *Wagon Roads West: A Study of Federal Road Surveys and Construction in the Trans–Mississippi West, 1846–1869.*

New Haven, Conn.: Yale University Press, 1964. Reprint, with a foreword by William H. Goetzmann, Lincoln: University of Nebraska Press, 1979.

Jamieson, Perry D. *Crossing the Deadly Ground: United States Army Tactics, 1865–1899*. Tuscaloosa: University of Alabama Press, 1994.

Judson, Capt. William J. "The Services of Graduates as Explorers, Builder of Railways, Canals, Bridges, Lighthouses, Harbors, and the Like." In *The Centennial of the United States Military Academy at West Point, New York, 1802–1902*. 2 vols. Washington, D.C.: Government Printing Office, 1904.

Kinevan, Marcos E. *Frontier Cavalryman: Lieutenant John Bigelow and the Buffalo Soldiers in Texas*. El Paso: Texas Western Press, 1998.

Kouch, Lena Clara. "Federal Indian Policy in Texas, 1845–1860." *Southwestern Historical Quarterly*, 28 (Jan., 1925), 222–234; (Apr., 1925), 259–286; 29 (July, 1925), 19–35; (Oct., 1925), 98–127.

Lackman, Howard. "George Thomas Howard, Texas Frontiersman." Ph.D diss., University of Texas at Austin, 1954.

Lambert, Joseph I. "The Defense of the Indian Frontier of Texas by the United States Army." M.A. thesis, St. Mary's University, 1948.

Lammons, Frank B. "Operation Camel." *Southwestern Historical Quarterly*, 61 (July, 1957), 40–50.

Launius, Roger D. "A New Way of War: The Development of Military Aviation in the American West, 1908–1945." *Military History of the West*, 25 (Fall, 1995), 167–190.

Leckie, William H. *The Buffalo Soldiers: A Narrative of the Negro Cavalry in the West*. Norman: University of Oklahoma Press, 1967.

Leach, John A. "Search and Destroy: Counter Insurgency on the American Plains." *Military History of Texas and the Southwest*, 9, no. 1 (1971), 55–60.

McChristian, Douglas C. *An Army of Marksmen*. Fort Collins, Colo.: Old Army Press, 1981.

_____. *The U.S. Army in the West, 1870–1880: Uniforms, Weapons, and Equipment*. Norman: University of Oklahoma Press, 1995.

_____. "Grierson's Fight at Tinaja del las Palmas: An Episode in the Victorio Campaign." *Red River Valley Historical Review*, 7 (Winter, 1982), 45–63.

_____. "Apaches and Soldiers: Mail Protection in West Texas." *Periodical: Journal of the Council on America's Military Past*, 13 (Aug., 1985), 3–17.

McKenna, Charles D. "The Forgotten Reform: The Institution of a System of Field Maneuvers in the U.S. Army, 1902–1912." *Army History*, 21 (Winter, 1991), 17–23.

Mahoney, Leo Edwin. "The Camel Corps: An Attempted Solution of the Problem of Western Transportation." M.A. thesis, University of Texas at Austin, 1928.

Marshall, Bruce. "Juan Cortina." *Military History of Texas and the Southwest*, 10, no. 1 (1972), 3–4.

Matthews, Jim. "Squarely Fought: Fort Concho and the Campaign against Victorio, 1880." *West Texas Historical Association Year Book*, 69 (1993), 34–44.

_____. "Twice Decorated for Gallantry and Distinguished Conduct: Sergeant William Wilson and the Medal Of Honor." *West Texas Historical Association Year Book*, 71 (1995), 96–105.

Miller, Darlis A. *Soldiers and Settlers: Military Supply in the Southwest, 1861–1885*. Albuquerque: University of New Mexico Press, 1989.

Morris, John Miller. *El Llano Estacado: Exploration and Imagination on the High Plains of Texas and New Mexico, 1536–1860*. Austin: Texas State Historical Association, 1997.

Neighbours, Kenneth F. *Robert Simpson Neighbors and the Texas Frontier, 1836–1859*. Waco: Texian Press, 1975.

_____. "Tonkaway Scouts and Guides." *West Texas Historical Association Year Book*, 49 (1973), 90–112.

Neilson, John C. "The Commanding Officers of Fort Concho: The Early Years, 1867–70." *Fort Concho and the South Plains Journal*, 23, no. 2 (1991), 127–146.

_____. "The Commanding Officers of Fort Concho: The Middle Years, 1870–75." *Fort Concho and the South Plains Journal*, 23, no. 3 (1991), 127–146.

_____. "The Commanding Officers of Fort Concho: The Grierson Era, 1875–82." *Fort Concho and the South Plains Journal*, 23, no. 4 (1991), 171–191.

_____. "The Commanding Officers of Fort Concho: The Final

Chapter, 1882–89." *Fort Concho and the South Plains Journal*, 24, no. 1 (1992), 17–37.

Pate, J'Nell. "United States–Mexican Border Conflicts, 1870–1880." *West Texas Historical Association Year Book*, 38 (1962), 175–194.

Pingenot, Ben E. "The Great Wagon Train Expedition of 1850." *Southwestern Historical Quarterly*, 98 (Oct., 1994), 182–225.

Porter, Kenneth Wiggins. "The Seminole Negro-Indian Scouts, 1870–1881." *Southwestern Historical Quarterly*, 55 (Jan., 1952), 358–377.

Prucha, Francis Paul. *The Sword of the Republic: The United States Army on the Frontier, 1783–1846*. New York: Macmillan, 1969. Reprint, Lincoln: University of Nebraska Press, 1986.

Rayburn, John C. "General Sherman Visits the Mexican Frontier, 1882." *West Texas Historical Association Year Book*, 38 (1962), 72–84.

"Record of Engagements with Hostile Indians in Texas 1868 to 1882." *West Texas Historical Association Year Book*, 9 (Oct., 1933), 101–118.

Richardson, Rupert Norval. *The Frontier of Northwest Texas, 1846–1876*. Glendale, Calif.: The Arthur H. Clark Company, 1963.

Rickey, Don Jr. *Forty Miles a Day on Beans and Hay: The Enlisted Soldier Fighting the Indian Wars*. Norman: University of Oklahoma Press, 1963.

Risch, Erna. *Quartermaster Support of the Army: A History of the Corps, 1775–1939*. Washington, D.C.: United States Army Center of Military History, 1962. Reprint, 1989.

Rister, Carl Coke. *The Southwestern Frontier, 1865–1881*. Cleveland: The Arthur H. Clark Company, 1928.

Robinson, Robert L. "The U.S. Navy vs. Cattle Rustlers: The *U.S.S. Rio Bravo* on the Rio Grande, 1875–1879." *Military History of Texas and the Southwest*, 15, no. 2 (1979), 43–52.

Rogers, Jerry L. "The Flint and Steel: Background of the Red River War of 1874–1875." *Texas Military History*, 7 (Fall, 1969), 153–175.

_____. "To the Canyon of the Tule: Colonel Nelson A. Miles and the Indian Territory Expedition, 1874." *Texas Military History*, 7 (Winter, 1968), 267–294.

_____. "Luck, Logistics, and Major Price: Problems of the Indian Territory Expedition, Autumn, 1874." *Texas Military History*, 8, no. 1 (1970), 27–53.

_____. "Indian Territory Expedition: Winter Campaigns, 1874–1875." *Texas Military History*, 8, no. 4 (1970), 233–251.

Schrader, Charles R. *U.S. Military Logistics, 1607–1991: A Research Guide*. Westport, Conn.: Greenwood Press, 1992.

Shook, Robert W. "Custer's Texas Command, 1865–1866." *Military History of Texas and the Southwest*, 9, no. 1 (1971), 49–54.

Skaggs, Jimmy M. "Military Operations on the Cattle Trails." *Texas Military History*, 6 (Summer, 1967), 137–148.

Smith, David Paul. *Frontier Defense in the Civil War: Texas' Rangers and Rebels*. College Station: Texas A&M University Press, 1992.

Smith, Thomas T. *The U.S. Army and the Texas Frontier Economy, 1845–1900*. College Station: Texas A&M University Press, 1999.

_____. "U.S. Army Combat Operations in the Indian Wars of Texas, 1849–1881." *Southwestern Historical Quarterly*, 99 (Apr., 1996), 501–531.

_____. "West Point and the Indian Wars, 1802–1891." *Military History of the West*, 24 (Spring, 1994), 24–55.

Steffen, Randy. *The Horse Soldier, 1776–1943*. 4 vols. Norman: University of Oklahoma Press, 1978.

Swift, Roy and Leavitt Corning Jr. *Three Roads to Chihuahua: The Great Wagon Roads That Opened the Southwest, 1823–1883*. Austin: Eakin Press, 1988.

Tate, Michael L. "The Multi-Purpose Army on the Frontier: A Call for Further Research." In Ronald Lora, ed. *The American West: Essays in Honor* of W. Eugene Hollon. Toledo, Ohio: University of Toledo, 1980; 171–208.

Temple, Frank M. "Federal Military Defense of the Trans–Pecos Region, 1850–1880." *West Texas Historical Association Year Book*, 30 (Oct., 1954), 40–60.

_____. "Colonel B. H. Grierson's Administration of the District of the Pecos." *West Texas Historical Association Year Book*, 38 (Oct., 1962), 85–96.

Thian, Raphael P. *Notes Illustrating the Military Geography of the United States, 1813–1880*. Washington, D.C.: Adjutant General's Office, 1881. Reprint, edited by John M. Carroll, with a foreword by Robert M. Utley, Austin: University of Texas Press, 1979.

Thompson, Edwin N. "The Negro Soldiers on the Frontier: A Fort

Davis Case Study." *Journal of the West*, 7 (Apr., 1968), 217–253.

Thompson, Jerry D. *Juan Cortina and the Texas-Mexico Frontier, 1859–1877*. El Paso: Texas Western Press, 1994.

Thompson, Richard A. *Crossing the Border with the 4th Cavalry: Mackenzie's Raid into Mexico*. Waco, Tex.: Texian Press, 1986.

Thrapp, Dan. L. *The Conquest of Apacheria*. Norman: University of Oklahoma Press, 1967.

Tudor, W. G. "Ghost Writers of the Palo Duro." *Southwestern Historical Quarterly*, 99 (Apr., 1996), 532–541.

Tyler, Ronnie C. "The Little Punitive Expedition in the Big Bend." *Southwestern Historical Quarterly*, 78 (Jan., 1975), 271–291.

U.S. Army Public Information Division. *The Medal of Honor of the United States Army*. Washington, D.C.: Government Printing Office, 1948.

Utley, Robert M. *Frontier Regulars: The United States Army and the Indian, 1866–1891*. New York: Macmillan, 1973.

_____. *Frontiersmen in Blue: The United States Army and the Indian, 1848–1865*. New York: Macmillan, 1967. Reprint, Lincoln: University of Nebraska Press, 1981.

_____. "A Chained Dog: The Indian-Fighting Army." *American West*, 10 (July, 1973), 18–24, 61.

_____. "'Pecos Bill' on the Texas Frontier." *American West*, 6 (Jan., 1969), 4–13.

Wallace, Edward S. "General John Lapham Bullis: The Thunderbolt of the Texas Frontier." *Southwestern Historical Quarterly*, 54 (Apr., 1951), 452–461; 55 (July, 1951), 77–85.

Wallace, Ernest. *Ranald S. Mackenzie on the Texas Frontier*. Lubbock: West Texas Museum Association, 1964. Reprint, College Station: Texas A&M University Press, 1993.

Webster, Michael G. "Intrigue on the Rio Grande: The Rio Bravo Affair, 1875." *Southwestern Historical Quarterly*, 74 (Oct., 1970), 149–164.

West, G. Derek. "The Battle of Adobe Walls (1874)." *Panhandle-Plains Historical Review*, 36 (1960), 1–36.

White, Lonnie. "The First Battle of Palo Duro Canyon." *Texas Military History*, 6 (Fall, 1967), 222–235.

_____. "New Sources Relating to the Battle of Adobe Walls, 1874." *Texas Military History*, 8, no. 1 (1970), 1–12.

Williams, Mary L. "Empire Building: Colonel Benjamin H. Grierson at Fort Davis, 1882–1885." *West Texas Historical Association Year Book,* 66 (1985), 58–73.

Wooster, Robert. *The Military and United States Indian Policy, 1865–1903.* New Haven, Conn.: Yale University Press, 1988.

_____. Nelson A. *Miles and the Twilight of the Frontier Army.* Lincoln: University of Nebraska Press, 1993.

_____. "Military Strategy in the Southwest, 1848–1860." *Military History of Texas and the Southwest,* 15, no. 2 (1979), 5–15.

A Gettysburg veteran, Maj. Louis Henry Carpenter began the Civil War as a regular army cavalry corporal and rose to colonel and regimental commander. As a post-war captain in the Tenth Cavalry in the frontier Indian Wars he earned a Congressional Medal of Honor in 1868 and led three companies in defeating the Apache leader Victorio at Rattlesnake Springs on August 6, 1880. Carpenter commanded Fort Sam Houston in 1897 and retired as a brigadier general in 1899. *Photograph courtesy Lawrence T. Jones III, Austin.*

INDEX

ABOUT THE AUTHOR

Thomas Tyree Smith is a native Texan and Regular Army Lieutenant Colonel. He served in Vietnam with the U.S. Navy and earned a B.S. in education from Southwest Texas State University, an M.A. in history from Texas A&M University, and is a graduate of the United States Army Command and General Staff College at Fort Leavenworth, Kansas. He commanded an infantry company in Germany, served as an assistant professor of history at the United States Military Academy at West Point, was the operations officer (S3) for the First Battalion, Sixteenth Infantry Regiment at Fort Riley, Kansas, and is currently assigned to Fort Bliss, Texas. He has published numerous articles on the nineteenth-century army, is the author of *The U.S. Army and the Texas Frontier Economy, 1845–1900* (1999), *Fort Inge: Sharps, Spurs, and Sabers on the Texas Frontier, 1849–1869* (1993), and is the editor of Emil A. Bode's *A Dose of Frontier Soldiering: The Memoirs of Corporal E. A. Bode, Frontier Regular Infantry, 1877–1882* (1994) and Mary Leefe Laurence's *Daughter of the Regiment: Memoirs of A Childhood in the Frontier Army, 1878–1898* (1996).

COLOPHON

This book is set in Granjon. Robert Granjon designed the face and it was introduced by English Linotype in 1924. It is based on a 1592 specimen sheet produced by Claude Garamond. The book was printed by Edwards Brothers on 55# Gladfeltter in Lillington, North Carolina.